Earnest Larsen, C.SS.R.

DON'T
JUST
STAND
THERE!

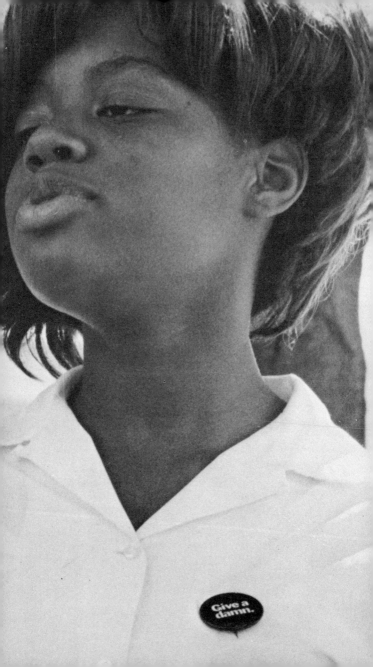

DEDICATED TO

Dr. Bernard Boelen

*WITH SPECIAL
THANKS TO*

My sister Carol

AND TO

*All who recognize the risk
And still take it*

ESPECIALLY

*My friends who sit
in the back row*

"It is absurd
when two masks
say to one another
'I love you.'
It is
very touching when
two human faces
look lovingly
upon one another."

(Malcolm Boyd)
BOOK OF DAYS

1: JUST OUT OF IT JUST OUT OF I

JUST OUT OF IT JUST OUT OF IT

"Then I read
a book by Albert Schweitzer.
He was another
fascinating cat. The man knew so much.
I really started wanting
to know things . . .
But . . . I couldn't see myself
going anyplace else,
because
if I didn't go to Harlem,
where would I have gone?
That was the only place I ever knew."

(Claude Brown)
MANCHILD IN THE PROMISED LAND

Did you ever feel—
Oh, I don't know, just

OUT OF IT? OUT OF IT? OUT OF IT

Separate
disconnected,
an outsider to everything?
Vance did,
and Vance was no dummy.
He was
a sharp San Antonio kid,
played football
went dancing
had a job
got good grades—
just knew the score.
But just now
down deep
he felt very much
out of it.
He was walking down Commerce,
buses rumbling and cars rolling
at his side
people
stores
newsstands
all around.

Signs on the windows
"Sale: buy now, don't miss it!"
A million magazines
sold by old men
all the same—
promising
hot sex, cool love
like a meat market.
Everyone he saw
was behind a kind of window
and he was on the outside
trying to look in.
It felt terrible.
How was it possible
to stand in the middle of
crowds—noise
stores—signs
and feel so **ALONE?**
It was weird
really
bad news!
Feeling like you're stuck in a desert
or stranded on an island
while your feet
pound pavement
and people's elbows and packages
and shoulders
bang against you.

Vance stood on a corner:
hurry up and change red light,
thinking about windows and deserts,
islands and feeling
alone.

He thought about that poem—
last semester in English—
the one about,
" . . . no man being an island . . . "

"No man is an island
entire of itself
every man is a piece of the Continent,
a part of the main.
If a clod be washed away by the sea
Europe is the less
as well as if a promontory were
as well as if a manor of thy friends
or of thine own were.
Any man's death diminishes me
because I am involved in Mankind.
And therefore
Never send to know for whom the bell tolls
It tolls for thee."

and he wondered if that guy who wrote it,
that John Donne,
knew what he was talking about.
I may not
BE an island,
Vance figured,
but I sure as hell know
I'm on one.
I don't like it,
I want off.
No one sees me
hears me
stranded here.
No one even knows
I'M here.
And worse,
much worse,
I don't know
if anyone ever
will.
I can't hear
see
touch
any other person.
My God
how I want to touch another
human being,
anyone
of the crowd around me.
But maybe
they are hung up
on their own islands
as far from me
as I am far
from them.
Maybe,
like me,
everybody
is stranded.

That feeling,
that sense of aloneness
Vance and so many
feel at times
has fancier names:
alienation
estrangement
isolation
they all mean the same
**I'M LOST, GOD,
SO LOST.**
Why?
That's the worst.
Not knowing why.

Sometimes
people feel this way
because they really are
alone.
Like Cheryl
when she was released after months in
the House of Correction.
She made a dress for the trip
back "home."
Not the latest style—
it didn't fit perfectly—
so what;
she made it and she
was going **HOME.**
Cheryl got off the bus
big smile
hope
bright dress
JOY
hugging the cardboard box
that was her luggage . . .
but
no one was there.
The bus pulled out
NO ONE WAS THERE.
Other travelers
kissing, hugging
being greeted,
"Thank God you're home"
"Did you have a good trip?"
"Your grandparents
will be so happy to see you"
"Dinner is waiting."
No one was there for her.
She just stood
holding the box
and her love,
for no one.
This is really alone!

lord tappo!

But sometimes,
feeling "out of it" isn't
because you're really alone,
like Cheryl,
but feeling
frustrated
depressed
discouraged
helpless
in the face of someone else's
suffering.
Like Lord Tappo.
Lord Tap
stands a bit over 6'4"
weighs in around 250,
a sharp kid
like Vance
but not like Vance
Lord Tap is black.
He leads a gang.
500 members march
in peace
or in war
at a word from Tap.

People listen
when Tap talks.
They stand aside
when Tap passes.
But one night in a ghetto shack,
standing by a sprung-through bed,
Tap said he cried.
A small boy slept on the bed
he had sores on his legs
dirt in his hair
an empty belly
hunger in his heart.
Today was dark.
Tomorrow—
a carbon copy of today.
And Tap cried.
What could he do?
Feed the boy—
man, his lieutenants could do that,
but what about his twin?
Thousands of them,
with the same
sores
dirt,
the same

hunger of belly and heart
in the same shacks
on the same
beds
in thousands of cities
just like
this one—
sharing the same dark
today,
promised the same
dark
tomorrow.

What if he did have
500 troops
or was the President
or the Pope?
WHAT IF HE WAS?
What about
THIS boy?
Here?
This Night?
What about it?
And Tap cried.
This is frustration.

And sometimes
aloneness—estrangement
—alienation
is just plain
Boredom.
One girl wrote a letter:
"Here I sit,
the middle of summer,
and I'm bored stiff.
Life,
my life,
couldn't be duller.
I come home from work
I do
nothing.
Nobody
has a car.
I pace back and forth
a lot.
I'm even so hard up
I cleaned my room.
Office work
is for the birds.
Everything
is just dull,
Dull
DULL.

How I'd love something
to get excited about,
involved in.
I shouldn't be sitting here,
wasting time.
I should be doing
something
really **great.**
But if I just
left the house,
where would I go?
I read,
I draw a lot.
But
that gets old.
I don't know,
guess
I'll go eat a banana
or something."

Just
blind—deaf—dumb
Boredom.
Nothing
means anything.
That's as good a way as any
to get uptight—just
to lose contact.

People get
boxed in
cut off
shut out
for lots of reasons.

It is **HARD**
to say a word that really
means something.
Easy to exist
not easy to
LIVE .
Maybe the problem
is me.
Maybe I have nothing
to say.
Or maybe it's
impossible
for anyone
to say anything.
Maybe Vance was right
and John Donne was wrong.
Maybe we have to settle for
islands
and like it.

But what if the
aloneness—frustration
—boredom
of all these islands
could be bridged?
What if a guy
could
and would
swim.
If he weren't
afraid
to be wet—cold—tired,
he could reach
any island
he wanted.
And what if Vance
and John Donne were
both
right?

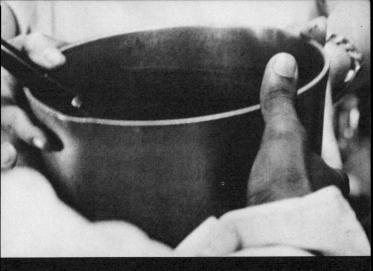

What if people on
islands
are rescuers
as well as
victims?
And that if everybody
waits
NOBODY makes it.
Of course you'd have to
know something
about swimming.
Like Paul Newman in
"Cat On A Hot Tin Roof."
He was Brick,
Burl Ives was his father,
Big Daddy.
They loved each other
deeply
but didn't know

HOW
to show it.
They looked
AT
each other
like all island people do,
over oceans.
They couldn't
I guess,
swim all that well either.

Looking At
is not
being With.
Maybe the problem
is a "between" thing;
the chemistry
of Interaction
BETWEEN people—
mixing
touching
so there is a chance of
understanding,
real understanding.
Bill Cosby sang about that
"Little Old Man . . .
Reach out your hand,
you'll understand."
Understanding in the heart
not just the head.
But if no one "reaches out"
no one understands;
and if no one understands
everyone is just—well—
w-a-s-t-e-d.
Like every day
maybe twice a day,
families gather around
family tables,
eating,
sharing food.
Far too often the
food
is all that is shared.
The stomach is all
that is satisfied.
No chemical
interaction—
understanding
among the people.
Nothing passes
between
them
but platters of meat
and bowls of vegetables.

"Pass the potatoes,"
"Who won the game today?"
"What game?"
"Man, it's hot."
"The meat tastes funny."
Bodies
filling chairs
don't make a family.
Hands meeting
on a salt shaker
aren't necessarily
communicating.

Hungry hearts
aren't filled
by
potatoes.

Funny, though,
this "between."
I can have words
with all kinds of people,
and smiles
and compliments
and congratulations;
and it can amount to
nothing
but phony
meaningless
noises.
It's between all right
but not real—
any more than
a stomachful of water
is a real
full stomach.
Something is missing if I
talk for an hour
a month
years,
and say nothing.

I can go to the inner city
or to a different church
or to a different school
and look
and look
and look
but see nothing.
I look
AT them;
they look
AT me.
But if nothing happens,
nothing between us,
it means nothing but
BLANK—
like Brick and Big Daddy.
I can give millions
to charity—
and have none;
I can read all kinds of books
about poetry—
without understanding a thing about it;
look at every painting ever done—
and see no beauty.
For all my effort
I can still be
empty
untouched
hungry,
because something that
could have
happened
should have
happened—
didn't.
It didn't used to be that way.
The island I mean.

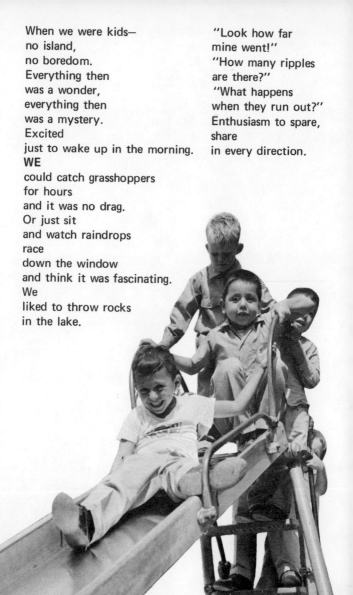

When we were kids—
no island,
no boredom.
Everything then
was a wonder,
everything then
was a mystery.
Excited
just to wake up in the morning.
WE
could catch grasshoppers
for hours
and it was no drag.
Or just sit
and watch raindrops
race
down the window
and think it was fascinating.
We
liked to throw rocks
in the lake.

"Look how far
mine went!"
"How many ripples
are there?"
"What happens
when they run out?"
Enthusiasm to spare,
share
in every direction.

Rocks,
dogs,
trees,
tin soldiers
made for a thousand
daydreams,
a million secrets.
It was a ball
to roll in the grass
watch airplanes
play "kick the can"
at night
under the streetlight.

Life didn't
stay like that
long enough.
Somewhere
the wonder was lost,
no more questions,
no real questions.

Now
only questions about how to get
here or there,
or how to solve a math problem
to get a good grade;
how to keep everyone
off my back.
But not **REAL** questions,
not important ones
like when I was a child.
What happened?

How did the joy of "we"
when I was
ONE
with the grass and rocks
sunshiny mornings and lamplit streets
other kids
toys
games
turn into the separation of "I"?
I don't
even feel
ONE
with myself any more!
Where
did all that sunshine go?
Where
did I lose touch with him,
that child
who used to be me?
Did I just outgrow him?
Like his cowboy boots?
Are wonder
involvement
oneness
the between things—
only for children?

Maybe it wouldn't
HAVE
to be that way.

Right now I feel something
deep down
boiling,
that wants to explode
like a volcano.
Because I am sick of being
shut out
cut off
from what is real.

Sick of being tied down
to a role;
sick of playing the game:
"Who are you?"
"Well, my folks have a boat . . .
drive a Caddy,
have a summer cabin . . . "
"OH—that's who you are."
Forget it!
No one **IS** what he has.
"Who is that man?"
"He's worth a million dollars—
that's who he is."
But only things
have worth;
people have
dignity
because they **ARE**
people,
not mansions
tree stumps
nor inboard motors.

I got to break away
from being a slave,
a slave to my fears
my doubts,
to what my friends wear,
or where they go
or what they do.
I'm sick of trying to fit a
groove
that doesn't fit me.
Because I'm not
a thing.
I don't have a price tag
or a label.
I don't want to
look like
think like
act like
everyone else.
I want to be
ME.

Dr. Seuss
writes for children.
But he knows lots of things.
Like he says,
"Today you are you!
That is truer than true.
There is no one alive
who is you-er than you.
Shout loud, 'I am lucky
to be what I am.'
Thank goodness I'm not just
a clam or a ham
or a dusty old jar
of sour gooseberry jam."

See,
I'm not a clam either,
and I'm not one of just
"everybody";
and I'm not
"nobody."
I'm
ME.
I really feel an urge to
be free.
But not just free **FROM**;
I mean free **TO.**
Not just free
from crawling—
that's not enough;
I want to be free
to fly!
free to choose
my own thing;
free to become
me.
To think what I think,
not
what I am simply
supposed to think—
and I know
I have to decide.
I can choose
NOT to choose—
think—decide
become.
I can see the
responsibility and
RUN—
oh man, how I can
RUN—
back to the herd
and fade into
everybody.

But I'm through with all that,
yes sir;
I want to escape
this crummy groove,
this cut off island.
I want to leap off
to swim away.
I want someone to show me
where
to find **REAL** singing
and crying
and blood
and sweat
and hopes—
meaning.
I want someone to teach me
how
to connect with it.
Connect so there might be
something going
between
me and my world again.
With no more
boredom
frustration
isolation.
I am called me—
Someone
special—
and I want to share
the Special-ness of
Me.
At least
that's how I feel
right now.

"With
all beings
and
all things
we shall
be as
relatives."

(Sioux Indian)

"Centuries ago,
civilization
acquired the
certain
knowledge
that man
had emerged
from
barbarity
on to the
degree that
he recognized
his relatedness
to his
fellow man."

(Martin Luther King, Jr.)
I HAVE A DREAM

"A man
was starving
in Capri;
He moved
his eyes
and looked
at me;
I felt
his gaze,
I heard
his moan,
And knew
his hunger
as my own . . . ."

(Edna St. Vincent Millay)
RENASCENCE

But sharing is,
has to be,
a between thing.

Ted
said the prayer.
Jill
said it was the first
formal prayer
Ted ever said.

This was a very different,
not like in
the slick magazines,
Thanksgiving dinner.
The table was
wobbly—
one leg broken—
borrowed silverware
peanut butter jars
for glasses.
"Sit easy on that chair—
it tips."

Jill's house.
She is
a volunteer ghetto worker
with Ruth and Donna;
they live poor
because
the people they love
are poor.
And they live with
these people.
It is their
daily bread.

Ted
and Jackie and Davida
have come 2000 miles to be
with
Jill;
they are friends.

Nate and Ralph are there,
each nine years old,
each homeless,
each loved
by Jill
and Ruth and Donna.
They're excited;
they've never come to a table where
anything more than food
was offered.
Jack and Gary are
there too.
They talk too loud
about getting drunk
about girls they conned
about how bad they are.
They run down
like clocks
because
no one is listening to their words,
only to the fear
which forges their self-hatred.
Their empty words—
like a blacksmith,
pound!
bong!
hammer in place.
They want to leave
escape
but Jill won't let them.
"This is Thanksgiving—
you'll eat with us."
Gary whispers to Jack
"We don't belong here,
let's split."

Jill seats them at table.
Three clergymen are there,
friends from the neighborhood,
present as friends
as ones who belong.

Dinner is served.
Cheap wine
poured with authentic
friendship
tastes like vintage.
A big ham
is placed on the wobbly table;
all is ready.
Then silence.
A holy moment.
Every faith
color
background
together at one table,
in reverence
as friends.

The food waits
the heart fills.
People from
Louisiana
New York
Nebraska
Missouri
California
gathered around this unlikely feast
in this unlikely place.
In each mind
in each heart—
thoughts.
For some
memories of oceans
of sun,
thoughts of plenty.
For others
memories of want
of hatred,
thoughts of hunger.

For some
memories of need
fulfilled,
thoughts of God.
All quiet now—
thinking.

Someone suggests a prayer.
"Ted
will you say the prayer?"
But "prayers" aren't
in Ted's line.
He has never said a "prayer."

"God"
is an alien word.
Pray to whom? To what?
FOR what?
The table waits.
Ted is embarrassed, confused.

He looks around
then softly says
"peace."
The meal begins—
the eating part, I mean.

Jill says she
loves
just **loves**
ham.
A clergyman, Father B.C.
laughs,
"A couple months ago
you mentioned it;
we remembered,
so we got ham."
Jill stares, amazed
humbled,
that someone listened
cared enough to listen and
remember.
Nate
reaches for seconds already.
Gary laughs,
the meal continues.
So different
than other Thanksgiving dinners
where so many people
eat big
talk little
finish up fast.
The whole meal
only for the stomach;
nothing else
between
the people gathered there.
No soul
no Spirit
included or invited,
I guess
to some Thanksgiving dinners—
each fancy place setting
marking off
the territorial limits
of each little island.

People,
like islands,
need bridges—
a way to cross over
speak
reach
see
over all that
dead water.
It is the only way.
Because
people aren't
people,
not real people
without that bridge;
and the only action,
the only real action,
takes place
on the bridge
"between" people.
So if I
wait,
you wait,
everyone waits.

When I don't start
you don't start.
Nobody arrives.
No builders,
no bridges.
The meaning of the world
doesn't change;
it always stays the same—
same hopes
same challenges
same tragedies
same fears and victories.
What does change
is my involvement with it—
my awareness
my understanding
my growth.
And growth is only
the deepening
of what passes
between
the World
and Me.

There is a difference
between reading about
a guy getting stomped,
and having the knocks
on your own head;
just like there is a difference
between hearing about the war
and being there—
shooting at
and
being shot at.
So much difference between
talking about love
and actually being able to love
and receive another's love.
It's a different thing to watch
a TV show about poverty,
and loving someone
who is actually poor
(which is the closest we can come
to understanding poverty
if we aren't poor ourselves).
You know—
the difference between

observing
and
participating.
So different because
one
only pretends
to care,
the other
prepares
to share.

It IS
the truth
the spirit
of what passes
BETWEEN
You
and the world
in which you live.
A man can only
"have"
by participating in.
Like
people say
"I hope you have
happiness."
But happiness
is not something you have;
it can't be counted
stored
programmed into a computer.
The harder you try
to have it
grab it
capture it
cage it
the more it slips away.
Happiness
is kind of like diving into
a cold pool
on a hot day;
you can only have the
cool—wet—experience
by letting the water
have you.
Happiness
isn't a question
of having
but of
being.

No one can give you
happiness
tied up
in a box,
but they can cause you to
BE
happy.

You are happy
if
between you
and that friend
that dance
that party
that school,
there exists
the chemical
interaction
which is called happiness.

If you
respond
to the possibility,
happiness happens.
Because it has been created
in you
and by you
for another
and by another.
Possibility
meets
possibility
on the bridge.
There is no other way.
People say you
have courage—
meaning to say you
are brave.

You are brave if
between you
and that challenge
that fear
that obstacle
that danger,
the call is heard
and a response is returned.
You can't have courage
or carry it around like change
in your pocket.
Real things
aren't like that.
Real things
are
Between things,
living things.

Most of all
you don't **have** love.
Love exists
between
you and another person—
reaching
creating
at both ends.
If love isn't given away
it dies;
if love doesn't create
it withers;
if it doesn't reach out
it falls.

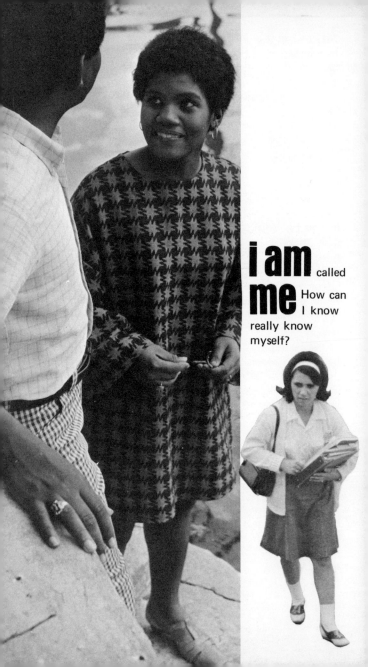

i am
me called
How can I know
really know
myself?

You must ask someone
who loves you.
Only someone who loves
you
can tell
you
who you are.
For only they **see** you—
see you as unique.
Not just another body
among billions of other bodies
at a beach on a hot day;
a face among a sea of faces—
two eyes
one nose
so what else is new?
When you are the
ONE loved
you are different,
different from all others.
Between you
and the one who loves you
something unique
in all the world
is happening.
Your love
has made that person
as different
as that person's love
has made you.
Without you
the whole world
is different.
The dance
is different,
the game
is different,
the walk by the lake
is different.

You have become part of
the one you love;
the one you love is part
of you.
Between you two—
who are now called
WE—
there are no longer
my things or
your plans,
my problems or
your good news.
Now only
our things, our plans—
ours
Ours
OURS.

Suddenly
it hits you—
how poverty-stricken
underprivileged
down and out
you were when all you had
were
my things.
How,
you wonder,
did I ever,
EVER
get along
that way—
on my little island, alone.
Now there is a new kind
of presence
in the world,
just born new,
first time new.

Now
the craziest things,
things you shared,
jokes
ticket stubs
a song
a meeting place in the park
take on gigantic
MEANING.
You leave the island
because somehow
in the mystery and wonder
of a child again
(but now different,
deeper, better)
the one you love
is
present in that
joke,
ticket stub,
song lyric,
meeting place
you shared
between
the two of you.
All of a sudden
these weren't things at all—
not just
paper stubs
sounds on a radio
a clearing in the park,
but a touchable,
tangible presence
of someone.

Because these things got
caught up
between
you and the one you love
and got
shot through
lit up
made valuable
with the love that
exists there.
To love
is to discover
who that person is
I call **ME.**

But saying
(and meaning)
"I love you"
is lots harder than saying
"Leave me alone."
Easier to say
"I have"
than
"I am."
Easier to
exist alone
than to
live between.
If between
you
and
me
nothing passes,
I make you
no one
as I am
no one.

If between me
and that beautiful
flower
or painting
or girl;
if between me and that
tragic
war
or riot
or murder
or suffering;
if between me and the
PEOPLE
who are
happy
or sad
or searching
or hurt,
nothing passes—then
I am not only dead,
I don't even
REALLY
exist.
Because life doesn't simply
dwell in me, but
passes
like blood
in a life-giving transfusion
between
me
and all that is.

We need others
not
so we can
"practice virtue"
as our
"ticket to heaven";

we need others
so we,
as individuals,
can grow
can become
genuine people—
able to make a
togetherness
with others.

Everyone needs
security,
recognition,
a sense of belonging
to make it at all;
but these things don't just
sprinkle down
from "up there" somewhere.
Islands aren't bridged
like that—
it takes people.

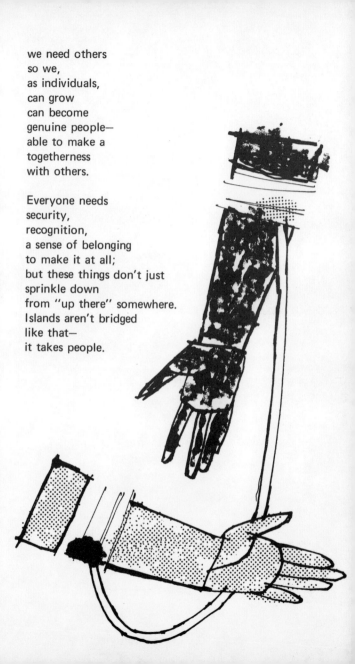

Once in Detroit
on a cold, miserable
Saturday night
in front of a TV
sat Charlie—
alcoholic
suffering
hands and feet wrapped in
puffy bandages
frostbitten fingers and toes—
pitiful sight.
Couldn't even hold
a cigarette.
Watery-eyed afraid
lip-quivering
sick—heartsick.
In walks the clergyman,
who runs the house
for Charlie
and the others.
He puts his arm around Charlie
lights him a smoke
makes small
but meaningful talk.
And between
them something passes.
Charlie changes.
He is secure
because someone
gave him security.
He needed
that arm
that smile
that cigarette
that word.
He needed that man.
One cigarette, one smile had
meaning
because they passed
between
two people.

always trying to
prove something.
Mr. G. works in East L.A.
he tries to cool things
prevent rumbles
help out.
He's tough, a good guy who
used to be a pro boxer.
He says,
"Why fight in the alley
for nothing, Chico?
The alley
is nothing.
I'll teach you—
get in the Golden Gloves.
For real."

recognition.
So who needs the alley any more?
Chico met
(looked at)
thousands of guys before;
nothing happened.
He met Mr. G. and
". . . who needs the alley any more?"
Something happened
because two people,
a "me" and a "he"
came halfway
to become a
WE.
They escaped out-of-it-ness.

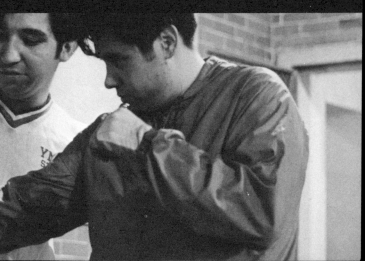

A sense of belonging?
Betty Lou
"belonged" to her mother
but she lived
at the orphanage,
because her mother
worked nights
slept days
somewhere downtown.
The court said
"No life for a kid,"
so Betty Lou—
age 12
sandy hair
freckled
blossoming—
waited on Sundays
like the other
unorphaned
orphans
for her family to come
at visiting hours.
Most Sundays
nobody came
to visit anybody.
And then
you told the other kids—
and they told you—
how busy,
very busy
their mothers, dads,
aunts, grandmas
were.
Or you said,
"Maybe they had an accident . . ."

That was it—an awful accident
on the way here—
because they said,
they **PROMISED**
they were coming.
They said "for sure"
this time.
"Something must have happened,"
you said to the other kids.
And they said to you
as you put away
your Sunday clothes,
"Grandma must be sick."
"Something must have come up
at the last minute—
something **important!**"
Strange
on those Sundays when the
two o'clock bus
didn't bring anybody
the cook always stayed late
to make ice cream.
So what if she did
miss her own bus?
So what if she did
have to go home in the dark?
Her little gift
of ice cream
was all she had to give
to Betty Lou
and the others
who waited
Sunday to Sunday
on the middle of the bridge;
and brother,
she was going to give it!
It mattered.

Look around.
Each happy
authentic
genuine
person who exists is
tangible evidence of
individuals who met
and touched
interacted
came to life—
became **we** by
creating a bridge between
themselves
and others.

People who
have sunk,
shipwrecked their lives,
are examples of
lonely "I's."
They never knew
or lost
or forgot
the certainty that comes from
"You better believe
someone cares!
That's why I'm
ME."

But sometimes it is so hard—
like impossible—
to connect
to form this
togetherness.
Why?
Maybe Shelley Berman
points to an answer.

He does a crazy routine about a
"great lover" who
uses all his charms but
gets nothing but the cold shoulder,
is mocked when he flashes his whitest,
toothiest
most winning smile.
Later he discovers—
oh no!—
a piece of spinach
caught in his front teeth.
Shelley forgot
to check out his mirror.
The people we come in contact with
are mirrors
in whom we can
recognize
judge
know
ourselves.
Don't look
and you
won't see;
don't see
and you won't know.
Just maybe,
if folks seem to be
unimpressed
disinterested
turned off
by us,
we should take a closer look
in the mirror
of other people.
They are saying something.

The only way
to know yourself—
which is to find meaning—
is to look

to reach
to go halfway
across the bridge.
Self
is found
BETWEEN
me and all else
that **IS.**
Unless
I become
we
in another,
I'm
a born loser.
We need
common-unity.
Need it
if our meals are to be
more than just
sessions of stomach-filling;
if our homes
schools
country
world
are to be more than just
lonely crowds
of people
living next to and
looking **AT**
each other;
fearing each other
using each other.
No one ever beat the odds
of island life—
only palm trees
make it alone.
Even that dude
Robinson Crusoe
had Friday.

man, there is just no other way!

"The real weakness of the idea
that God will do everything
is its false conception of both
God and man. It makes God
so absolutely sovereign that man
is absolutely helpless . . . .
Our age-old and noble dream
of a world of peace may yet
become a reality, but it will
come neither by man working alone
nor by God destroying the wicked
schemes of men, but when men
so open their lives to God
that he may fill them with love,
mutual respect, understanding
and good will."

(Martin Luther King, Jr.)
I HAVE A DREAM

3. god's

thing

So then
who needs God?

If the possibility
of real meaning
exists "between"
you
and
me
who are brave enough to risk
sharing
and become
a we,
then
who needs God?
WE
can do it alone.

"Okay"
lots of people say.
"We prayed,
gave God His due.
Now let's get down
to the old nitty gritty.
Let's talk about
the real world—
things like money
for poverty programs,
more police to stop riots,
more soldiers to fight the war,
more foreign aid to
poor countries . . . ."
BUT
regardless of wealth
power
force,

the only revolution
that will ever make
any real difference
is one of the heart—
inside.
Without this,
everything planned
or promised
by presidents
or prophets
is no go.

In the real world,
what is real?

Money?
How many billions
have we spent "fighting poverty,"
building
huge high rise housing complexes
that couldn't be homes—
so we ended up with
billion-dollar poverty
instead of penny-ante poverty?

How real is power?
It takes how many police to stop a riot?
But squashing a riot doesn't squash
hatred—
from which riots spring.

What about **force**?
How many soldiers
will "win" a war?
How many soldiers
and civilians have
died
violently
in all of human history—
from Cain
to the latest Vietnam casualty—
all for their own cause
their own reason
their own purpose?
Millions are destroyed;
and violence and war
are still
with us.

We send money
grain
farm equipment
personnel
thousands of miles away
to gain the friendship
trust
good will of our million
faraway brothers
who accept all we give—
then
stone our embassy.
Money alone can't buy it—
trust and respect
I mean.

Once you think on it
you
feel like
EXPLODING!
"Let's do something
REAL,
something
HONEST,
something
that **MATTERS.** "

What is real?
God is.
"Yeah?
What can God do?"

Do?
God doesn't just
do things.

He **IS** someone.
Someone who
IS
here and now—
always was—but
we have held God off,
pushed Him away
put Him
"out there"
in the furthest boundaries
of human life.
"We have fashioned Him,"
as Martin Luther King
said so well,
" . . . a cosmic bellhop."
Need a cure?
Ring up for God.
Want sunshine for your picnic?
God handles weather problems.

Nervous about your algebra finals?
Have a word with the Super Tutor.
Whenever our own power
looks shaky
or runs out
we look "up there," and
call for
the God who fills in the limited
power gaps
of human beings doing
things.
He is
beyond
over
around
life,
never IN life.
For emergencies only,
like a fire extinguisher.

As man's power grows—
his understanding
technology
scholarship—he
becomes increasing master
of his world;
and God
like a blacksmith
faced with the Model-T
is slowly
drummed out of business—
another victim of
automation.
We don't need to do
a rain dance
to God
or even pray
for rain.

Instead,
send up a plane
salt the clouds—
rain for sure.
(More efficient;
easier on the knees.)
And someday we'll control
earthquakes—
all of nature.
And technology
and genetics
and science will
retire God.

Who needs God?
Maybe,
for all our smart, handy, ingenious
mastery of the world
we got God
all wrong
to start with.
Maybe God
isn't just "up there" after all.
(. . . "Hey, man, I think I see His feet
sticking out of the clouds" one turned-off
kid said.)
Maybe He doesn't just
wait for us to push the old
panic button,
ring Him up
when we need more muscle.
Maybe for all our shouting and grabbing
"out there"
He has been
right here all the time.
INSIDE life—
inside where bridges are made,
where the **between**
of you and me becoming
we
makes existence **LIFE**,
not just survival.
Maybe God has something to do
with nitty gritty
REAL things
like
friendship
like
love
like
trust—
with people becoming more like
people,

instead of half-human hermits
barricading themselves behind their
hang ups
on their little islands.
Maybe God's "thing"
isn't so much to decide when
the winds blow
or rain falls
or who wins the football games
or passes a test,
but more with
"Why don't some people ever get a break?"
"Why is my home so miserable?"
"Why are reform schools always so full?"
"Why so many riots and wars?"
"Why does the word 'brother' make so many people
gag?"
Maybe this
is more God's thing.
Yo-yoing nature
is simple stuff.
Maybe His real business
is Big Time stuff,
really hard things like
"Reach out your hand—you'll understand"
and planning island escapes.
Like enabling us **NOT** just to
look **AT** people,
but to **SEE** them as
unique individuals
who have pride—and need pride,
dreams—which may or may not come true,
fears—to meet each day,
secrets—that are theirs alone;
to see each man
each woman
each child
as capable of fantastic growth.

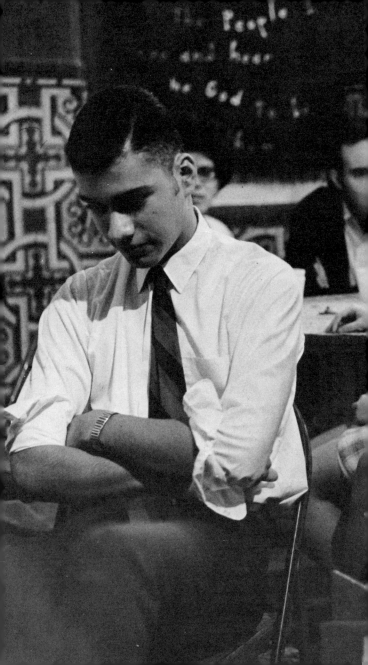

"This little fella here's gonna be President someday!"

Maybe.
But even if he doesn't
he can stand as tall as any man—
with pride—
no matter what he does.

Maybe this is God's
thing—
not looking down from above,
pulling our puppet strings,
causing all the ups and downs
in our life,
ready to strike fast
if we goof.

Yet,
we still say
"Why does God do it?"
But is it God who does it?
God doesn't want
war
or riots
or starvation.
It isn't God's will that man
destroys man.
It isn't God's will
that cities burn
and wasted people
keel over from hunger.
God doesn't make cannons smoke.
He makes people **FREE** to choose.
God breathed
His Spirit
into man,
spoke to man
His Word—
who is Light
Truth
the Way;
and God said, "Choose!"

It is man
and man alone who
chooses
to make war, create
human misery.
God's thing is making
possible
another way.
God
challenges
calls
inspires
lifts
influences man
in the world
TODAY—
on the narrow bridge
between you and me
where **WE** become us:
brothers,
who will not
would not
could not
destroy one another.

****

"Life is something of a great triangle.
At one angle stands the individual
person, at the other angle stand
other persons, and at the top stands
the Supreme, Infinite Person, God. These
three must meet in every individual life if
that life is to be complete." Martin Luther King, Jr.

****

God
can never fit
in a picture frame
or in someone's words
or totally in one person's experiences.
He just isn't the answer
to some teachers' questions.
For some
He is so **REAL**
they can't even start
to talk about Him.

Yolanda met the Indian
on the midnight run.
Greyhound Express
heading north.
Strange pair.
Neither
would have "chosen" the other
to sit next to.
Yolanda—pretty
smartly dressed
bright eyed
a college sophomore majoring in sociology
going back to school.
The Indian—a laboring man,
his clothes said so
ageless,
(hard to tell about Indians).
Someone had told him
they were hiring
up north.
Side by side amid the stale smoke,
squirming sleepers,
drone of the humming engine—
each heading north
toward his own
hopeful tomorrow.

Too much to think about
so neither slept.
Yolanda studied the Indian
out of the corner of her eye,
decided he was safe,
so she spoke first—
small talk
going back to school
the weather.
Things.

The Indian listened,
but didn't say much.
What did he know
about talking to city girls,
rich, talkative girls
who went to college?
He didn't read books
didn't even like to chitchat
with anyone.
He wished she would pick on someone else
or just look out the window.
But Yolanda
was interested in people,
and not one bit tired,
so on she went.
The Indian listened.

Two a.m.—Yolanda
is talking theology class now:
about God.
The Indian stared
into the silent darkness
listening and wanting,
wanting so much
to tell this girl
about the reservation.

He **WANTED** to say,
"Last year
on the plains
in a place you can't imagine,
an old man froze to death in his
tar-paper shack;
a young boy got tuberculosis—
they took him away.
We have no doctors, no medicine,
out there.
Packs of dogs run loose—
wild dogs.
Our good school teachers
wouldn't stay.
Our food goes bad; so everybody
is hungry
all the time.
Our babies
don't look like babies—
they look old right from the start.
What does the God,
your God,
the God you study
say about this?"
But he didn't
say anything
because what could this rich girl,
this student of God
know about
wild dogs and moldy meat?
What could she know,
sitting there in her fancy clothes,
about cold wind and bare arms,
about needing practically everything
and having nothing?

If
he had the words
he would tell her about
his God;
the God who is like
the burning sun setting
behind the rim of the earth
each night;
like the wind
always blowing on the prairie—
the Spirit who makes all things
one—
the rabbits and coyotes
and never-young babies
and heart-crippled men.
The God who always
moves a man on,
going somewhere,
going home.
But she wouldn't know about this;
and he—
he didn't have the words.

Yolanda tried
to look into her silent companion.
He seemed faceless—
dark skin
black hair.
His manner said nothing,
revealed nothing.
Just a drifter she decided,
not very friendly,
nothing on the ball.
Five a.m.
silence.

Sun just bursting,
(the Indian greets his friend).
The long night ride is over.
Everybody out.
Yolanda to school,
off with her red alligator luggage,
off to her books, her friends,
her real life.
The Indian too—
off with his carefully tied bundles,
off to find a cup of coffee and then
the "man who is hiring."

God
does not fit into a frame.
God
is not just answers in a book,
or court of last appeal,
or super wizard—
know what I mean?
He is real,
and He asks real
personal communication
with us.
It is **great**
to gain scientific control
of the earth,
to learn the parts of things
and how
to make them work.
But
people are not things.
Things are meant
to be controlled.
People are not.
We keep forgetting this.

So many shake their heads,
"Man,
we put three guys in orbit
around the moon—
why can't we stop the war?"
But
they are
two different ball games—
one involves things
made of parts,
the other involves man
who is more than just parts.
If we treat people
as things—
things that present
problems—
then we
can never
discover
their
true dignity.
People are endless mysteries,
not problems—
mysteries made up of
honor
dreams
vision
the door
to countless other doors,
to endless meetings,
the temple of God.
Maybe
this is why
there are so many
messes
in the world,
why so much
doesn't make sense.
Because we forget
man is living
and must reach out

on the bridge
between God and man:
to his brothers.

Ann,
such a beautiful girl,
a doll,
brimming over with light
stood waiting for a bus.
A car drove up.
Six boys
gawking.
Out to prove their manhood.
The door opens,
"Get in
we'll give you $10."
Ann moves away.
The boys get out.
Ann runs to safety,
terrified
shaking.
"How much
are you worth?"
they had asked.
$10?
$20?
$50?
But only things
have price tags.
People have dignity,
beyond price.
Ann—
more beautiful
than any spaceship,
more wonderful
than any orbit—
treated as many people are
as less
than a thing.

EVERY TIME
we do this,
look out,
here come more messes!
Because something is missing:

the something that allows us to
control nature
beautiful days
plenty of rain—
yet still kill our
brothers
on these perfect days;

the something that is missing
when we can
analyze murder
theorize endlessly about broken homes
about juvenile delinquency
about violence—
and always have another riot
to suffer through;

the something that is missing when we can
cure polio
transplant organs
greatly prolong life—
and yet perfectly healthy men
stockpile atom bombs;

the something that is missing when we have
better job training
more parks
head-start programs—
but the crime rate goes
up and up.

All these scientific victories
are not only
noble,
they are necessary.
Because
they are human.
But something is missing.
The something that
makes man—
you
me
him—my neighbor
more than his parts;
that makes **ME**
an essential element of
WE.

Without this
"Something that is missing"
(the ability to create bridges)
I look at
but do not see,
and not seeing I do not love,
and not loving I do not understand
because
"I only understand what I love."
That is why men
still make perfect days
on which to shoot each other;
build supersonic aircraft
to fly over
burning cities of hate;
whisk men to the moon
for a faraway look at this earth
where thousands starve each day.

"Brother,"
we are told
"build up the earth."
With what?
Just bricks,
just steel,
just cement
just super space-age plastics?
These can't do the job.
This is
to eat a meal that is just
food
and nothing more.
This is
to come away hungry,
unsatisfied
aching
for something else—
but
for what?

For God
Who
IS
and illuminates
the Limitless in Man,
calling from deep to deep—
from man to himself;
calling the separateness
of islands into the
Oneness of himself.
God, who
doesn't just sit
on the world's sidelines
waiting
for man's power
knowledge
control
to fail and in failing

make Him necessary.
God, who
is not at the
end
of man's rope,
but where the glory
the mystery
the wonder
of man **begins**
and reaches out
to another man,
another island:
people together
instead of
things alone.
That
is what we are doing—
all of us
every day in
every act—
building a world.
"Me alone"
is an impossibility
anyway.
I affect
and am affected
by all around me.
The world has shrunk,
Mr. Jones;
you **ARE** involved
like it
face it
accept it
or not.
Someone
in Southeast Asia
starts a war
and I may
die.

A thousand miles away
a switch is thrown,
a fuse blows
a generator breaks down
and my city's lights go out.
India or Italy or Iceland
are not so far away.
Turn on the TV and see
people there **NOW**,
TODAY,
prospering, partying
or
starving.
A steel strike ups prices—
all prices.
So fewer buy—
less money around;
harder to borrow—
higher interests.
I don't know steel from
cornflakes;
I don't know
the persons responsible,
but they have affected me.

Someone in Paris
has an idea—
the hemline is **here** this year;
buy accordingly.

The world shrinks,
converges
more and more
every day.
I am part of that world,
for better or worse;
I don't want it to blow up
and
I don't want it
ONLY
not to blow up.
I want our world
to be all
God had in mind
when He made it
in the first place—
GOOD.

" . . . They asked him,
'Is it against the law to cure a man on
the sabbath day?' hoping for something to use
against Him . . . He said to the man, 'Stretch out
your hand.' He stretched it out and his hand
was better, as sound as the
other one. At this the
Pharisees went out and
began to plot against
him.''

(Mt. 12:10-14)

4 Jesus
tore
'em up!

Ever peel the hide
off a baseball?
Bands and bands of rubber
or twine
inside.
Golf balls, too—
the core makes the ball.
Seeds
are the life center of apples and
tungsten
in light bulbs
produces light.

BUT
HOW CAN A GUY
GET WITH
GOD'S ACTION?

Even celery has a heart.

The world, too,
converging,
drawing in on itself,
must have a
center
core
heart—
around which it evolves and
from which it draws its life force.
But
where is it?
And what is it?
Maybe the real question is not
where
or
what,
but
who?

The world is not a
grapefruit and
people are not
seeds and
What
indicates **things.**

The world isn't just a global mass of
continents and oceans which are only
things;
the world
is
People
who are created to become
human beings
(as caterpillars to be butterflies,
as tadpoles to be toads).
Beginnings are not endings
any more than oaks are acorns.
As surely as seeds must
burst
into life,
people must
burst
into the fullness of
common-unity
which is
life
together.

Pulsating
Breathing
Bleeding
Warm
Conscious
is the world:

"My brother went to Vietnam today;
I feel like crawling in a hole."
"These riots scare me to death."
"Let's have a party tonight!"
"My friend snubbed me today."
"I hate school."
"Not meat loaf **again tonight?!**"
The world is that
kind of scene—
HUMAN.

The world operates
as humans
operate—
because the people of the world
are not objects
dotting the globe like waterways
or palm trees
or apples
or any other
thing.
So maybe the question isn't
where or
what.
The world's core of life may be
something more **personal** like
in whom
does this core of life exist?

Man needs God
to be man,
for man is
of
God.

Is it God, then?
Is He the "in whom"?

But how can I get to God, or
how can I know what He wants me to know?
How does He bridge the gap
between himself and us
in order that
We
may bridge the gap
between
each other?

His name was
Word,

The Word,
spoken by God to
man.
Jesus—He
did the business.

It's possible,
really possible,
to have 20/20 eyesight, and
hear snow fall
but to be deaf and blind
to the Word.
When Jesus first came,
teaching,
working,
shaking folks to honesty,
they were deaf and blind to Him
who is the Word.
They missed Him
not because they all needed glasses
and hearing aids,
but because
they were looking for something else—
a general
lots of power.
"Smack the Romans down."
"Let's build a nation
The nation,"
"Nobody will touch us!"

Jesus said
YES.

But not to what they wanted.
Creating just "a" nation wasn't enough;
Jesus created
a whole Kingdom
for **all** mankind;
He didn't conquer,
He converted.

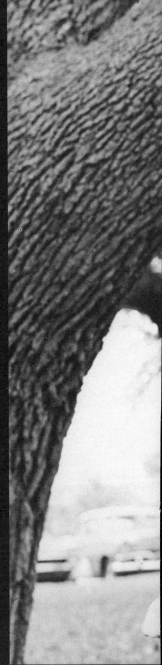

He called the Little People—
the quiet ones
who were meek enough to listen;
the poor ones
who didn't have so much
they had to spend all their time
protecting it,
and He said:
"I have news for you.
Good News.
God
is your Father,
so don't make light of it.
Believe me, I know.
I come from the Father
and I tell you it is true.
He
IS
Father.

And I'll tell you
something else.
Your phony
sacrifice and offerings
aren't good enough
for the Father.
That's why I took that
whip
and kicked the crooks out
of the Temple—
My Father's House.
They were making it
a slaughterhouse,
a supermarket.
My Father's House!

"This business of saying,
'Here God,
take this dove I offer—
it's good, pure—
but don't look at me'
has got
to stop.
It reeks.
Give yourselves
or give nothing,
because that's just what
empty sacrifice is—
Nothing.
You have memorized
a billion complicated laws.
I'll give it to you in one—
LOVE GOD.
And in **really** loving God
you'll have to love
your brother.
Because you
abide in him,
as you abide in me.

I have come to make you
strong,
fully strong.
Stronger than your dreams
of what you'll do to those
Roman soldiers
with those knives.
Yes, **those** knives,
hidden in your belts—
I see them.
I will make you so strong
that men will cut you,
throw you to animals,
kill you—
and you will march
to your death
singing
happy
Free.
And your tormentors will say,
'I don't believe it;
they are either crazy
or
they are
out of this world.' "

And Jesus said
"**Yes**
out of **your** world—
selfish man
proud man
hard-headed man—
out of **Your** world
because that prison
you call your life
is only big enough for one—
an empty
isolated
you.

"But
I have come
from your Father and mine
to speak
of the Real World which is
People.
Real People,
not rubber stamps
and
yes men
and
sellouts,
but Real People who can
Be
a Real Family—
because that's what you **ARE**:
a family.
We
are brothers
We
are sisters.
I
am the first-born of the brethren.
Abide in Me
as I in You
and We in the Father—
a family!

"Look in your hearts!
Whoever heard of brother
cheating brother?
What does your heart tell you
of cruelty,
selfishness,
blindness?
So much I see around here—
taking root in a family!

"We are
Together.
Happy is the one who
doesn't think
he is so big
so smart
so self-sufficient
that he doesn't need
or want
his family members.
There is only **one way**
a family can work.
You know it's true—
just look around.
I bring you the possibility
of Peace.
Not the slavery
of the weak,
not the tyranny
of the power-mad
but the peace of real men
who are free.
Accept it and
live—or
refuse it and
die.
Put away your greed,
your selfishness
your hatred
your hardness of heart.
This is my World.
This is **The** Kingdom.
It is your world
if
you will take it,

if
you will hear the call
to Become
Children of God,
to Be
My Brothers."

So easy to miss Jesus—
to miss the Father,
to miss man.
So easy to go on
creating perfect days
on which we shoot each other;
perfecting fabulous satellites
so we can see
the day's war wounded carted off
in living color;

to build gorgeous houses
which will never be real
homes
because the people living there
don't know how to
speak
to one another.
Every day
we add on to
get the bugs out
spruce up
our incredibly doted-on world of **things,**
without improving
one bit
the people gap.

Ever see one of those
last-two-people-on-earth
AFTER-THE-BOMB
movies?
Without
other
people,
the whole magnificent world
and everything in it
could be
all yours;
BUT
you would truly
have
nothing
because
without people
the real meaning of this magnificent world is
wiped out.

Jesus got His hands dirty
His clothes sweaty, and
no doubt had headaches and tired feet
while working hard to
show

people how to be
real individuals
so they could join
other real individuals and become
a real family.
He wasn't taken in by
titles
degrees
or social position.
He took twelve of the
least likely
most ragged
uneducated men, and
showed them **who they were;**
revealed them
to
themselves;
hinted to them of their own
boundlessness;
taught them that true greatness is
the power of service.
He
breathed the Spirit into them—
set them on fire.
He
told them to go out and
make a Family
of mankind.
He gave them a **new** birth—
from death to life,
darkness to light.
He gave them a vision—
a Kingdom
a Way
the Truth.
He told them that,
as Children of God, they were

Precious,
Dignified,
All of them,
together,
of One Father.

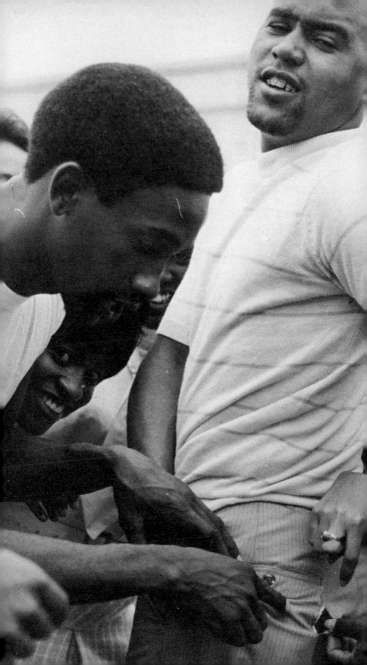

was what Jesus said
to those
first
twelve.
And that's not all.

He told them that
His
Their
Kingdom
was not "out there"
someplace, but
WITHIN—
like a fire in a hearth
that spreads,
warms,
transforms.
Within
is what He told them.

The elements of the world
come together,
converge until
"the world is our oyster"—
managed
controlled
by us
toward a point
of scientific perfection.
The people of the world
crowded up tight,
feel the squeeze
of the "small world"
they masterminded
until they are so close
there is no choice but to

rub elbows
brush hands
meet each others'
eyes.
ABIDE IN ME.

We look at our world
as we look at
a wide-screen movie—
detached, uninvolved,
strangers
not able or
not caring
to distinguish
the make-believe
characters
from the real-life people.
ABIDE IN ME.

"Who are you?"
"Your neighbor.
I live upstairs."
"Oh yeah?
I don't remember seeing
you around before—
are you new here?"
"This is my fifteenth year."
ABIDE IN ME.

"And today's ball scores are
6-3
5-2
1-0—
The week's war fatalities:
S. Vietnam—173
N. Vietnam—305
American—50
Others—59."
Click.
"So much for the scores;
guess I'll go to bed."
Like a game!
ABIDE IN ME.

"I always feel so alone—so
powerless
to change anything . . . "
ABIDE IN ME.

"Give 'em the Mace!"
"Set the dogs loose!"
"Get that guy!
   Get him!
   GET him!"
"We need more guns
   more guns
   more guns!"
ABIDE IN ME.

"Smash that window!
Grab that TV set
that liquor
that ring!"
"Shoot 'em from the windows!"
"Burn it, man, burn it!"
"Rip it apart!"
"Tear it down!"
"We need more ammo
more knives
more fire bombs
more guns
and guns
and guns."
More hatred, more fear,
more violence.
ABIDE IN ME.

The world shrinks.
Skin
touches
skin.
The elements unite and
so must brothers.
But how?
Standing alone
as on far-flung islands
yelling out
hopelessly
to each other?
Or
coming together as
the People of God,
abiding as a family
hooked-up
tuned-in
involved
building
through the first-born
of our family,
Jesus?

But how do we love
or even
see
Christ **in** someone?
How can He be
in there?
Is He floating around
with the breakfast bacon?
Or is He a little golden glow
like Tinkerbell
who skitters around hiding and only
peeks out
now and then?
How then?
Maybe it's better
to understand Christ's presence
as occupying that space
between
you and me—us.
Between Us
in unity—as a family.
Without coming together,
we don't make it.
No family;
no Presence.

We are present to Jesus
In
His Family;
He is present to us
In
our family:
Present as people who really
are
who really understand
who really care
are present to each other at a
genuine meal.

Not just filling chairs,
filling time,
filling stomachs
but **totally present** with
the between filled full up,
too—
no gaps,
no spaces,
no oceans
separating brother
from brother.
Present in the acceptance
reverence
respect
shown the weak
family member
by the strong,
shown the youngest by the oldest,
shown the sick by the well.
Present
on the bridge
which comes into being
only
when brothers yearn
for such a bridge to be.

To see Christ in someone
is to see that person
in Christ.
Special, that person—he's
one of us,—my
family;
To love Christ in someone
is to love that someone in Christ—
same family
same name
same life
same Father.

To love them
for who they are
and who
they are becoming—
in my family
which is our family
which is
God's family
gathered together
in Christ.

What is **In Christ**?
Nitty gritty like,
what does it really
mean?

The room was big but not big enough—
bursting with people
who were not just bodies but
real people.
First name basis, this group,
friends,
nobody ignored.
Father Tom started off,
"I am an alcoholic.
I know I am.
I thank God for it . . . . "
One of the visitors laughed,
"Come on!—you're kidding!
You can't really be
THANKFUL.
You're a dr---
I mean
an alcoholic!"

Father Tom smiled—
"You started to say 'a drunk,'
meaning a bum
a mess;
and that's right,
I was.
Down in the gutter, face down,
15 years of it.
As much as people hated me
I hated myself more—
GOD,
how I hated myself—
so much I chose
to run,
to stay drunk rather than
face myself.
I know what 'down' is.

I know
without God—
my 'power greater than myself'—
I'd be right back in the gutter,
'down.'
All right, be polite.
Call me a turned-on alcoholic.
It adds up the same:
God
is between me and that first drink,
which will never be my last.
I KNOW
I need God;
my alcoholism reminds me.
But you need Him, too, Mac—
everyone does
just as much as I do—
but you don't know it."

God—
in the distance
between.
The people in that packed room,
together
as Family
walked one night deeper
into that distance.
Each one
alone
had been 'down'—
tried everything from
pills to
hiding to
running to
ignoring—
everything but openness
to the power,
God

who takes His place in the **CENTER**
of life,
which is their life.
The God made present
through His Word—Jesus—
in whom we **ARE.**
Together
these people knew and understood
as family
what they had never
known or understood
as individuals
that they
NEEDED each other
even if at first they didn't
WANT each other.

Sometimes
what we want most
is what we need least.
"I stole shaving lotion to drink,"
one man said.
Sometimes
what we need most
we lose
because we wanted something else.
"My family threw me out,"
said the elderly fellow
with holes in his socks.

                    Trust
                    acceptance
                    humility
                    were present—
                    with Christ—
                    in that crowded room.

"I lay there in the park for two days."

                    No one looked superior,
                    condescending.

"My kids were ashamed to bring
their friends home . . . ."
No one faked "forgiveness,"
trying to play God.

"I never fixed dinner,
took care of the house—
nothing."
No one raised eyebrows.
Just a family
trying to live in God,
to seek Him
in each other;
to talk to Him,
through each other.

They drank coffee,
each cup filled to the brim
with the honesty
the security
of each other's presence.
Now
as family,
coffee was enough. It was, in fact,
just fine.

Pillars of the community, this group?
Oh no.
Good candidates for local office?
Not this term.
Not a fashion doll or business tycoon
in the room.
But common-unity?
Yes. Togetherness?
Oh yes!
Maybe **this** is the kind of thing "In Christ" is.
Not just strangers standing on top of
each other **AT** church services;
not just bodies filling chairs
around a silent
dinner table;

not nose-in-the-air
individuals
so carefully avoiding
bumping elbows
brushing hands
"minding their own business,"
going their own way—
at school or
in the neighborhood or
on the street or
at home.
That doesn't make it.
Christ isn't there.

But how can I
possibly
love Christ
in that person I don't like—
in that sour-tempered teacher,
in that grumpy, screaming neighbor,
in that stingy old man,
in that dirty, stinking old bum,
in that weird-looking classmate
with whom I have nothing—
but nothing—
in common?
How can Christ be in
them?

And what about
the other ones—
the people I really connect with?
You know—
my friends!
Do I love
them
or Christ **in** them?
Or what?

Maybe I can love
Christ in the people I don't like;
and the ones I do—
well,
no problem there—
I don't need Christ
to love them.
Does that sound okay?
ABIDE IN ME.

If Christ is the Special Life
in **all** of us,
then no one—
no matter how he looks
or acts
or smells—
should be cut off from the
trust
security
acceptance
due him
as a member of our family
born through Baptism
into Christ.

Why is it, then, that
(and it is true—just think)
there is nothing more
meaningless, more
hollow sounding
than saying
"Jesus loves you"?

But isn't Christ
in
all of us
like **life**
is in all of us—
but a
Special Life—
(the kind that is different
than the life, say, of a
dandelion or a salamander)
made deeper,
fuller
through the Word,
Jesus,
explaining to us what it's
all about?

Maybe I can love Christ
in that crabby teacher,
that malicious neighbor,
that smelly bum,
by loving **that person**;
and through him and
with him,
learn to love Christ
as part of my family—
whether that person is
up or down,
friend or enemy,
ugly or beautiful.
Maybe that person
Is the other half
of my bridge.

Why?
Why has the Truth
about our Family,
about our Way after the First-Born,
about our capacity to make
peaceful days
out of "perfect days"
become so
up-in-the-clouds remote?
So fuzzy and vague?
So funny-sounding to talk about?
Why doesn't it
GRAB?

Maybe because we SAY it
too much,
live it
too little.
How we love to theorize! And
theory is great
but
you can't eat it
wear it
feel it.
Theory won't make your ears warm
in a blizzard.
Theory can't put its arms around you
when you're discouraged
and
feel like crying—
only **PEOPLE** can.
People who make things happen
between
them.
People who don't mess around
trumpeting theories
but
put it on the line.

People like
Lincoln
Ghandi
Dr. King
Tom Dooley
the Kennedys,
and millions of others
not in the history books.
People!
whose lives—what they say and do—
maybe don't make any sense
except
"They're out of this world."
People!
whose very talking and walking
raise big questions,
irritating, persistent questions.
"Why is he doing that?"
"What's in it for him?"
"He must have an angle—but what?"
People!
who are possessed of a great secret
and a secret source of greatness,
daring to say with their lives
"Don't tell **me** it can't be done, Mac!
LOOK—SEE
I'm doing it
with my life!"

Maybe
these skyscraping people
are the reason
it seems so weird,
so uncomfortable,
to say
or to accept—
with simple sincerity—
"Jesus loves you."

Maybe
most of us stopped growing
when we started
talking so much.
Maybe
simplicity
only comes naturally to the
big guys;
and it is all of us—
who aren't that big—
who make the world so slow
to catch on,
to understand,
to **live**
the Supreme Simplicity of
"Jesus loves you."
And you know what,
Mrs. Robinson;
He really does.
The **WORD**—
Jesus—
walked our earth so long ago,
so perfectly,
Hurling the Challenge
Raising the Question
Offering the genuine possibility.
Maybe we—
you and me
our Church—
who live in the world today
don't
hurl a challenge or
raise a question or
offer a genuine possibility
for family life
in Christ.

" . . . the Church seeks but a
solitary goal: to carry forward
the work of Christ . . . And Christ
entered this world to give witness
to the truth, to rescue and not
to sit in judgment, to serve
and not to be served."

> (Document of Vatican II)
> THE CHURCH TODAY

"Every generation has its central
concern . . . today's young people appear
to have chosen for their concern the
dignity of the individual human being."

> (Senator Robert Kennedy)
> TO SEEK A NEWER WORLD

"Take up your quarrel with the foe;
To you from failing hands we throw
The torch; be yours to hold it high.
If you break faith with us who die
We shall not sleep."

> (Lieut. Col. John McCrae)
> IN FLANDERS FIELDS

S. DON'T JUST STAND THERE!

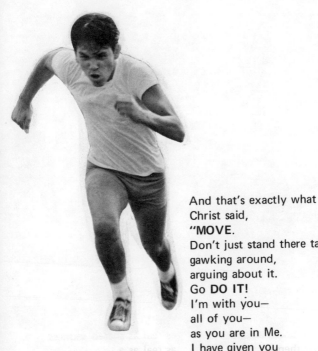

And that's exactly what
Christ said,
"MOVE.
Don't just stand there talking,
gawking around,
arguing about it.
Go **DO IT!**
I'm with you—
all of you—
as you are in Me.
I have given you
everything you need:
a Father
a home
a dream
a vision
a mission;
and not just "a" mission but
THE mission,
the only one that really counts

Now go make it work!
Make that man
that woman
those sinners and saints
understand
not only in their heads but
in their hearts
that they are not alone
on islands,
not forsaken at all.
Show them—
so they'll believe it—
that they are a family
In Me.
MY FAMILY!
(They have to know.)
I won't leave you
orphans
as you were before,
for I have claimed you,
all of you,
as My own.
I remain with you
in the Spirit
where it really counts."

His presence in the Spirit
is
REAL—
as real as shared sadness
as real as a
broken-in-half candy bar
as real as when
He pulled together
11 (Judas was a drop-out)
individuals,
homely and handsome,
quick and slow,
and made them a unit

because they dared to
count on each other.
Like a football team:
"Get that big dude!"
"I can beat that guy
in the flat—
hum it over his head."
They dared to
trust each other.
"Get behind me when
you run back that punt—
we'll rattle some bones!"
So they became winners
together.
It was spirit—
THE spirit—
that hooked up,
fueled up,
made champions of
11 very different individuals.

His presence in the spirit
is as real as
the tangible brotherhood
at a party,
a **real** party,
a real celebration
where people meet,
not just where
bodies congregate.
At real gatherings of
real people—**I AM THERE.**
We go together,
my brothers,
my family—
I in you and
You in Me.
We give out the good news:
All Men One.

He talked to them like that
one day—for the last time—
and then He,
Jesus,
(who had **promised** to stay)
was lifted up . . .
"Where did He go?"
Amazement.
"Where did He go?"
Fear.
"Where did He go?"
Anguish.
"Even He has betrayed us! I'm
cutting out."
"Now they'll kill us, too!"
And they gathered together
with His mother,
Mary . . .
alone again, doubting, despairing . . .
"I'm not going to get murdered.
Forget it!
I'm going home."

But then a great commotion
like wind
and fire
and noise
all at once shook them,
jolted and crashed and electrified
them.
"He's **HERE**.
I can't **see** Him—but for real
He,
Jesus,
is **HERE!**
Present among us, in us,
BETWEEN us,
we are **ONE**
In Him.

How could we have doubted?" But
wait!
"What are we doing in this room?
Didn't He,
Jesus,
tell us to move out,
march on,
go out and get lost in the thick of
man's life
in all men's feelings and
problems and fears and hopes?
Didn't He say
to make of all men
a Family?
So why are we hanging around **HERE**?"
And they tore the door down,
marched out into the city,
climbed up on hay carts and tree stumps—
before so many different people from
different places, you
WOULDN'T BELIEVE IT!
And they said,
"Look, brothers
We have news for you . . . . "

Two thousand years later
(seems like an awfully long time)
another man—
same job
same mission
same vision—
stood before a group of young people.
But there was sadness in his heart, because
the Word was spoken so long ago,
seems as if everyone would be
clued in by **now**—but no.
"What's your name?" he asked the blond boy.

"Bob."
"How long have you been in the Church?"
" 'In the Church?' . . . well, ah, I don't
know . . . all my life, I guess . . . 17 years."
"What's it all about?" the man asked.
Bob hesitated, looked around,
what kind of question was **that**?
Who knows, who cares "what it's all about,"
and besides—
it wasn't in the book!
But he feels kind of dumb anyway.
(After all,
he's been "in it" for
17 years.)
"I don't know,
get us to heaven, I guess . . . . "

The word wa

"How about you," the man asks a different boy.
"What's your name?"
"Pete."
Pete's a bit scared he'll get the
same dumb question—
what a stupid question!
He's thinking,
hard.
"What do you say, Pete? What's it
all about?"
"You mean the Church?"
"Yeah, the Church . . . . "
"Well, it keeps you out of hell and
teaches you how to do
right things,
you know, good things,
so you don't sin."
A hand shoots up.
"What's your name?"
"Steve, and I think . . . the Church is for
giving you grace
so you can keep all the laws of God."
Steve sits down, grinning.
How can you miss—
it's **got** to be grace!
Every religion book from the
first grade up
talked about grace!

poken so long ago!

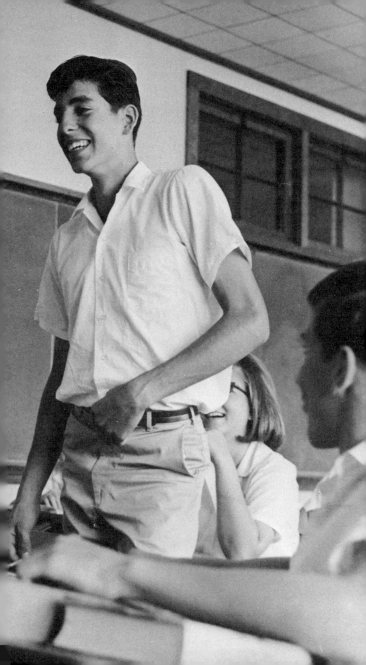

George figured the Church was a
building—
walls, a roof, fancy windows—
where people went to services.
And George
had a lot of company.
Most everyone there
figured the Church was a building,
usually too expensive
always too boring
never any action;
just a building—
like the Post Office or maybe a museum.

The Word was spoken so long ago!

But
the Church **lives**, Brother; it
LIVES
or it isn't the Church.
The Church is
NOT
a pile of bricks, and it is
NOT
just another institution or organization
like the Red Cross or
ladies aid society, and it is
NOT
a bunch of old men in purple robes
sitting around in ivory towers
making up
kill-joy laws regarding just
YOUR sins,
YOUR grace,
YOUR doing good things—
NEVER!
The Church is People,
the Church
is
US—

our family,
the family of Man
come together, standing present
to each other
IN Christ.
WE
are God made present
through Christ—
on earth,
HERE
NOW
in this life.
WE
are the unit now, the team
(the first 11 have been gone a long time);
the ball has passed into
OUR
hands—
Christ's colors passed on to
OUR
backs—
It is
OUR
individuality, separateness,
that is being called up
NOW
HERE
to lose itself in the One,
Greater
Spirit
that makes a **Team.**
It is **OUR DAY, OUR TURN**—
to either grab the ball and
run with it
or
to fumble, fall,
or even worse
just warm the bench,
keep the jersey clean,
refuse to play
at all.

The Church doesn't
live
or move
unless **we**
live and move;
the Church is only as
boring
as we
are boring.
(Only bores are bored,
anyway.)

The Church
would be easier to
"take"
maybe,
if it **were** just
a "pile of bricks."
Nothing very unsettling,
disturbing,
demanding
about another pile
of bricks.
But that definition
is as cheesy
inadequate
just plain insulting
as if someone
neatly described
you
as " . . . oh, that guy?
He's just
96 cents worth
of chemical material.
A hank of hair
and a piece of bone,
that's all that
guy is."

Without the Spirit—
which is Life—
nothing
amounts to
anything.

If the Church
isn't **US,**
it is
NOTHING.
And "us"
doesn't only mean
the neighbors on our block,
or
the kids we like best, or
even all the people
we happen to know
personally.
"Us" means
ALL
of us—**everybody.**
"Us" includes even "them"—
(Hurry up, lock the door;
I don't like this guy coming, so
don't answer if he knocks—
who needs him, anyway?)
"Us" includes
rioters—
and the victims of rioting
the well-fed—and the starving
Eagle Scouts—
and reform school kids
the geniuses—and the retarded.
Families don't
bar the door to
one—or any
of their "own."

The Church
is the Family of God
In Christ.
And Christ said
**DON'T JUST STAND THERE,
MOVE!**
Make it work.

Two thousand years ago
our brothers—
same family
same Father
same Spirit
In Christ—
tore the door off the wall and went
OUT—
because they had too much fire
WITHIN
to sit out their lives "on the bench."
They said
"Brother, listen to us . . ."
and the Church moved;
it grew,
because the **spirit wouldn't be stilled**:
mankind **HAD** to know
it was a family
In Christ.
The Church's beginning
was strictly high gear.
It was important to those men and women—
so down-deep important they
would die for it—
to make their brothers understand:
"Don't stab that man in the back
love him.
Don't use that woman
reverence her—
she is your sister.
Don't cheat those people
honor them.
(You know very well
that old sway-backed camel
isn't worth a nickel;
yet you pass it off as a good deal
on your own brother
just because you can get away with it.)

Don't sit like stony statues
at that meal—communicate!
Don't be a slave to the
measly
piddling
third-rate
ideas called "popular opinion."
Use your head
Use your heart
Think,
act,
BECOME!

Don't be afraid; be yourself.
There are no outsiders here,
no spies for "them."
WE
you, me, all of us
are a family.
The Spirit is here with
you, me, all of us.
HERE,
not as a booming voice from the
heavenly echo chamber
not as an ultra-exclusive brain
who whispers only to saints.
He
the Spirit
was present in their brotherhood—
right there
with Paul and Barnabas as they
marched down the long roads
into the strange cities
talking to people who couldn't care less.
("I got a good thing going, pal;
don't come around here making waves.")

The Spirit was **right there**
with them
as they ran, hiding
from their persecutors.
Right there
marching with them
singing with them
as they were herded into the arenas.
The Spirit was there, too,
in the hearts of those who killed them
who watched them die
who said,
"Those Christians are something else;
they are out of this world."
The Spirit was
right there
with them
as they collected the bodies,
buried them in the catacombs,
celebrated Communion
TOGETHER.
He was present to them,
among them,
between them.
For they were together
in Christ
in the Family
where everyone belongs—
not as blobs among many blobs
but as real people
with honor and dignity,
moving in communion
with their brothers and sisters
remaking the world.

What about now? Today?
"What does the Church mean to you,
Bob . . . ?"

The Church is God—
with man for man.
And man is that odd bird who is
smart enough to make perfect days
but
ignorant enough to shoot his brother.
At times he makes some
pretty good messes.
He misunderstands, doesn't listen;
he forgets.
One thing he can't seem to remember is that
the Church is not a "what"—
not a Linus blanket
tucking us **in**
and not a brick fortress
walling "them" **out**.

The Church is a
"who."

People,
and people's ideas,
can,
in time,
suffer the hang-ups of old age.
Arteries can harden
arthritis can cripple the joints
cataracts can cloud the eyes.
It's so easy,
over such a period of time:
to get hung up on the Laws
but forget what they mean;
to throw up a new building
and figure the building

automatically makes a new church;
to worship together elbow to elbow
without ever communicating
eyeball to eyeball;
to pray for the Spirit to "Come,"
then rest in the pews waiting for Him—
forgetting, forgetting, forgetting
that He is restless
that He sets men on fire to
storm the world
that He once got
11 men killed
because they spoke His Name, saying,
"Brothers, we have news for you . . . . "

Some were boiled in oil,
some nailed to a cross,
one was even thrown off his own
temple
because he wouldn't let the temple
become a slaughterhouse
or noisy convention center.
And those who killed them were
relieved;
they said,
"Now that's that;
we got rid of those troublemakers
once and for all—no more problem."
But it didn't work out that way.
The Spirit said,
"For everyone of my
true witnesses you kill
I'll raise up twenty
to take their place.
Because
I AM Truth—
and you can't kill truth—
it conquers all. "

We can forget
that since the Church is a **WE**
it is **ALIVE!**

And living things must either
grow
or
die.
**Number growth alone
is not going to make it**.
(Big numbers don't automatically
make real families.)
Only growth of the Spirit,
in love,
in unity,
in Christ
will.

We can forget
that real, living families must be
creative.
Not artsy-craftsy creative in the big
magazine's manner
but the kind of creativity that
thinks
makes
does.
People in love are enormously creative;
they take the ordinary ticks of the clock
the ordinary pages of a calendar
and make an extraordinary
creation
of ordinary time.
Time is their servant;
it races when they are together,
drags when they are apart;
is valuable, precious, priceless
because it is used creatively.

We can forget
that living things aren't static, but
moving.
A family
or school
or club
or business
that sits on its hands, never moves;
it will either petrify
or disintegrate.

The Church must
GROW—MOVE—CREATE
to stay alive.
It must be faithful to the Past—
to Jesus
the Word, who said
**DON'T JUST STAND THERE—
Make it work!**

But to be faithful to the past is not to
LIVE
in the past
(that is to choose death—for it does
not create).
Jesus sent us the Spirit
so that we could
grow, be deepened and
be faithful to the past by
growing into the future;
not to retire to an ancient rocking chair,
brick fortress, or
Linus blanket,
listening to our arteries harden,
watching our joints buckle up
with arthritis,
dozing as the cataracts get thicker
and thicker.
"Do not go gentle into that good night!"
the poet Dylan Thomas said
to his dying father.
"Rage, rage against the dying of the
light!"
We, too—
We, the Church—
must "rage"
against the inhumanity, the
terrified island dwellers
the separate-ness—
that has no place in a redeemed world.
The Family of our Father,
the Church,
needs the blood, breath and will
of its **every**
family member
working in the shops,
sitting at meals—
open, everywhere, to the Spirit
present among them
in the brotherhood of Christ.

This is to be "available"
to each other—
available for listening and talking,
available for giving and taking,
available for sharing whatever grief—
or joy—
our brother brings to the family.

History brings us to a critical point;
we can destroy ourselves in so many ways.
We can push the button—
BOOM!
All over.

We can run together in a herd,
run scared,
away from the islands, maybe,
but to a worse place,
a place fit only for a half-wild mob
where no one dares to be anything but
"average,"
where everybody wants to be faceless,
be just alike.
(Being "yourself" is a terrible
responsibility.)

But who **IS** "average"?
"Averages" are numbers—
statistical center points.
You
are not a number.
You
are **You,**
someone unique,
special.
(And so is everyone else.)
We can refuse to recognize this;
we can go on making perfect days
for shooting at each other,
and if this happens it is because
we didn't let the Spirit in—
we didn't allow for the "Between"
to make you and me
a **WE.**
If we do this
we are refusing to
be alive,
refusing to tear the door off the wall
and shout,
"Brother, we have something to tell you . . ."
refusing
to remake this world the only way
it can be remade—
humanly—
in Christ
as a family-Church
through the Spirit.

A decision will have to be made
pretty soon:
either hang tight to our ear plugs,
our blinders
and exist together instinctively—
a school of know-nothing fish,
a cage of skittering white mice—

or
get rid of the ear plugs and blinders, and
open up
reach out
get with
BE ALIVE to
our brothers and sisters,
our family
in Christ—
coming together
as He told us to do
two thousand years ago.

"See dem red flowers?"
the tiny tot said;
"Dem's **bluebells!**"

But tulips
aren't
bluebells
just because a little kid **thinks** they are.
And the Church
isn't
a building
or boring services
or a social club
even if a whole lot of people
think it is.
It is **Us**
hearing the Word:
"DON'T JUST STAND THERE!"
It is **Us**
doing something about it—
together.

"For the apathetic . . .
existence itself
is a mistake
or a failure.
For the enthusiasts . . .
not only is it
better to be
than not to be
but it is always
possible,
indeed it is their
supreme interest
in life
to grow toward
ever more being."

(Teilhard de Chardin)
A CELEBRATION
OF LIFE

"We do not know
the time for
the consummation
of the earth and
humanity.
Nor do we know
how all things
will be transformed . . .
But . . . God is preparing
a new dwelling place
and a new earth
where justice
will abide,

and whose blessedness
will answer
and surpass
all the longings
for peace
which spring up
in the human heart."

(Document of Vatican II)
THE CHURCH TODAY

"And when
I am lifted up
from the earth
I shall
draw all men
to myself."

(John 12:32)

6
BUILD
BABY
BUILD!

Lots of people figure
heaven
is going to be **TOO MUCH!**
Keep your nose clean and someday,
Oh, man
SOMEDAY—
you'll have it made!
The Indians called heaven
"that great watering hole in the sky";
The Vikings said
"Valhalla!"
Cowboys used to sing about
"that last roundup": and
heaven,
in Tom and Jerry cartoons,
is a nice blue sky full of
super fluffy clouds and harp-
twanging angels.
No matter
how you think about it—
any way you cut it—
heaven will be—well, just
"heavenly!"
" . . . paradise up above . . . "
the song goes
de-dum, de-dum, de-dum.

Would you believe that
some people
don't want
to go to heaven?
"Keep it!"
said Lord Tappo
"I hate your heaven.
You guys think you
'get heaven'
by rattling off prayers and trying
to look holy.

But what about
this little kid
on this cruddy bed—
the bed **here**; the kid **here**—
what about him?
This little squirt
never learned prayers
and he doesn't look
one damn bit 'holy';
he looks dirty
hungry
sick—
what about him?
Does he 'get heaven'?
You'd better believe
he don't **want** heaven, and
he don't **need** it!

He needs something more
something better
than some dumb clouds
and sappy angels
to dream about.
He needs **HELP**
and he needs it **NOW**—
today—
not when he's an old man
about to kick off.
You guys think
'getting heaven'
is a big deal because
then you get sprung
from this stinkin' world;
but, Baby,
I GOT NEWS:
this stinkin' world
is crumbling
under your feet.

Can't you **hear** it, man?
Can't you hear this baby crying?
Ain't you got eyes to look
up and down this crummy street?
Ain't you got a nose to
smell the **stink**?
That's **DESPAIR** you smell, man—
black despair—
ugly, ain't it?
So why don't you holy Joes just
get on out of here and go home?
THIS—
this smelly, noisy, funky street
is all I got time to think about.
THIS
is my world.
And take your daydreams
about 'getting out'
right along with you.

Even if there **was**
such a place as your 'heaven'
(and I don't believe a word of it)
I wouldn't want to spend no time
AT ALL
there,
with folks who spent their lives dreaming of
copping out and
getting sprung; folks who
hold their noses when they walk down
my street;
folks who wrap their prayer books
in silk
and could care less about this sick baby
wrapped in rags;
folks who jabber about tomorrow
all the time
and never think about doing anything
today.
I figure them kind of folks to be
bad company."

Heaven
doesn't sound "heavenly"
to everybody.
"The pie-in-the-sky bit?—
Who're you trying to kid?"
said the shiny-haired
clear-eyed college girl.
"The whole idea
of heaven
is just too corny,
too preposterous,
too—**medieval**!

Heaven is the Easter Bunny
and Santa Claus
the Big Rock Candy Mountain
you wave in front of little kid
(or hold over their heads)
to keep them in line:
'Brush your teeth, kiddies;
clean your plates and
don't twirl your rosary beads
do everything
big daddy tells you
just as you are told—

and you'll get that many more stars
in the Big Book!'
Don't con **me**, Jack!—I've heard
that routine before:
'Heaven' is **leverage**—a trick
to get kids
who don't know any better—
to shape up.
Probably
heaven is okay
for real old-timers
in black shawls—
what have they got to lose?
Everything's over for them, anyway.
Might as well
dream about a never-ending resting place,
a once-and-for-all vacation
from their aches and pains—
whether it's true or not!
But
I'm not a washed-up old lady
or a gullible kid.
I'm twentieth century!
My generation
doesn't buy
that old-fashioned cartoon.
How dumb do you think we are?
We're **on** to you mind benders;
we see what you're trying to do!
Forget it!
The people under 30—the people I know—
aren't just putting in time
twiddling thumbs
treading water
fiddling, like Nero,
while the world burns.
We care about what's happening
on **this** side of the sky!

And your Christian heaven
(at least the way I heard it)
is full of eyes-up types who
thought
it didn't really matter
WHAT
happened here on earth.
They hid
wore hair shirts
ducked out;
kept **their own thing** going with God,
going like mad,
and to hell—literally, to hell—
with people who didn't see it
as they did.
Who knows? Maybe they were right—
it's just not our way.

"We're on
to the world we live in right now.
We're **INVOLVED,**
TUNED IN
COMMITTED
to the way things were **right here**
when we came on the scene.
Maybe
(and who can be sure of anything?)
we'll miss out on the goodies,
if there **really is** a
Big Book
for tallying up hits and misses.
But at least
we won't be sitting on the sidelines
watching the show
and tsk-tsking.
We are up to our elbows—
up to our necks—
in making history!

We're **watching** nothing, Mac; we're **DOING**—we're

but not

part

ims

of the world.

If it turns out
in the end
that we didn't accomplish everything
we set out to—
well, too bad.
But it won't be
because we spent our lives nit-picking
over pluses and minuses in the Book.
It won't be
because we didn't try
or didn't **care**
or ducked out
on the hellishness that exists
in so much of **this** world.
Maybe **that's** what
my generation
could accept as 'heaven':
this very world we're living in—
but
transformed
by our
knocking out as much ugliness
as we can
in the time we have.
Yes, I like that.
Heaven,
for me,
would be old mother earth
with all her heartbreak knocked out.
Just that
would be a 24-carat paradise.

"You know,
I'm not a believer—not really—
like you are.
But I still go for—
even more
than when I was a kid—
what I read about Jesus.
He,
your Savior,
was so real,
so genuine.
He blasted
when blasting was called for;
He cared about
and comforted
even the people who hated Him.
It always seemed to me
that He went around
doing things especially on the
SABBATH—
curing people
picking grain
tying that guy in a knot
about getting his ox
out of the ditch
on the Sabbath . . .

That was a **real** thing to do,
a really humane thing—
and to hell with
the letter of the law.
Everything He said—
even if He did
think and act unlike
the rest of His own society—
proved how
GENUINE, how
REAL
the Man was.

Like calling the bluff on
those hypocrite Pharisees:
Jesus **KNEW** better
than to be taken in
by a bunch of phonies.
And Jesus
CARED.
'Why not cure this man?'
He said.
'No matter the day.
This man is suffering,
you know.
SUFFERING,
so I'm going to cure him.'
Does that say anything to you?
When His men were hungry
they saw the grain there,
but it was Sabbath
and against the law.
Jesus said
'**EAT**
that's what it's here for!'
He cared. He knew.
He didn't say
'Hold off
someday
things will be great . . . . '

"Jesus
was a holy man.
I love the way
He was always talking about
KINGDOM—
talking as if
it were on its way
or here
or at least not
two billion miles
straight up.

Jesus
was with it
moving
going somewhere;
and He wasn't
any stony-face pickle puss
while He was on His way,
either.
Jesus
didn't 'save himself'
or play it safe
like so many do
who call themselves
by His name.

He jumped right in—even
threw himself to the dogs,
kind of.
Jesus was
well, 'with it!'—**all the time.**
I guess that's why
your 'heaven'
turns me off.
What you do 'down here'
doesn't add up
to what you expect
'up there.'
There's no relation between
the life you've **got**
and the life
you're **waiting for.**
Me, I want
to be alive **all the time!**
I don't have time for waiting.
Your way of looking at it
means nothing to me—
but nothing.
So I guess I'm out of it."

To some people
heaven sounds
only a shade better
than hell.
But maybe
heaven
isn't really like a lot of people think it is
at all.

Maybe heaven "up there"
really does have something to do
with "down here."
Down here
where Christ revealed His Father,
God;
down here
where Christ lived,
got busted,
rose and said, **FOLLOW.**
Maybe Christ meant
not only for us to **keep** the laws
but to **fulfill** them
as He did;
not only to follow negatively
controlling our tendency to
mess things up—
but to follow positively—to
do a little building.
And maybe
He meant the doing to begin
right now
down here.

A first step might be
to check out what the hang up is
when we have plenty of money
plenty of food
plenty of almost everything

BUT
still kill our brother—
kill him with
hatred
suspicion
indifference
and bullets.
It might be making the
"Burn, Baby, Burn" thing
sound
something like
"BUILD, BABY, BUILD."
(Now that would be a **real** revolution!)
Chanted with the same
intensity—
same soul!
And since we have **already** built
computers
communications satellites and
bigger bombs
we might try
beginning at the beginning
this time.

We might try building a
"We" World—
a real WE WORLD,
where people would be safe.
A world where a fireman—
good man,
honest,
likes his job—
doesn't have to put on a helmet
with a bulletproof visor
and pack a gun
when he goes out
(in the middle of the night,
to fight fire,
smoke and falling bricks)

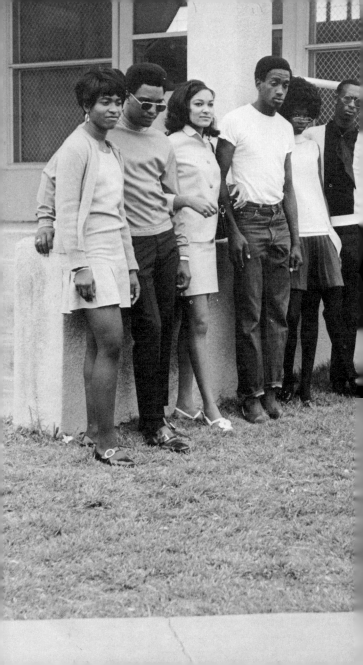

and have to worry about getting
SHOT IN THE BACK
because he's putting out the fire.

A **real WE WORLD**—
where nobody gets dumped
(his brothers wouldn't stand for it)
before he even gets started.
Like the guy who gets a
tenth-grade education,
maybe gets kicked out of school,
then steps out into a specialized society,
fails, and
gets labeled a bum,
because
" . . . he won't work."

BUILD, BABY, BUILD
but
not just more cars, more TV sets,
more high-rise housing.

No matter how many
things
we grind out,
something is still
MISSING.
Something Important
(as important as blood is to a body).
What needs building is that
bridge
between
YOU and ME,
between cities and nations,
brothers and brothers.
BUILD, BABY, BUILD.
Build it!
This is the **same** bridge
that links
"up there" with
"down here."
Not just
"**me** getting **there**,"
but
"We" on our way
together.
"We"—or—
nobody goes.
Because **YOU** are
part
of **ME.**
Each tick of the clock
expresses motion;
time moves, and we
move with it
and in it.

Either in circles
or across that bridge to
the area **BETWEEN:**
that space in our togetherness
that wilderness
that no man's land
where so few have dared go before.
Only here,
between brothers,
is there light enough to see
what causes the hang ups,
the contradictions,
the messes we find ourselves in.
Only on the bridge
(which we alone can build)
will the root causes of poverty,
crime,
war,
hatred
rear their ugly heads **for the last time.**
Only on the bridge—so—
BUILD IT, BABY, BUILD IT!

Because it's **not**
"just a bridge";
it's **HEAVEN**
we're beginning to build—
right here.
And it isn't a matter of
ignoring or
making peanuts of
our life down here;
it isn't a matter of
finding an "out"
or "escaping"—
like tunneling out of a concentration
camp or something;

rather
it is a matter of
throwing the vision of **MAN**—
on his way to the Father in Christ—
WIDE OPEN.
Open enough so that
all may see!
The building
HAS BEGUN.
The work
IS OURS.
It isn't finished yet; but one day, we,
like starry-eyed immigrants,
will end our bittersweet work and
agonizing trip.
We,
US,
MANKIND
will arrive—together—
as **ONE**
on the shores of the Promised Land.
As **ONE**
we will complete that life
the hand of God
Started,
the total life of Christ
Redeemed, and
Renewed in the presence of
the Spirit.
Heaven is
not entirely "other than"
the hopes and joys
anxieties and grief
of Man on earth.
Heaven is
the fulfillment of them,
the Finally Realized Kingdom
established by Christ
two thousand years ago.

"Abide in Me,"
He said.
" . . . have Life—
have it more abundantly."
"I am the Vine,
you the branches."
This is **IT,**
The Kingdom.

"But
I don't have time to wait,"
the college girl said . . . .
She made a mistake
putting heaven down
as "leverage."

BUT
she had something there
about not being content
to wait this life out.
How could waiting—
just **waiting**—
possibly prove anything?
WAIT?
Wait while the world
burns?
Wait while brother
shoots brother?
Wait while people starve?
No.
The starving—quite literally—
"don't have time to wait"
either.
And neither do any of us—
not hands folded
eyes up
passively.

Our "waiting"
is the sweat-streaming
blister-popping
"waiting"
of a construction crew who
"wait"
for the completion of a
structure

THEY ARE BUILDING.
And construction crews
are made up of
metal workers,
excavators,
electricians, plasterers,
carpenters—

different people
different trades
different skills—
who join their individual efforts,
like the brass and woodwinds
of a symphony orchestra,
in harmony
toward the triumphant execution
of the finished **whole.**
A major work
isn't polished off in a single day
or by a
single man;
or even by a whole bunch of men—
if they are only concerned with,
turned on to
their **own** brick-laying or bass-thumping.
Members of a team
MUST
have a vision of the **WHOLE**
and not be
pounding nails or
blowing a trumpet
whenever and wherever
the mood strikes them.
Those who do, spoil the whole shot
not **only** for themselves
but for everybody else;
and members of a team
can't lay down on the job.
The building just won't go up—
not one stone
not one foot—
if the crew sits around dreaming
" . . . how nice it would be if that cement
would pour itself,
if that ironwork would rivet itself,
if those power lines would connect,
all by themselves."
They **WON'T.**

The building
is the work of the workers—
not of the raw materials.
There are sure to be snags,
problems,
a million hours of labor
a full ocean of sweat spilt
before the building is completed.
But that is the price.
If you're not willing to pay it you
can curse the empty lot that
MIGHT
have supported a building;
you can curse the unfinished building
because it isn't
YET
finished;
but curses
never
got a job done.

Mankind is building.
Mankind is on its way.
Slowly,
painfully,
in darkness and in sorrow
in joy and in light.
You can curse
the uncompleted job
(which is
to give up, not care)
or
you can wait with busy hands
by building,
thrilling
(because **YOU** are invested there)
in the joy of each new stone
each new window
falling into place.

The joy
belongs to the builders.
The knothole peepers
the loafers
the cursers
never know
the joy.

To wait is to
YEARN; and
dead-souled people don't yearn.
To wait is to
CREATE;
living souls call out to all creation
THAT THEY ARE ALIVE.
To wait is to
GROW
because all living, precious things
need time to
stretch out,
to deepen,
to mature—
something like a seed which must
grow or
die.
Like a friendship
or love
or trust
or simple willingness
to be involved—
which are living things that will
either flourish or fizzle.

Time is the tool
of those who wait creatively.
If you didn't wait for a crop to ripen
(it couldn't if you didn't plant it);
if you didn't wait for your savings
account to grow
(it couldn't if you didn't put anything
in it),
there would be nothing to look forward to
in life—no hope, no excitement.
(No investment—no return).
The same is true
in every area of life, and
MOST true
of the investment **only you** can make in the
BETWEEN,
for it is in this area that
you
and the rest of Mankind
have a chance
for completion.
You must yearn for that completion
crave it
wait for it—
which means you must **build it**
YOURSELF
stone by stone,
inch by inch.

Sure, to wait—even to wait creatively—
leaves you open to
setbacks,
frustration,
failure.
This is the hard part;
this is where the blisters and
sweat come in.

Because if you want to taste the
JOY
of building a world that makes sense,
you will also have to taste
the vinegar
which delays **your building.**
Your "baby"
your "investment"
into which you are pouring your very life
will be vandalized by the ignorant,
impeded by the loafers
mocked by the cursers
threatened on every side;
but you will have to forget about
the bitter taste
of vinegar
and go on building
in spite of those who would ruin your work.
Go on building
because
the vision
of what this building **could be**
is sweeter,
greater,
than the hard fact—
the sour taste—
of what the building happens to look like
right at this moment.
Because
just now
the building site
(burning cities, violent mobs,
international hatred and suspicion)
is a pretty big mess.
But—
besides your vision—
this is all you have
to go on.

Do you want it?
Is it
better to be
outside
peeping through a knothole
laughing
jeering
laying odds
against the building
ever going up?
Then
you wouldn't have to wait
for anything
because
there won't **be** anything
to wait for.
(A foolproof bet—
if you could find any takers.)
OR
is it better
to leap over the fence
grab your tools
and get to work?
No matter how hopeless
the job looks;
no matter
who says
it can't be done.
Is it worth it
to be a Creative Waiter?
Is it worth
the blisters
the sweat
the frustration?
(Onlookers don't sweat.)
One choice hurts,
the other choice doesn't.

One is a wearisome journey—the other is
rest in the tomb;
one is the song of brothers in unity—
the other is the silence of strangers;
one sows seeds of sweat—reaps
a harvest of joy;
the other sows only the wind
—reaps nothing.

Is "heaven" worth it?

Is earth worth it?
Even Christ
found vinegar hard to swallow;
but Christ's triumph
was our
ticket.
"Heaven" was born
right there
in the majestic
"out of this world"
YES
of the crib
of Calvary
of Easter Sunday.
Mankind
the earth
and "heaven" were
worth it
to Christ.

"Heaven" isn't like supper dessert.
It isn't stashed away in the clouds for the eternity
after
human life ends.

Heaven is the fulfillment
of
human life—
the last brick finally in place,
the ultimate coming to maturity,
the final
full-throated
beautiful shout
not now in agony, but in victory:
"It is consummated."
Heaven is
arriving.

TREASURE CHESTS™

KNIGHTS

The Age of
Adventure, to Unlock
and Discover

CONTENTS

Marilyn Tolhurst

WHAT'S IN THE TREASURE CHEST

Your treasure chest is packed full of amazing items. There is a stand-up castle with castle characters, such as archers and armored knights, and a siege catapult to assemble and attack your castle with. The kit also contains a signet ring with attachable initials and clay to seal your proclamation.

The Castle and Siege Catapult

Inside your secret drawer there is an instruction sheet which shows you how to assemble these models. Then, you can use your catapult, ammunition, and castle characters to lay siege against your

castle! You can position your castle inside your treasure chest, to give it extra stability. Use the nine men's morris gameboard as the floor of your castle.

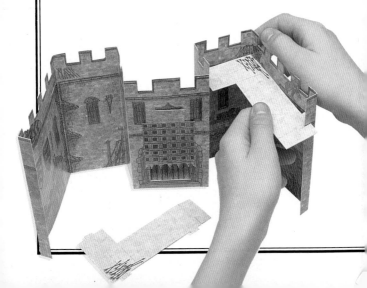

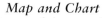

Map and Chart
A map of the crusades
and a chart showing
you all the pieces that
make up a suit of armor are in the
drawer. Each of these has a companion sticker sheet
which you will also find in the drawer.

Proclamation and Signet Ring
Your royal proclamation is in the drawer. You
can seal it with the medieval signet
ring which has attachable initials.
To do this, take a piece of clay (the
rest will harden once the bag has
been opened). Place the ribbon under
it, and lay them both under your

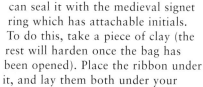

signature. Pick out
your initials from
the alphabet
selection and
attach them, one
at a time, to your
ring and press into
your clay.

Nine Men's Morris
and Stained Glass Window
There is a board game with
instructions under your book.
The playing pieces are in the
secret drawer. There
is also a stained
glass window to
color in.

BECOMING A KNIGHT

One of the squire's tasks was to help his lord in and out of his armor.

To become a knight was no easy matter. A young nobleman was put through arduous training to prepare him for the task. Knighthood was regarded almost as a religious order, with its own rules and codes of behavior.

Squires had to serve food gracefully, offering each dish first to those of highest rank.

A squire had to know how to groom and train a warhorse, a knight's most precious possession.

To become a knight meant starting young, for there were many things to learn, not only about arms and warfare but about courtesy as well. The son of a nobleman was sent away at the age of seven to the castle of a neighboring knight to begin his training as a page, doing menial jobs such as fetching and carrying. As he grew older he learned the use of arms – the sword, lance, and the axe. He also practiced wrestling and leaping into the saddle in full armor without touching the stirrups.

One way to learn the use of a lance was riding at the quintain, a wooden structure shaped like a soldier.

At the age of 14 he became a squire, a role that required him to learn about hunting and the management of hounds and hawks. He also had to take care of his lord's armor, brushing away rust and repairing it when necessary. Above all, a squire had to learn good manners and the meaning of honor.

The Dubbing of a Knight

When the time came for him to be made a knight, or dubbed, the squire was ceremonially bathed and dressed in white robes. He spent the night in prayer with his sword and armor on the chapel altar. It was called keeping vigil. The following morning he made an oath in church to devote his life to the service of God and chivalry. Knighthood was conferred by another nobleman who struck a blow on his shoulder with the flat of a sword. This was called the *collée*. Then, fixing on his spurs, the young squire rose as a knight.

Many successful warriors were knighted by other knights on the battlefield.

This illustration from the 1338 poem, Romance of Alexander, *shows a king accompanied by his knights.*

6

FEUDALISM

An early 16th century illustration of a farm laborer cutting wheat.

Between about 1270 and 1490, a period known as the Middle Ages, countries were organized differently than they are today. Europe was divided into a number of small kingdoms that were often at war.

Kings granted huge areas of land to their most faithful followers in return for a promise to supply mounted knights in times of war. These men in turn granted part of their land to their own loyal followers. Society was organized in this way from top to bottom in a series of services paid for land. The peasants paid back their lord in labor, animals, and food in return for his protection. This system is known as feudalism.

This illustration (above) from the Très Riches Heures by Jean, duc de Berry, shows how the feudal estate was organized. At the bottom were the peasants who farmed the land.

Poverty and disease were rife in the Middle Ages. The Church dealt severely with offenders, as shown in this illustration.

Lords and Vassals

When a king, or a great baron, wanted to wage war on his neighbors, he called up an army made up of his vassals. A vassal was a man who pledged his loyalty to another in return for a grant of land called a fief. Loyalty was seen as a great virtue in the Middle Ages and for many, a tie of loyalty between a lord and his vassal was as important as a tie of blood. Sometimes, if the king was weak, his barons could use their armies of knights against him.

In a feudal state, the king was the most powerful man in the land, since he was the greatest landowner. This illustration shows a baron pledging loyalty to his lord.

Acts of Homage

When a vassal pledged his loyalty to his lord, he did so in an act of homage, a word which came from the French word *homme* for man. It meant that one man had declared himself to be the "man" of the other. There was generally a ceremony in which the man swore loyalty to his lord and the promise was sealed with clasped hands and a kiss. The vassal was handed a sword or even a clod of earth or a bunch of corn as a symbol that he had been given his fief.

Bertrand du Guesclin, a famous 14th century French knight, is shown being given the Sword of the Constable of France by King Charles V. This made him commander-in-chief of the whole French armed forces.

CASTLES

Small windows prevented enemy soldiers and arrows getting in.

During the Middle Ages, castles were common throughout Europe. The land was a patchwork of small kingdoms almost permanently at war with each other. To protect themselves and their possessions, rival kings and barons built castles.

The earliest European castles were built by French knights to defend their conquest of England. They were thrown up at great speed and consisted of a wooden lookout tower on top of an earth mound. To one side was a defended area surrounded by a ditch and a fence or a row of wooden stakes. As soon as time and money allowed, they were strengthened with stone. Soon, this pattern was repeated all over Europe. Castles were built wherever there was a need to guard bridges, to defend harbors, and to protect frontiers.

Defense from Attack
Whether in France, Germany, or Spain, castles

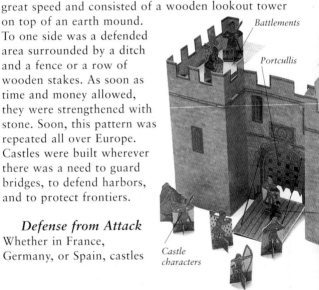

Battlements

Portcullis

Castle characters

Battlements and projecting wall towers allowed defenders to shoot at the enemy without exposing themselves to fire.

Kings and lords ruled their lands from castles, which served as both military fortresses and palaces.

had the same basic construction, consisting of a series of defenses, one inside the other. The inner stronghold was called the keep or donjon. It had massive stone walls and an entrance on the first floor to make it difficult to storm. Inside there were living quarters for the troops, storerooms, a chapel, and most importantly a well.

Projecting wall towers

The gatehouse, or castle entrance, was thought to be the weakest point. It was protected by a drawbridge and an iron gate called a portcullis.

Drawbridge

The castle model in your secret drawer *(left)* is of a gatehouse with a portcullis and a drawbridge to protect the entrance over the moat. *(See the instruction sheet inside your drawer which tells you how to put it together.)* Castles as well fortified as this one were difficult to capture, except by treachery or trickery – or a siege. Use the model soldiers to try and storm your way in!

No castle could withstand cannon fire. Fewer castles were built after its invention in 1450.

WEAPONS AND ARMOR

A knight on horseback, armed to the teeth and encased in full armor, was a fearsome sight. In battle, he charged at the enemy with his lance lowered, and attempted to knock the opposing knight out of the saddle with the force of the blow.

It took a lot of strength to pull the longbow. A skilled archer could fire 12 arrows a minute.

Knights in battle were under attack, not only from other knights, but from foot soldiers armed with a variety of weapons. Massed infantry with a "hedge" of pikes or spears could break up a cavalry charge. Archers with powerful longbows could shower the enemy with arrows, causing havoc, especially among the horses. The crossbow was slower to load since it had to be mechanically wound back, but its deadly bolts could pierce plate armor at a hundred paces.

The weight of a suit of armor, between 50-70 lbs, was distributed over the knight's body. This German suit (right) dates from c. 1520.

The crossbow had advantages over the longbow. Its arrows traveled farther and crossbowmen needed less strength and skill.

Siege Warfare

A castle might be assaulted with scaling ladders or siege towers. Battering rams were used to smash down the gates. If the castle was not moated, tunnelers might try to collapse the walls by undermining them. If this failed, a siege engine was sometimes the answer. In your kit is a model of a mangonel, one of the earliest catapults that was used to fire boulders. *(Inside your secret drawer there is an instruction sheet which shows you how to put it together.)* Since elastic was unknown in the Middle Ages, lengths of rope twisted with a lever were used to hold back the arm. When released, the rope would unwind, jerking the arm upright and hurling the boulder forward.

This illustration is of a 15th century siege tower. At the top are the archers, who attack the castle defenders as the tower is wheeled toward the wall. Then, the men below rush up the ladders and over the wall.

Body Armor

The earliest type of armor was chainmail, a flexible fabric of interlinked iron rings worn over a leather tunic, or hauberk. Gradually, the hauberk was adapted to carry plates of metal to give extra protection. By 1450, armorers had joined these plates together into suits of armor. Your secret drawer contains a chart telling you more about the history of armor.

This suit of armor, c. 1350, shows a combination of full chainmail and plate armor.

THE CRUSADES

In 1095, Christians throughout Europe were called to fight a Holy War. Their mission was to win back Jerusalem and other places of Christian pilgrimage from the Turkish Muslims, know as Saracens, who controlled the Holy Land.

Crusaders wore a white tunic with a red cross on it to show they were fighting for Christianity.

The First Crusade went overland across Europe. Many in the crusading army of 40,000 died of sickness

Traveling was far more hazardous to the crusaders than doing battle with the Saracens, although the sea route was generally safer.

or starvation on the way. The second wave of this crusade was much more successful and took a safer route by sea. The strength of the crusading army was the mounted knight who wore heavy chainmail and was armed with a sword and lance.

Richard the Lionheart

Perhaps the most famous crusader was King Richard of England. His exploits won him the title "Richard the Lionheart". He led the Third Crusade of 1191 against the Saracen leader, Saladin. After much bloody fighting it ended in a truce.

After his coronation in 1190, Richard I swore to raise enough money to go on crusade. He said, "I would sell London if I could find a buyer."

An illustration from the Siege of Antioch in the First Crusade. Unlike the crusaders, the Saracens wore little body armor. They carried a light bow and a long curved sword called a scimitar.

A Lasting Legacy

Over a period of 200 years, eight crusades were launched against the Saracens, but few achieved any success and most ended in disaster. Their most lasting legacy was the wealth of new ideas in science and culture that reached Europe from the civilizations of the east. Inside your secret drawer you will find a map which tells you much more about the crusades.

The art of the siege was developed during the crusades because Saracen castles were heavily fortified. This crusader castle in Cyprus is in ruins.

HERALDRY

The fleur-de-lys is France's heraldic emblem.

Once a knight was encased in plate armor it was difficult to tell one from another. This could prove dangerous in battle, so from the late 12th century knights adopted the patterned shield as a way of telling friend from foe.

The herald who carried messages between kings and their armies on the field became an expert on the designs of shields, and in due course the practice became known as heraldry. Once established, it soon came to have a complex language of its own and an elaborate set of rules. Each part of the shield was given a name and only seven colors were allowed, each of them with a special heraldic title. Tournaments, splendid mock-battles that were staged in times of peace, became the occasion for knights to show off their colors, badges, and crests. Birds, beasts, flowers, fishes, crowns, and castles appeared on shields.

These vestments hang above the tomb of the knight known as the Black Prince. They bear his coat of arms (left).

Heralds drew up a list or register of knights who took part in tournaments or battles. It was called a roll of arms.

A knight wore his coat of arms on his shield, surcoat, and his horse's caparison, or decorated covering.

The lion was the first beast to appear on a shield and was used to signify strength or valor. The lion might be upright, sitting, lying, facing backward or forward, and each posture had its own heraldic description.

This lion is in the rampant position.

Quartered Shields

The first designs had only a single band of color on a contrasting background. But as the fashion grew, designs became more complex. A knight passed on his title and coat of arms to his children. When noble families intermarried, their shields combined in a process called quartering.

In your secret drawer there is a sheet of heraldic stickers. Match them with the shields on your armor chart (right).

Quartered shield from Richmond Castle, England.

THE AGE OF CHIVALRY

A knight saw himself as a cut above other men. Not only did he excel in the arts of war, he also prided himself on his honor, loyalty, and courtesy.

Playing an instrument was one of the skills expected of a courtly knight.

A sense of brotherhood developed between knights, aided by the crusades which brought many of them together. This expressed itself throughout Europe in a code of behavior combining military, Christian, and courtly virtues. This code was called chivalry. The word chivalry came from the French *chevalier* meaning a mounted soldier or knight.

A maid gives her heart to a youth in this 14th century illustration from the Romance of Alexander.

This 15th century tournament shield (above) shows a knight kneeling before his lady. The words on the long scroll above him mean "You or death".

Perdigon (below) was a troubadour of humble origins. He was knighted and granted lands of his own in return for his services.

Troubadours

The songs of the period began to reflect this new mood amongst knights. Instead of songs of battle and the slashing off of heads, love songs became popular. Troubadours came from the south of France. They traveled from court to court singing about beautiful ladies and gallant knights. Some were of noble birth and their songs were highly thought of.

As courtly virtues became popular, fashionable knights and their ladies dressed in fine clothes and spent time listening to poetry and music.

Fact or Fantasy?

The image of the knight in shining armor was largely a myth. Many knights in the crusades proved themselves to be greedy and cruel. And the women of the Middle Ages were as tough and capable as any.

This 15th century illustration shows a lady receiving a game bird as a gift. Most medieval women had little time for such romantic pursuits.

MEDIEVAL CLOTHING

For ordinary people, clothing changed very little during the Middle Ages. Clothes were designed for useful wear and tended to be simple. But for the courtly knight and his lady, fashion was very important because fine dress was a mark of status.

Babies were wrapped in swaddling bands in the mistaken idea that this would give them straight limbs.

 Poor people wore rough woolen clothes. Shoes were made of heavy felt or leather with wooden clogs for wet weather. A pointed hood, called a capuchon, covered the head and shoulders.

In the late Middle Ages, the fashion for pointed shoes became very exaggerated.

All over Europe, peasants wore similar clothes. A wool or linen tunic, called a cotte, was belted in at the waist over a pair of woolen tights called chausses.

High Fashion

The nobility spent large sums of money on imported cloth, such as silk from Italy, velvet from France, and intricately patterned linen or silk, called damask, from the city of Damascus in the Holy Land.

This illustration from the Très Riches Heures by Jean, duc de Berry, shows a betrothal between a richly dressed lord and his lady. Ladies decorated their hair with fine jeweled bands and feathers.

The Knight

When not on the battlefield, the knight wore a tunic of fine cloth, sometimes buttoned down the front. His tights, or chausses, were of fine wool and his shoes had long points. His belt was jeweled and generally held his dagger.

The Knight's Lady

The knight's lady wore a long tunic covered with a surcoat of rich cloth. Sometimes long wide sleeves, called tippets, were added from the elbow. Fur trimmings and fur-lined cloaks were common.

Early 15th century costume. Both men and women wore purses that hung from the belt.

Headdresses became very ornate. They were made from stiffened fabric, sometimes pointed, with a fine gauze veil hanging down the back. Others were molded into a horn-shaped roll, encrusted with jewels and hung with fine cloth.

An early 15th century costume. Trimmings and linings were made from squirrel fur or ermine, a type of mink.

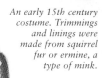

Headgear was an expression of high fashion. This 15th century illustration shows two ladies admiring a new headdress.

BANQUETS

In noblemen's houses there was often a fool or jester who entertained the guests at mealtimes.

Medieval banquets were spectacular occasions announced with trumpets. The host and chief guests sat at the high table and washed their hands in basins of water scented with rose petals. Lesser guests sat, according to rank, at tables down the hall.

T he medieval noble did not regard fruit and vegetables as proper food, so meat was the staple food at his table and was served in astonishing quantity and variety. Beef, mutton, pork, venison, wild boar, and even bear meat was served. Chicken, goose, duck, swan, and peacock were also commonly served. Several courses were provided and little distinction was made between sweet and savory dishes. Many meats were cooked with dried figs, prunes, or raisins, sweetened with honey and heavily spiced. The nobles drank fine wines; the lesser guests, beer or cider.

In royal courts, plates might be of gold or silver. Spoons and knives were provided for the guests but most people ate with their fingers.

Medieval jug used to store water or wine.

The kitchen was attached to the hall and was incredibly hot, in both summer and winter, from two great open fires – one for roasting meat and the other for stewing or broiling. Sauces were cooked in small containers inside cauldrons of hot water hung from tripods over the fire. In the stifling heat, cooks and lowly servants toiled and sweated, glad for a break between courses. Outside the castle gate, hungry and hopeful beggars waited for the leftovers.

14th century illustration (right) of a cook stirring a sauce.

Joints and poultry were roasted on a spit and turned by a boy.

This is the first course of a banquet given for Catherine of France. Two equally elaborate courses followed!

Boar's meat with mustard
Eels in sauce
Frumenty (porridge)
Pike with sea bream (fish) Trout
Pickled lampreys (type of eel)
Large crabs
Codling (small cod fish)
Meat en croute Fried merlin fish
Lombardy pork slices Small pies

A special sweet dessert in the shape of a tiger

TOURNAMENTS

Tournaments began in the 11th century as practice for war. They were mock-battles fought between opposing teams of knights. It was a dangerous but spectacular sport for knights with lots of money to spend on expensive arms and equipment.

There were two main events at a tournament: the joust and the mêlée. In the joust, one knight rode against another with his lance and tried to knock him from the saddle. The mêlée was a team event fought on foot with real weapons. Early tournaments were very like real battles and often ended in injury or even death.

A tournament was a pageant of noise and color with trumpeters and cheering crowds.

Rules of Play

The church disapproved of tournaments and often tried to stop them. Eventually, rules were laid down to make them safer. Contestants fought in an enclosure with a fence or a tilt down the middle to keep the knights apart. Lances had to be made of wood that splintered on impact and sword blades had to be blunted.

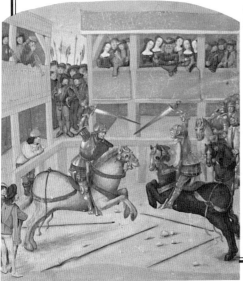

This late 15th century illustration shows knights jousting before King Arthur. Their discarded lances lie on the ground.

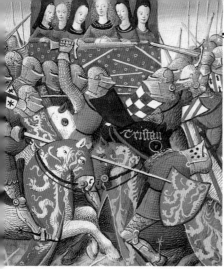

Despite this, the tournament remained very dangerous. A knight who was knocked from his horse at full speed could break his neck in the fall. At the very least he could get a concussion and loosened teeth.

Illustration of Sir Tristan, a legendary knight, fighting in a mêlée and watched by the Queen and her ladies. He was considered a great warrior, second only to Sir Lancelot.

Prize-fighters

Many knights tried to make their reputations at tournaments. One such knight was William Marshall, a knight of humble beginnings who later rose to be Lord Protector of England in the reign of Henry III. At his first tournament he had to ride a borrowed horse, but by the end he had won four horses and a great deal of equipment. He traveled around Europe as a prize-fighter, winning fame and fortune for his skill.

The horse was a knight's most expensive possession. The destrier was a stallion used for jousting as it was both strong and nimble.

MEDIEVAL PASTIMES

War was the knight's favorite pastime. But when he couldn't play on the battlefield or at a tournament, he played on the gameboard. *Chess and nine men's morris were favorite games of strategy and skill.*

Children's games were similar to those of today. This game involved whipping tops to make them spin.

These ladies are playing nine men's morris, a popular medieval game.

Many of these board games are ancient games and have their origins in the Middle East. They were brought to Europe by knights returning from the crusades. In your kit underneath this book there is a gameboard and instructions for playing nine men's morris. Try your skill with a friend.

Playing games such as chess was considered a great accomplishment of the courtly knight.

Sports

Most games were
rougher than those of
today. Boisterous ball games
were popular over the ages.
One village might compete
against another in an early
form of football which was
played with an inflated pig's
bladder stuffed with peas.
There were few rules and
lots of foul play. 'Games of
wit' included sessions of
silly questions and answers.
One game was called St.
Cosmo and involved trying
to present a gift, without
laughing, to someone who
was pulling faces.

Hoodman blind involved one player being blindfolded by his hood. The others tried to hit him without being caught.

Hawking was very popular and developed into an art form with manuals on hawking written by knights from all over Europe.

On The Hunt

Hunting and
hawking parties
were popular with
the nobility and
usually included
picnics and dancing
in the open air. In
the evenings there
was time for music
and courtly songs of
love and honor.

*Hunting was an
important knightly
activity. A stag,
shown in this
illustration, was
considered one of
the greatest prizes.*

LETTERS AND LEARNING

During the Middle Ages very few people – including the average knight – could read or write. The Church played a major part in medieval life and learning took place in the monastery, where books were written and the first libraries were kept.

Books were copied by professional writers called scribes.

Pens were made from goosefeather quills trimmed at the end.

Printing was not invented until the end of the Middle Ages, so books, letters, and documents were written by hand. Most books were about religious subjects. They were written on sheets of parchment or vellum, which was made from sheep or calfskin. Lines were pricked onto the parchment to keep the scribe's handwriting straight.

Manuscripts

Most books were written in Latin, since it was understood by scholars all over Europe. A manuscript could take a year to complete. It was then bound with decorated leather. Such a book was expensive and might be chained to the shelf

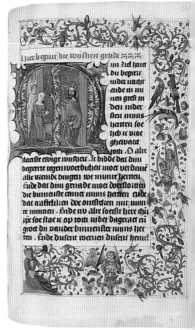

Late 15th century Dutch manuscript depicting the coronation of the virgin.

in a library. Monks often mixed their own inks using ground minerals. Red could be made from ground copper and salt, mixed with honey.

Sometimes, the capital letters of each page were illuminated with colored inks.

A Royal Proclamation

An important message from a king to his subjects was "proclaimed" by the herald who brought them. In your kit there is a proclamation. Sign it and then read it aloud like a herald. Stamp it with your seal which you will find in your kit. A seal was like a signature. A knight might have a signet ring which bore his initials or it might be a larger metal die as shown in the picture below. He would press it into warm wax to put his mark on a document. *(See pages 2-3 for instructions on how to use it.)*

Medieval books also had little pictures in the margins called drolleries, which were added to enliven the text.

This is the Great Seal used by King Richard I of England, also known as Richard the Lionheart.

enry, by the grace of God, Lord of this great kingdom, hereby do restore all Lands pertaining to his most loyal subject, the holder of this document.

Moreover, as befits a noble and courageous warrior, and because we wish to see Justice done, he shall be dubbed a knight by our hand. Let him be bathed and cleansed, as our custom demands, and wrapped in fine linen. Let him keep the vigil in prayer and contemplation. Then shall he be fitted with a cuirass second to none, that no lance or sword can pierce. After he be made a knight, gold spurs shall be set on his heels and he shall be raised up and take his arms, banner, and his shield.

As a sign that he do pledge loyalty to his liege lord and his kingdom, let him sign his name here below and seal it with his seal.

This photograph of the proclamation (above) has already been signed, sealed, and decorated.

DEATH WITH HONOR

Life was dangerous in medieval times. Medicine was crude, and hygiene almost unknown. Many people died of illnesses such as measles, flu, or smallpox, that are rarely fatal today. Babies had to be tough to survive common childhood ailments, and it was taken for granted that many of them would die.

Brass monument of a knight in full armor.

For the knight, death from fever or infection was as likely as death in battle. A rich knight would therefore plan his own memorial before he went to war. Many European churches contain splendid monuments to medieval knights.

Charlemagne, a powerful 9th century king, is shown mourning at the tomb of his nephew, Roland.

Full-sized carvings in wood or stone, called effigies, were popular with the very wealthy.

Wooden effigy of Sir Robert du Bois, c. 1335.

The Church was an influential force in people's lives. This stained glass window shows a knight praying at a statue of Mary Magdalene.

Stained Glass Windows

Windows of stained and painted glass were another way of remembering the dead. These might show pictures, rather like cartoons, of a knight in battle or in a religious scene. There is an image from a stained glass window in your secret drawer to color in. Look on page 31 for ideas on what colors to use.

Many effigies show the knight in full armor, or in the act of drawing his sword. Others are more peaceful, with the knight in an attitude of prayer.

Monuments of brass were also popular as memorials. These were made using sharp tools to cut a picture into a sheet of brass. They usually showed the knight in the full glory of his youth.

Prince Edward, the Black Prince, was knighted at the age of 16. He became known as the Black Prince because of the color of his jousting armor. His effigy (above) shows him wearing the arms of England (lions) and of France (fleurs-de-lys).

The tomb of St. Swithin, a ninth century bishop, became a famous shrine. According to tradition, whatever the weather on St. Swithin's Day (July 15th) it will remain the same for the next 40 days.

THE MAKING OF LEGENDS

King Arthur and his knights were the storybook heroes of the medieval world. It is not known if Arthur was a real person, but it seems likely that he was a fifth century warrior. Whatever his origins, stories of his bravery became so exaggerated that they soon became legendary.

In 1590, the Spanish author, Cervantes, wrote Don Quixote, *the story of a foolish old man who is an avid reader of chivalric romances and who, like the knights of old, attempts to put right the wrongs of the world.*

The story of Arthur was first written down by a Welshman, Geoffrey of Monmouth, in the 12th century in a book called *A History of Kings of England*. It told the tale of Arthur from birth to death, including his marriage to Lady Guinevere and his fight with the evil Mordred, who tried, and failed to take over his kingdom. Arthur's faithful company of knights included Sir Kay, Sir Gawain, and Sir Bedivere. The magician Merlin also made his appearance. The book was written in Latin and was instantly popular. Arthur was re-invented as a medieval king with a court of noble knights. In many ways, Arthur and his knights personified the ideal of chivalry.

This famous scene from the legend of King Arthur shows him mortally wounded at the lakeside. Sir Bedivere casts the sword, called Excalibur, into the lake, where it is caught by a mysterious hand.

The French author, Chretien de Troyes, added more to the story with the adventures of Sir Lancelot, his courtship of Lady Guinevere, and his quest for the Holy Grail. In your secret drawer there is a stained glass window of Sir Lancelot and Lady Guinevere *(right)* for you to color in.

Color in your stained glass window and hold it up against the light.

Dragon Slayers

The Church regarded the knight as her defender against evil. The dragon was often seen as the symbol of evil, so many stories of this period told of brave knights doing battle with dragons.

Illustration from the romance, Sir Gawain and the Green Knight. Sir Gawain does battle with a lion, a giant, a dragon, and a troll.

This 16th century illustration shows St. George slaying the evil dragon and rescuing the princess. In fact, St. George was a soldier who was killed by the Romans in A.D. 350.

A FEMALE KNIGHT

In medieval times, power lay almost entirely with men. Women had few opportunities to prove themselves. One rare exception was Joan of Arc, who changed the outcome of the war between France and England in 1429, at the tender age of 17.

Joan of Arc, like most girls of 15th century France, never learned to read or write.

Joan of Arc believed she was inspired by visions of the saints to go to the aid of the king. She dressed in men's armor and set out to lead the French into victory.

Joan of Arc is the national heroine of France. She was declared a saint in 1920. She is also known as the Maid of Orleans.

She was completely fearless in battle and managed to inspire the roughest fighting men with confidence. She turned the tide of the war, but she was later captured by the English and put on trial for heresy and witchcraft. She defended herself with wit and courage but still had to suffer the fate of the alleged witches – death by burning.

**A Home Subscription! It's the easiest and most convenient way
to get every one of the exciting Coventry Romance Novels!
...And you get 4 of them FREE!**

You pay nothing extra for this convenience: there are no additional
charges...you don't even pay for postage! Fill out and send us the handy
coupon now, and we'll send you 4 exciting Coventry Romance
novels absolutely FREE!

SEND NO MONEY, GET THESE
FOUR BOOKS
FREE!

━━ ━━ ━━ ━━ ━━ ━━ ━━ ━━ ━━ ━━ ━━ ━━ ━━

C0281

MAIL THIS COUPON TODAY TO:
COVENTRY HOME
SUBSCRIPTION SERVICE
6 COMMERCIAL STREET
HICKSVILLE, NEW YORK 11801

YES, please start a Coventry Romance Home Subscription in my name,
and send me FREE and without obligation to buy, my 4 Coventry Romances.
If you do not hear from me after I have examined my 4 FREE books, please
send me the 6 new Coventry Romances each month as soon as they come
off the presses. I understand that I will be billed only $10.50 for all 6 books.
There are no shipping and handling nor any other hidden charges. There is
no minimum number of monthly purchases that I have to make. In fact, I can
cancel my subscription at any time. The first 4 FREE books are mine to keep
as a gift, even if I do not buy any additional books.

For added convenience, your monthly subscription may be charged automatically to your credit card.

☐ Master Charge   ☐ Visa

Credit Card #_____

Expiration Date_____

Name_____
                              (Please Print)
Address_____

City_____State_____Zip_____

Signature_____

☐ Bill Me Direct Each Month

This offer expires March 31, 1981. Prices subject to change without notice.
Publisher reserves the right to substitute alternate FREE books. Sales tax collected where required by law. Offer valid for new members only.

THE
TARRANT
ROSE

Veronica Heley

FAWCETT COVENTRY • NEW YORK

THE TARRANT ROSE

Published by Fawcett Coventry Books, a unit of CBS Pub-
lications, the Consumer Publishing Division of CBS Inc.

ISBN: 0-449-50163-9

Printed in the United States of America

First Fawcett Coventry printing: February 1981

10   9   8   7   6   5   4   3   2   1

Chapter One

The traveling coach rumbled steadily along the bottom of the valley, drawn by six matched bays. The crest of the gilded Swan on the door panels, and the green and gold liveries of the coachmen, guards and outriders identified the owner of this magnificence as the Earl of Rame. It had been dry of late, and the ruts in the road, although several inches deep, had been hardened by frost, so that they made good progress. Leafless trees climbed the slopes of the hills on either side of them, up to the darkening sky. The Earl and his entourage had set out from London the previous morning, stayed overnight with a relative of his, and expected to reach the Earl's manor of Hamberley before another night fell. Dusk was beginning to deepen the shadows in the valley, but the coachman did not stop to light the lanterns. He did not know this road, but the postboy had assured him that Hamberley lay round the nearside hill. The bitter winds of March and the fatigue of the long journey kept both coachman and outriders silent. Their thoughts were on the log fires, hot punch and roast meats that awaited them at their journey's end.

The occupants of the coach were also silent. Chivers, the valet, sat with his feet neatly together in a corner, holding his master's jewel-case on his knees. Mr. Denbigh, who had once been tutor to the Earl and now fulfilled that office to the Earl's son and heir, sat opposite his master, and tried not to fidget. He was not an old man, having entered the service of the Earls of Rame when he graduated from Cambridge,

5

but his muscles were protesting at his having sat still for so long. Also, he fretted about Thomas. It was all very well for the Earl to say that doctor and nurse would be perfectly capable of looking after the boy for a few days, but Thomas had not been well for months. Mr. Denbigh, like most over-conscientious people, was sure that his charge would take a turn for the worse as soon as his back was turned. Had it really been necessary for him to accompany the Earl to Hamberley? Could not the Earl have decided for himself whether or not the place was suitable to house Thomas for a few months? Normally, the boy would have spent the summer at the Earl's great house in Rame, but an outbreak of smallpox there had rendered that scheme impossible. But Bath would surely have been a more suitable place to send the boy than this desolate valley?

Yet when the Earl had requested Mr. Denbigh's presence on this trip, the tutor had not seen fit to demur. Philip Gervase St. John Rich, fourth Earl of Rame, never found it necessary to raise his voice in order to have his orders obeyed. Tall and slim, the Earl's figure was set off to perfection by the brocaded coats, ruffled shirts and massive periwigs that were de rigueur at Court. He was wearing Court dress today because the relative with whom he had spent the previous night had held a position at George I's court years ago, and still believed that a man was in a state of undress unless he were painted, patched, bewigged and clad in the latest fashion.

Mr. Denbigh thought it was typical of Philip to have donned Court dress in order to please his host, when everyone knew that the Earl found such fripperies a nuisance, and that he would far have preferred to dress plainly and foreswear powder and paint. Once Mr. Denbigh had worried about this tendency of Philip's to defer to the wishes of others at the expense of his own inclinations, but he did so no longer. Philip had been born with a sense of duty, and his parents had reinforced this trait. It had been impressed on him also that to be an Earl of Rame was to be the equal of any man alive, and only slightly inferior to the King. It was almost entirely due to Mr. Denbigh's humane influence on a reserved and lonely boy that the Earl's chief characteristic nowadays was a sense of duty, rather than pride in his position.

Philip had been obedient to his parents' wishes during their lifetime; going on an extended Grand Tour of Europe

6

with Mr. Denbigh, and then marrying the heiress selected for him. Pretty but captious, his wife had found little to interest her in her handsome, silent husband, but had presented him with four children before death removed her and her last, stillborn child from the fashionable world which she had loved so much.

Freed of constraint by his parents' death in an epidemic shortly after, the new Earl had at long last decided to follow his own inclinations. Despite objections from family and friends, he had left London to fight in Flanders with the British Army. Mr. Denbigh had been recalled from a tedious position in Cornwall to take charge of the nursery at Rame, in which were lodged the motherless children. None of them had ever been strong, and in spite of Mr. Denbigh's anxious care, there was only one ailing boy left by the time that Philip was invalided home from Flanders.

Before Philip had been back in England a month, Society was pairing him off with this heiress or that beauty. Everyone was agreed that he must marry again, yet he seemed in no hurry to do so. His broken arm had healed well enough, yet the amusements of the Town failed to divert him. His sojourn abroad, far from doing him a disservice in the eyes of the King, had brought him to the notice of His Majesty. George II was a straightforward person with three great passions in life—for his dead Queen, for the genealogies of the crowned heads of Europe, and for his Army. It was his greatest triumph that he had led his troops into battle at Dettingen, and his greatest sorrow that his ministers would not let him repeat this action. He welcomed Philip back to Court and appointed him Gentleman of the Bedchamber.

It surprised most people in the fashionable world that Philip should accept such a position, which was supposed to be beneath the dignity of an Earl. However, the pundits said that there was more to the appointment than met the eye. Had not the King also appointed Lord Lincoln a Gentleman of the Bedchamber? Lord Lincoln was one of Philip's closest friends, but his chief claim to fame was that he was nephew to the all-powerful Secretary of State, the Duke of Newcastle, who now headed the Government. George II detested Newcastle, although he liked young Lincoln, and forgave him for being related to the Duke. Newcastle represented a new trend in politics which took no account of the King's love of Hanover, the land which had given him birth, and which he

7

always regarded as his real home. The King would have preferred to continue seeking counsel from his ex-minister, Lord Carteret, who shared his views on European politics. Although Carteret had officially fallen from power, he was often to be found at the King's elbow and, this was the significant point, Philip was Lord Carteret's nephew.

It looked as though the King was seeking to counterbalance Newcastle's influence at Court by making Philip Gentleman of the Bedchamber.

Mr. Denbigh had often discussed politics with Philip, but he did not know his erstwhile pupil's mind on this matter. Philip had not chosen to confide in him of late. It had crossed Mr. Denbigh's mind that his master had commanded the tutor's presence on this journey to unburden himself of whatever it was that troubled him; for it was clear to Mr. Denbigh that the Earl was worried about something. It might, of course, be the affair of his projected marriage to Lady Millicent. . . . Mr. Denbigh feared the lady was as shallow as the Earl's first wife had been.

He sighed. The Earl lowered his gaze from the silk-lined roof of his carriage and smiled at Mr. Denbigh.

"Are you very tired?" he asked. "We must nearly be there." He took a gold watch from his pocket, opened the case and flicked a knob. The watch chimed the hour, and then the quarter.

"I confess I shall be glad to arrive," said Mr. Denbigh. "It looks like snow."

"You are cold?" Chivers had laid a fur over the Earl's knees, not because his master felt the cold, but because Chivers deemed it proper that the Earl be smothered in furs when he traveled. Mr. Denbigh was about to admit that he did feel a trifle chilled when the sound of a shot rang along the valley. "What was that? Highwaymen, do you think?" He peered out of the window.

"We have two armed men with us," said the Earl soothingly. "No one would dare to attack us." Nevertheless the thought was present in both men's minds that it was some time since they had passed any signs of human habitation. The Earl's dress sword hung in a loop from the upholstery beside him. The hilt was adorned with gems which glittered as the coach swayed. They were not riding as smoothly as they had been before the shot had been fired. No doubt the horses had been startled by the sound. The Earl caressed the

8

hilt of his sword and then let go of it, as if he had thought better of an impulse to arm himself.

Chivers cleared his throat. "Begging your pardon, my lord, but that shot sounded as if it came from somewhere on the road ahead of us."

The Earl's hand dropped onto the small pistol which traveled in a concealed pocket beside him. Without hurrying, he checked that the pistol was primed. He smiled apologetically at his companions. "A sportsman in the woods, probably. Perhaps a poacher? I daresay we shan't see or hear anything more of him. Do you know, I haven't had a gun in my hand since I left the Army?" His grin was boyish. Mr. Denbigh and Chivers relaxed, as he had intended that they should.

There was a change in the rhythm of the horse's hooves. The coachman's whip cracked overhead, and he shouted something in a hoarse, surprised voice. Another shot rang out, this time nearer to them. The coach jerked, as the coachman's whip cracked above the horses. Above them, someone screamed. Chivers put his master's jewel-case on the floor between his feet.

"Put it under my rug," said the Earl. With his left hand he threw the rug away from him, onto the seat at his side. His brocaded coat shimmered in the dusk, and the lace at his throat and wrists gleamed as white as the paint on his face. He kicked his feet free of the fur, and the diamonds on his buckled shoes flashed fire.

A shot rang out close to them. Someone above them was shouting for them to stop, for God's sake! The coach swayed, bucking as it was driven over rough ground. The trees were close to them on their left. They were being driven to the side of the road.

"Was that our guard who fired?" Mr. Denbigh's hand sought his neatly starched cravat. Another shot resounded through the valley, this time from above. They could hear the coachman cursing, and another man babbling that he was hurt. Another shot...a cry...a heavy object fell past the window of the coach and disappeared.

"He's dropped his gun!" Mr. Denbigh half rose in his seat.

"Sit down, and keep still," said the Earl. He cocked his pistol.

One of the horses whinnied with fear. The coach shuddered to a halt. The silhouette of a man in a tricorne hat appeared at the window next the Earl. The newcomer's gloved hand

9

held a blunderbuss, and his face was masked with a triangle of dark material.

"Stand and deliver!" The dreaded words lifted Mr. Denbigh's hands above his head. Chivers looked at his master for instructions. The Earl's face showed neither surprise nor fear.

"Open the door. Get out!" ordered the highwayman. He seemed impatient, glancing from the occupants of the carriage to the road ahead of them. The Earl nodded at Mr. Denbigh, who lowered his hands and felt for the handle of the door. The highwayman pulled his horse back, so that the door could swing open and allow the occupants of the coach to descend.

The highwayman's head and shoulders made a good target against the skyline. The Earl put out one hand to prevent Mr. Denbigh from leaving the coach, and raised the other, with the pistol in it. He shot the highwayman through the head. The man threw his arms wide, his horse reared, and slipped the man off the saddle and down onto the road. Before the highwayman's body had settled into its last position, the Earl had leaped from the coach, without waiting for the steps to be lowered. He stooped over the robber, in order to collect the man's weapon, which luckily had not been discharged in the fall. The horse, riderless, reared again, and then galloped off down the road, stirrups and reins flying loose.

The Earl ran forward, towards the horses' heads. A warning shout from the coachman, and he whirled, brocaded skirts swinging. The coachman was still in his box, supporting one of the guards...there was blood on both men's faces...the second guard was furiously trying to reload his weapon...the grooms and the postboy were struggling with the horses, which were plunging and rearing in fright...the off-leader entangled in the traces....

A second highwayman, dressed like the first, edged his horse round the back of the carriage, blunderbuss levelled.

"Halt, or I fire!" cried the Earl, raising his newly-acquired weapon.

"Fool!" said the second highwayman. He swivelled his gun from the Earl to the coachman and back. "Drop your weapons, I say!"

The Earl pulled the trigger. Almost at the same instant, the highwayman fired, and the ball parted the curls of the Earl's peruke. The highwayman was not so fortunate. He was hit in the right arm. With an oath he dragged his horse's head round and set spurs to its flanks. Horse and rider thundered off up the hillside between the trees and were soon lost to sight.

"The Lord be praised!" exclaimed Mr. Denbigh. "You are not hurt, Philip?" In moments of stress, Mr. Denbigh was still inclined to address the Earl by his Christian name.

"My lord!" The coachman pointed to the road ahead.

The Earl turned to see what was the matter. Two men were struggling in the middle of the road. A fine black stallion, which showed signs of having been ridden hard, lay at the side of the road, kicking feebly. Nearby stood another horse, shifting nervously this way and that. As the Earl began to run towards the struggling couple, there was a muffled shot, and the strength seemed to go out of one of the men. He slithered to the ground, clutching his breast. The victor straightened himself, a smoking pistol in his hand. Hearing the pad of the Earl's feet, he glanced over his shoulder. His hat had fallen off, and his mask been torn from his face, but the dusk was kind to him, so that the Earl only caught a glimpse of a pleasant, plump face under a neat tie-wig. The murderer's head turned further, assessing how much assistance the Earl could muster. The servants, released from fear now that two of the highwaymen had been put out of commission and the third had discharged his pistol, were leaving the coach and advancing along the road.

"You are under arrest!" cried the Earl, while still some way from the scene of the crime. The murderer looked around him, as if wondering what had become of his accomplices. A shrill whistle sounded from the hillside above them. A signal? The murderer stooped over his victim, and made a grab into the pockets of his greatcoat. Then, as the Earl was almost within reach, the murderer ran for his horse, leaped on its back, and was off and away into the woods, whistling shrilly as he did so.

The Earl halted, scanning the dark woods above him. Those trees could be hiding a hundred dark-clad figures. There was a crashing sound, and a riderless horse galloped down the hillside and bolted past them, wild with fear. One moment he was there, and the next he was gone. What had frightened him?

The Earl hesitated. He was now unarmed, and he did not know how many more men the highwaymen could muster.

11

If they chose to return now, in force, the occupants of the coach would be at their mercy.

"*Au secours!*" The faint cry came from the wounded man. He was not dead, but failing fast. Blood welled from a wound in his chest. His greatcoat and clothing beneath were blackened with powderburns, and his gloved hands were soaked with blood. A diamond clasp glinted among the laces at his throat, and the head of his riding crop nearby was of chased gold. Undoubtedly he had been worth robbing.

Mr. Denbigh caught up with the Earl, bringing his master his dress sword.

"My lord, return to the carriage, I beg. Who knows what will happen next?"

The coachman, too, came panting up to make his report. The off-leader had been cut free; but could not be ridden. The postboy swore this valley had never before been frequented by highwaymen, but he was probably lying; or maybe in league with the thieves...the one guard had a bad head-wound, which was being bound up by Mr. Chivers...the second guard—a useless fellow, begging your pardon, my lord, but why you ever took him on is a mystery to me!—he was blaming everyone but himself, because it appeared that his powder was damp and therefore they could not reload any of their guns.

"We will proceed as quickly as we can. I have a small flask of powder in the coach. Reload as many guns as you can from that. The postboy must lead the lamed horse, and one of the outriders walk along with him." The Earl glanced up at the sky, and from that to the leafless trees around. A heavy silence had fallen on the valley around them, but they felt that they were being watched. The moon was rising, but there were too many clouds in the sky to hope for a clear night. "Light the lanterns, and send me one here. We cannot leave the highwayman's body. We must take him with us, and this poor man, too."

"Not in my coach, my lord!"

"If you please," said the Earl.

The coachman sighed. "Oh, very well, my lord." He began to retrace his steps.

"Send Chivers to me." The Earl called after him. "And brandy."

The Earl dropped to one knee beside the wounded man, and raised his hand from the ground. The man's clothes were of good quality and he wore a fashionable wig. The horse he had been riding gave one last kick and expired. Mr. Denbigh leaned over his master.

"My lord," he whispered. "I think the man is French!"

"You think we should refuse him aid, because we are at war with France?"

That was precisely what Mr. Denbigh had meant, but he did not like to say so. Chivers ran up with a flask of brandy and the Earl's dressing-case. One of the outriders followed more slowly with a lantern, which he set down on the road beside the dying man.

"I beg, my lord," said Chivers, "That you will permit me to hold the man for you. Your coat..."

"The stains will give you something on which to exercise your art," said the Earl, continuing to support the Frenchman. Chivers set the brandy to the Frenchman's lips, and his eyelids fluttered. He began to pant out phrases in French and English. The Earl jerked his head at the outrider, who retired to the coach.

"I beg you...last request....*Dieu vous remercie...très importante*...a matter of life and death...." The man's hand dropped to his boot, and he tugged feebly at it.

"Take his boot off," said the Earl to Chivers. "The man is carrying something of importance inside. The highwaymen may have taken whatever was in his pockets, but it seems he has outwitted them."

Chivers eased off the dying man's boot. Within lay a letter, heavily sealed, which he handed to the Earl. There was no superscription on the letter.

"Êtes-vous catholique?" asked the Frenchman, his eyes fixed on the Earl's face.

"You want a priest?"

"Oui...mais ce n'est pas..." The dying man tried to lift himself, and failed.

"We are not Catholics," said the Earl. "We would carry you to the nearest Catholic household if we knew where one might be found, but we are strangers in these parts. We are traveling to Hamberly. It is not above a couple of miles from here, I believe, but..."

"I will not live to see it," gasped the Frenchman. He pointed with a trembling hand to the letter. "The letter.... *jurez*...promise me you will deliver it?"

13

"Only tell me where it is to go, and I will see that it is delivered."

The Frenchman mouthed something, but no sound came out. The Earl bent his head. Mr. Denbigh began to whisper the Lord's Prayer. Darkness shrouded the woods, but the lantern lit up every feature of the group in the road. The Frenchman's face had become waxen with the approach of death. He put up a wavering hand. He tried to sit upright. The Earl aided him.

"At the sign of the Ram and Rose." All three men heard the whisper. The Frenchman tried to repeat the words, but though his lips moved, no further sound came from them. His eyes were wide, expressing the agony he felt in trying to make himself understood.

"I understand," said the Earl. "The letter is to be delivered at the sign of the Ram and Rose."

The Frenchman tried to say something more. His body arched, and an expression of pain contorted his features. Then he seemed to become boneless. He hung slackly in the Earl's arms. Philip let the lifeless body sink to the ground and stood up.

"Lay the man in the carriage. The highwayman's body can travel outside, but this man deserved something better. He was an inside passenger in life, and we will accord him equal respect in death. Wrap his body in one of my cloaks."

A shrill whistle sounded from the hill above them. The three men stood in the road, awaiting attack, but none came. All was silence, except for the wind, which had begun to rustle the dead leaves of the trees.

"Hurry," said the Earl, dropping his voice. "The sooner we are away from here, the better."

The morning after the Earl's arrival at Hamberley dawned dark and gloomy. The Earl and Mr. Denbigh made a quick tour of the manor house, and then sat down for breakfast in one of the small, wainscotted parlors. The silver and china on the gate-legged table set close to the fire bore the Earl's crest, and glistened in the firelight, but everything else in the room looked shabby. The Earl's butler, who had traveled down ahead of his master, together with the riding horses and a picked band of servants, signalled to a footman to serve the hot chocolate, and continued his report.

"The nearest magistrate is one Sir John Bladen. Your note advising him of the contretemps with the highwaymen was sent to him first thing this morning, and a servant has just now returned with the information that Sir John will wait on you at noon. I do not know where you will wish to receive him, my lord. There is not a single room capable of holding a decent company in this house, the situation is damp, and the chef unhappy with the kitchen range. The furnishings have moths, the staircases woodworm, and there is dry rot in the hall."

"You've forgotten something," said the Earl, "There is nothing but the yard of a farm to be seen from the windows of the reception rooms. You are quite right...this is no place to bring my son. We will move on to Bath as soon as the horses are rested."

"Very good, my lord." The butler managed to express approval in the depth of his bow. "There is one other thing I should mention, my lord. There are two casks of French brandy and a chest of tea in the apple loft. I would not normally draw your attention to such a trifling matter, but this is Sussex, and..."

"Smugglers, by Jove!" cried Mr. Denbigh. "You think they left the contraband for our consumption, as a bribe?"

"No, sir. We think they may have been using the outbuildings here to store their goods, seeing that the house has been empty for so long. Two men were seen lurking in the yard last night near the staircase which leads to the apple loft, but they ran off when they realized that their presence was observed."

"Awkward." The Earl extended his cup to be refilled. "We don't want to become embroiled with local smugglers. I suggest we leave both the brandy and tea where they are, and pretend we haven't noticed them."

"We could report the matter to this local magistrate when he calls."

"Ten to one, he's hand in glove with the Free Traders. But perhaps you are right. We will tell him about it. I daresay he will be very surprised and indignant and promise to have something done about it at once; and the contraband will duly disappear. One thing more," he said to the butler, "A friend of mine said he might put up locally for a few days,

15

at the sign of the Ram and Rose. Will you make enquiries where the inn may be?"

The servants withdrew, and Mr. Denbigh scowled at the fire. He was sure that the sheets on his bed last night had been damp, and there was an ache in his left shoulder which boded no good. The Earl yawned. He was dressed in a brocaded morning gown and wore a silk cap on his closely-cropped head. Without powder and paint, he looked barely older than on the day when Mr. Denbigh had first met him, so many years ago. His sandy hair and eyebrows might be a shade darker than then, his skin more sallow, and his smile readier; that was all. Only, his eyes were no longer those of a trusting boy. Mr. Denbigh thought the Earl looked tired.

"It's a pity this place is unsuitable," Philip said. "My late wife inherited it from an uncle. I believe she only stayed here two or three times herself. Judging by the proximity of the farmyard, her uncle must have been more interested in the production of pigs than I am. But my bailiff should have seen to the repairs." He strolled around the room, tapping the woodwork. "I see little enough of the boy as it is. I thought that if we could have had a couple of months here, in good hunting country, before I had to go to Hanover with the King....I wonder if I could hire a suitable place hereabouts. But that would all take time. You had better make arrangements to take Thomas to Bath yourself."

"But what are you going to do? Do you not come with us?" The Earl had recently concluded a spell of duty as Gentleman of the Bedchamber, and was on leave from the Court until May.

"I wish I could, but I must stay here until our little mystery has been cleared up." The Earl sighed. "I wish I had not killed the man."

"He was only a highwayman. His fate would have been worse, if you had captured him. Hanging or transportation would have been his lot."

The Earl peered out of the window. "What on earth possessed them to build a house in this valley? There is no outlook at all. They ought to have built on the south side of that hill there." He turned his back on the outside world. "Did you hear what Chivers said to me last night when he helped me out of the coach? He said, 'How shall we dispose of the Jacobite gentleman, my lord?' A most acute rogue, Chivers."

"Jacobite?" Mr. Denbigh breathed the word. He went to

16

the door and opened it sharply, as if expecting to find someone listening at the keyhole. He looked out, closed the door, and stood with his back to it. "No one there. Philip, are you serious? You think that the man we tried to help last night was a Jacobite? On what grounds?"

"Circumstantial evidence. He was French, and traveling to a part of the country which has always had strong Jacobite sympathies, at a time when France is at war with England. He was carrying a letter which was a matter of life and death, and yet the letter bore no superscription. He was attacked by a number of masked men who were unusually well accoutered for highwaymen. One of the highwaymen had sufficient nerve to grab the contents of his pockets, but ignored a valuable diamond clasp at the man's throat, and his gold-headed riding crop. Also, there have been rumors in government circles of a Jacobite conspiracy originating in this part of the world."

"Gracious heavens!"

"That is partly why I came here. Only partly, of course, for I did hope that the place would be suitable for Thomas; but I was actually asked to come here, if I could do so without causing comment."

"By whom?"

"My uncle Carteret, of course. If anyone has his finger on the international pulse, it is he. He thought I might pick up some local gossip about local Catholic families. He had no idea that I would fall over a Jacobite courier before I'd even got here."

Mr. Denbigh had his hands to his head. "You think the highwaymen were after the Frenchman's papers, and not his valuables?" The Earl nodded. "How could they know that he carried important papers?"

"I don't think they were highwaymen, at all. I think they were Government agents, who had been set to watch for a courier. They would probably have had orders to let the man get to his destination before they arrested him and whoever he delivered the letters to, but...who can tell what went wrong? The courier may have become suspicious, turned to face them, to fight it out with them, rather than risk taking them on to his destination. He did not lack for courage, did he?"

"But if they were not highwaymen, why did they hold us up?"

"How could they avoid doing so, once we had stumbled on their ambush?"

"If that is true, you killed a Government agent last night."

"I think I probably did." The Earl made a moue of distaste. "Of course, only you and I and Chivers suspect that the man was anything other than he appeared to be. Certainly he deserved to be shot for his bungling of the affair."

Mr. Denbigh tried to laugh. "Oh, this is all nonsense. The letter will be found to be a love missive, and the man you shot really was a highwayman."

"We shall see. I agree with you that it all hangs on the letter." The Earl touched a handbell, and when a footman appeared, asked him to request his valet's attendance. "Chivers is a man of parts," said his master, when the footman had departed. "I suspect he has not always kept good company. He volunteered the information, this morning, that he knew how to remove the seals from letters and replace them without anyone being the wiser. The seal on the letter which the Frenchman was carrying is impressed with someone's personal crest. I dare not break it, and therefore shall be glad to avail myself of Chivers' offer."

"How could an honest man have acquired such a skill?" demanded Mr. Denbigh.

"I haven't the slightest intention of asking him," said the Earl.

The valet appeared, bearing a candle in a tarnished silver holder. The Earl produced the letter given him by the Frenchman, Chivers lit the candle, heated a thin-bladed knife in the flame and then edged it between seal and paper. He repeated this operation over and over until the wax finally parted from the paper, and the letter fell open.

"You need not go," said the Earl to his valet. "Sir John Bladen will want to take your deposition as to the events of last night. It would be as well if we decide together on what we are to say to him." He smoothed out the letter, read it, and then handed it on to Mr. Denbigh. Chivers peered over the tutor's shoulder at a discreet distance.

"So, it is all true," mused the Earl. "A letter from Charles Stuart, the Young Pretender, addressed to the Chief of his Company of Friends, inciting him to rebel. Therefore, the Frenchman was a Jacobite courier, and the man I shot was a Government agent and no highwayman."

"Treason!" exclaimed Mr. Denbigh. "It is treason to correspond with the Pretender, or either of his sons. Anyone who does so risks death, and the forfeiture of his estates."

"Which is probably why the letter was not addressed to any one specific," said the Earl. "The courier knew to whom it was to be delivered, and he has given us a clue to the man's name. Leave the letter on the table, Chivers. Mr. Denbigh must make a copy of it before you reseal it. Now, who should I send to London with my report? A pity that guard was wounded. Now that reminds me, I haven't seen him this morning. Is he all right?"

"Well enough, my lord, and pleased with the sovereign you gave him. But he won't be fit to ride inside a week."

"The other guard—the one who allowed his powder to become damp—what is his name? Greenwood or Greenwich, or something like that. Was he drunk? He acted like it, and it's not the first time I've seen him the worse for wear on duty. He might have got us all killed," said the Earl. "See that he is dismissed, will you? Give him enough money to get back to London, on top of whatever wages are due to him, and get him off the premises before he does any more damage. We will send one of the grooms to London—the one whose mother lives at the lodge at Rame. He's quick and willing and knows where my lord Carteret lives."

He sat down and began to mend a quill. Chivers consulted his watch.

"My lord, it is nearly half past eleven, and Sir John Bladen waits on you at noon."

"I had not forgotten," said the Earl, beginning to write. "We will tell him nothing about the traveler being French, or about the letter, or what we may have surmised concerning the 'highwaymen.' We will simply make a report, a factual report, of what happened. We will say that we interrupted some armed and masked men in the act of robbing a solitary horseman, that we shot at two or them, wounding one and killing another. We are informing him of this so that he may take the usual steps, as Magistrate of the Peace, etcetera.... Then we hand over both bodies to him. There was no identification on either body, was there?—and give him a glass of wine, and that will be that."

Mr. Denbigh interposed. "Ought we not to ask Sir John if there are any Jacobites in the vicinity?"

"Sir John may be the very man to whom the letter is addressed. It is possible. We know nothing of him. Country magistrates have been known to commit treason, and to smuggle contraband before now. Even if he is not a Jacobite, he may be a fool, or worse still, have a loose tongue in his head. If I confide in him, he may give his friends a nod here and a wink there, saying 'I could a tale unfold....' The news would be all over the country within the hour, and our Jacobite warned that we are on his track. Let us tell Sir John what he needs to know in order to give the dead men a decent burial, let us report on the matter to Lord Carteret, and then let us forget the whole thing."

"Yes, my lord, I quite agree. But what I meant was that you have very little time to dress before Sir John arrives, and knowing these country gentry, he will arrive early."

"I do not intend to dress."

Chivers drew himself up. "My lord, with all respect—I beg of you to remember what is due to your rank. This may be the country, but it is not Rame, where everyone knows you. Sir John may only be a gentleman in a small way, but he is the local magistrate, and is waiting on you in his official capacity. It is only fitting that you receive him in a manner becoming your station." The Earl threw down his quill, and Chivers smiled. "I have already laid out your clothes, my lord."

"One of these days I shall decline to be bullied into dressing when I do not wish to do so," said the Earl. "Denbigh, will you copy out this letter for me, and draft a report on the matter to my uncle? Also, if there is time before Sir John arrives, will you find out whether any of the other servants have heard of the inn we seek?"

"I anticipated your wish," said Chivers, "And have already made enquiries. There are two Rose and Crowns in the vicinity, three Boars of different colors, one Queen's Head and a White Hart. There are smugglers everywhere and a witch or two, but no one has heard of the inn you seek."

Even before Sir John Bladen had greeted his host, the Earl had formed an unfavorable opinion of the man. It had taken Philip some time to dress, and when Sir John arrived, Mr. Denbigh had been sent to make his master's apologies, and offer Sir John refreshments. It seemed, however, that Sir John had considered himself insulted by Mr. Denbigh's

20

company. As the Earl entered, he heard Sir John say that he would not demean himself to discuss matters of importance with a mere tutor. Since Mr. Denbigh was not only highly esteemed, but also loved by the Earl, Sir John's dictum was not likely to please him, and the visitor's subsequent conduct merely reinforced the Earl's first impression of the man. Sir John was not tall, but he was overweight and overdressed. He fawned on the Earl and ignored Mr. Denbigh. In this Sir John proved himself to be not only insensible to Mr. Denbigh's feelings but unaware that the Earl did not share his low opinion of his "inferiors." Before the matter of the highwaymen was broached, the Earl had formed the opinion that Sir John was an ill-educated fool with a high opinion of himself, who despised all branches of learning save those connected with the chase and the cockfight. He had inherited a fortune and believed it entitled him to consort on equal terms with the highest in the land. Sir John did not lack a certain degree of animal cunning, but this was counterbalanced by a tendency to boastfulness. Moreover, his person was offensive to the nose, and his manners and language coarse. Philip conducted his business with despatch, and got rid of the man. Sir John Bladen, he had decided, was definitely not the man to entrust with delicate investigations into the affairs of local Jacobites, although the Earl did not think it likely that the man was one himself.

The second day after the Earl's arrival at Hamberley dawned misty, but with a promise of better weather to come. After a morning spent with his bailiff, the Earl called for his favorite horse to be saddled. Despite his valet's protestations, he had discarded his fashionable clothes and periwig in favor of one of the plain but good broadcloth suits, and the neat tie-wig he liked to wear when riding about his estates at Rame. In vain Chivers protested that the Earl did not do himself justice dressed "like any Tom, Dick or Harry." The Earl smoothed a darn in his sleeve—this was one of the coats he had worn campaigning in Flanders—and picked up his riding crop.

"One patch," begged Chivers. "And allow me to darken your eyebrows."

The Earl smiled at his valet, and walked out. He took a

deep breath of farmyard air, and hastily put his handkerchief to his nose. Once more his eyes wandered over the undulating landscape and settled on the wooded hill which had attracted his attention from the parlor window. The bleak sun laid a clear wash of color over the hill. Yes, that would be a good place to build a house.

A gig was driven into the farmyard, and the driver alighted from it. He was hatchet-faced, of mature years, and had the air of a gentleman. The new arrival swept off his hat and made a leg.

"Good morning, sir. Carramine's the name, from Carramine House, on the far side of the village. Have I the pleasure of addressing—?"

"Rame, at your service."

Mr. Carramine's eyes were light and lively. Philip had the impression that the newcomer was taking an inventory of everything he wore, and of every item of live and farm stock in the yard.

"Delighted to have caught you at home, my lord. A small matter of business...extremely tiresome...no need for you to trouble yourself if you are on your way somewhere."

The Earl looked hard at the gig, and thought that if Mr. Carramine had been making an ordinary morning's call, he would have ridden and not driven over.

"No trouble at all," he said politely. "You will take a glass of wine with me?"

"Delighted, my lord. Some other time, perhaps? Business first, eh? I believe you have been the embarrassed recipient of some goods which were not intended for you. Local smuggling very prevalent, I'm afraid. Came to my ears—being J.P., you know—came straight over to relieve you of the contraband...if you will be so good as to tell your servants to let me have the goods?"

"So Sir John told you about the contraband, and you came straight over to collect it? Mr. Carramine, the wind is very sharp. I insist that you have a glass of wine with me."

Once the footman had poured out their wine, the Earl dismissed his servant, so that he could be alone with his guest. An intelligent man, the Earl thought as he scrutinized Mr. Carramine. A man of decision, a man of action, and a man who enjoyed life. Was he also a smuggler? It seemed very possible. The Earl leaned back in his chair and put up his quizzing glass. Mr. Carramine smiled blandly at his host, and waited to hear what the Earl had to say. Now, the Earl's quizzing glass was a weapon which he could use with deadly effect on nervous people. It seemed that Mr. Carramine had strong nerves.

"So you are yet another of the magistrates hereabouts?" the Earl asked. "I met one of your colleagues, Sir John Bladen, yesterday. I had to ask him to take charge of the bodies of a highwayman and his unfortunate victim. You heard of the matter?"

"It's all over the county."

"Sir John was horrified that such a thing should have occurred locally. He said he could not remember any instance of highwaymen being in this part of the world before. Can you?"

"I can't say I can."

"Before he took the bodies away, I showed him the contraband we had found in the apple loft. He seemed equally horrified about that. He declared that he had never heard of such a thing, in these parts." The Earl contrived to give the impression that although he had given Sir John the benefit of the doubt in the first matter, he believed Sir John had been lying when he had disclaimed all knowledge of smuggling locally. Mr. Carramine ironed out a smile with the ball of his thumb.

"I formed the impression," continued the Earl, "That Sir John was blind, deaf and dumb on certain subjects. Perhaps this is an affliction which descends on everyone around here when the word 'smugglers' is mentioned?"

"It might well be." Mr. Carramine gave a short bark of laughter.

"I would like to make it clear that I have no interest in smuggling. I detest the Trade because it is undermining the economy—every piece of contraband is paid for with good English gold, which goes into the pockets of our enemies—but I am not here to do anything about the Free Traders."

"You have been asking questions about this and that. Naturally, we wondered why you had come here."

"I have been trying to locate an inn called the Ram and the Rose." A blank expression settled on Mr. Carramine's face. The Earl took another sip of wine and noted that Mr. Carramine knew more than he was prepared to divulge.

"I know of no such inn."

The Earl withheld a sigh. First Chivers, and then Mr.

Carramine, had denied knowledge of the existence of the place. It was a blow. He must think again about the disposal of the letter. In the meantime, Mr. Carramine was a pleasant companion; which was more than the Earl could have said about Sir John Bladen.

"What makes a gentleman take to Free Trading?" he asked.

"A gentleman like me, you mean?" Mr. Carramine grinned. "I suppose there are as many motives as there are gentlemen involved. For a gentleman such as myself, I suppose the answer would be the boredom of country life. I am comfortably off, my estates are in the hands of a good bailiff, my wife—God bless her—is dead, and my children married. My neighbors are only interested in hunting and cockfighting and fishing. I find it difficult to converse with them, except with the aid of the Country Interpreter—the bottle! I find nothing to interest me in the fashionable pursuits of London Town. I like the country hereabouts. I'm too old to serve as a soldier. Oh yes, a gentleman like myself might find it very exciting to run a cargo now and then, to fool the Preventives....are you sure you don't care for brandy?"

"Thank you, no. If I want brandy, I'll pay duty on it. You may think it very odd of me, but there it is. You see, I have been a soldier. I fought in Flanders, and I can't help remembering that we are still at war with France, and that your contraband is putting money into the pockets of our enemy."

"I hadn't looked at it that way," said Mr. Carramine. "Perhaps I ought to have done so." He stood up. "You were on your way out. I will not trespass on your hospitality any longer, but perhaps you would care to dine with me one night, when we may discuss the matter more fully? Any night. Send a man over with a note. Now, if you will allow me to remove my property? The house has been uninhabited so long that they thought it safe to leave contraband here...tried to retrieve it...alarm given...have to do everything yourself, if you want it done properly." He sent his host another shrewd glance. "Then you are down here on another business?"

"I'm trying to run a Jacobite traitor to earth." Mr. Carramine blinked. Yes, thought Philip, he does know something.

"I know of no Jacobite traitors in the neighborhood," said Mr. Carramine slowly.

"Yet you do know something about the Ram and the Rose?"

24

"That's different. Queen Anne is dead, and so, I think, is the traitor you seek. I think your journey has been for nothing. In any other matter, I am yours to command. Your servant, my lord."

He bowed, and left.

Chapter Two

The Earl rode through the village of Hamberley at walking
pace. He was stared at a good deal, and he heard one woman
saying to another that the Earl must think a lot of his tutor
to let him ride a good horse like that! Philip doffed his hat
and smiled at the women, at which they looked confused, and
bobbed a curtsey. As he passed along he heard one say to the
other that she thought he had a pleasant way with him. Far
from being annoyed at being mistaken for Mr. Denbigh,
Philip was amused, and made a note to share the joke with
his tutor. He was far from wishing to enlighten the villagers
as to his identity; it suited him very well to take an afternoon's ride without being called upon to fulfill any of the
social duties of a landowner. He was beginning to wonder if
Mr. Farrow, his bailiff, was a rogue or not. Mr. Farrow had
had a reasonable if not lavish sum to hand to the Earl by
way of rents collected, and he had accounted for the balance
due by saying it had been spent on necessary repairs in the
village. Rising costs, Mr. Farrow said, had been responsible
for the fact that money went such a little way. Now the Earl
could see for himself that several cottages in the village were
in urgent need of attention, but nowhere could he see evidence of recent repairs having been done to buildings. Several
houses had roofs which looked, even to a casual eye, as if
they would leak as soon as it rained again, and there were
broken windows here and there, either boarded over or
stuffed with rags to keep out the weather.

Here was a new problem for the Earl. Some landowners could conveniently overlook evidence that their bailiff was doing his job badly, but he was not one of them. It seemed he must exert himself to investigate Mr. Farrow's conduct of affairs, as well as find the elusive Ram and Rose.

He checked that Hamberley did not contain an inn of the name he sought, even while he told himself that it would have been unlike Chivers to have made a mistake. Then he trotted out of the village in the direction of the wooded hill he had seen from his parlor windows. Prince was skittish, and needed a gallop. They came to a crossroads. Which way should he go? A road, little more than a track, wound up the wooded hillside on his left. Some way up the hill he caught a glimpse of the twisted, Jacobean chimneys of a house. The view from that house, on that hill, would be pleasant. The road which led up to it was broad enough for a gallop and deserted. He turned Prince's head and dug in his heels. He was a good horseman, but rarely had the chance of a gallop such as this...the thunder of hooves...the broad, gently winding track...dense hedges...the air whipping past...the exhilaration....

Something large and red dropped from nowhere onto the track just ahead of them. Prince reared, pawing the air. Philip's face was raked by a bramble dangling from the hedge. A jerk on his bad arm, and he felt the reins burn through his fingers. Prince bolted. Philip clung on to his back. A sharp bend in the track ahead...Prince could not turn in time...they must jump...they could not jump that high...he bent lower over Prince's neck, urging him up and over...what a sensation, floating free! A jar in mid-air, a twist of the horse's body...they were going down....He kicked free of his stirrups and jumped clear, putting out a hand to save himself....

All was quiet.

He opened his eyes. He was lying flat on his back on the hard ground. A woman in a scarlet cloak was kneeling above him, between him and the pale blue of the sky. She was undoing the buttons of his waistcoat. He tried to sit up. The earth cartwheeled around him, and pain knifed across his shoulder and down his arm. His bad arm. He gasped.

She pressed him back to earth. "You have broken your collarbone. Lie still."

His collarbone. Yes, it was broken. He tried to breathe

lightly, so as not to disturb the broken bone, and in the hope that he would not be sick. He moved his other arm presently, and then his legs. He did not seem to have broken anything else, but his head ached.

"Prince...my horse?"

"Your horse is all right. He's up and moving about." Her hands were strong, larger than was ideal for a woman. She wore a plain gown of dark blue woolen stuff under her cloak, just like a farmer's daughter, but the fragment of lace on her dark hair looked good, and she had the air of one used to command. "Can you stand a little discomfort?" she asked. "I want to get your arm out of your coat and waistcoat."

He sat up, to show how easily he could bear "a little discomfort," and nearly fainted. The woman put her arm under his shoulders. He told himself he was not going to be sick in front of a woman, not for "a little discomfort." He wondered if he were suffering from concussion. She bent his arm across his chest, and buttoned waistcoat and coat over it, holding the arm into place. At once the pain in his arm receded to manageable proportions, although he still felt dizzy.

"Can you walk? If not, I'll fetch someone to carry you. It's not far."

He told her he could walk, but he had to lean on her to get to his feet. He had lost both wig and hat. His hand trembled as he touched the back of his head. There was mud on his fingers, and blood.

"You're not badly hurt," she said. "A graze, that's all. Nothing to make a fuss about. This way. One step, and then another. That's a good boy."

"Madam, I am not a..."

"You are doing very well. Sit on the stile while I fetch your hat and wig."

He sat, and looked about him. They were in a field which sloped uphill to a hedge. The stile on which he was sitting gave access to the lane up which he had galloped a short while ago. Prince stood, shivering, some yards away. The horse made a pass at a clump of grass, and began to eat. Yes, he looked all right, which was more than could be said for his master. The Earl put a hand to his aching head.

"It serves you right, if you have a headache," said the lady, returning with his wig. She picked strands of grass from the curls deftly setting the wig back into shape. She had strongly-marked eyebrows and deep blue eyes. She was not a beauty, but hers was a face that would stand out in a crowd. "You have no business galloping up our lane like that. You would have run me down if I hadn't heard you in time and pressed back into the hedge. Just because you are in the service of the Earl of Rame, you think you can act as you like."

"I beg your pardon?"

"Don't put on airs with me. This is private land, and you are a trespasser."

"You appeared from nowhere. You startled my horse, and he bolted." Something dropped onto his hand. His cheek was bleeding. What a ragamuffin he must look! If it were to get out that he, the Earl of Rame, had allowed his horse to bolt and throw him into a field...how everyone would laugh!

"I entered the lane by means of the stile at the bottom of our kitchen garden. I was on my way to the village to see Granny Grout, who is not at all well. Now, I suppose Granny will have to wait for her broth while I spend the rest of the afternoon putting you to rights."

He got to his feet with the intention of sweeping her a bow which would annihilate her. He found he had lost the heel of one of his riding boots. It is difficult if not impossible, to appear dignified when you have lost your wig, your hat, and can't stand straight, but he did his best. "My apologies, madam," he began, and bent his head to bow. The pain in his shoulder increased and he stopped.

"There, now!" she said, setting her shoulder under his good arm, and helping him to stand upright once more. "Never mind your apologies for the moment. Let's get you to bed first."

He did not protest. Indeed, he didn't think she would have heeded him if he had. She had the uncouth strength of a farmhand, and no consideration at all for his pride. She treated him as if he were a small boy who had fallen down and hurt himself, and must be smacked and sent to bed to consider his failings. Of course, she had reason—he had been thoughtless in riding at a gallop along a private road. He was willing to admit his fault, if she would treat him as a man, and not as a child. She almost threw him over the stile, and as for the way she pressed her body close to his as she dragged him along the lane...he preferred not to think about that. She was not wearing so much as a corselet under her gown....

29

"I am putting you to a good deal of trouble," he said.

"That's what women are for." Her tone compounded weariness and amusement. He wondered what her experience of life had been. A brutal husband, perhaps? She had none of the conscious look of women on the marriage market.

They turned the corner of the lane and the large house, whose chimneys he had seen earlier, came into view. It was a hotpotch of buildings; of stone, of brick, and of wattle and daub. The Earl's attention was engaged by the crest over the gatehouse under which they must shortly pass. An animal's head, carved in stone, looked out over the lane. The animal had horns which curved round its head, and there was a sort of ruff behind the head—or was it a stylized rose?

"What is that over the gateway?"

"Our family crest. The Tarrant Ram."

A babble of voices surrounded them, from servants all talking at once. The girl in the blue gown silenced them; one was sent to bring in the stranger's horse, another to fetch the basket she had dropped in the lane, and a third to warn "Aunt Nan" that a stranger from the Manor had been thrown from his horse on their land, and was hurt. Yet another ran off to find "Master Jasper." A burly man in a dirty smock offered to take "the gennelman" from the lady, whose name appeared to be "Miss Sophia," but she would have none of him. She guided Philip under another ram's head carved on the lintel of the porch . . . and then he was in a dark hall, the flicker of a fire on the hearth drawing his eyes and then receding into the distance. . . .

". . . only fainted," a voice was saying. "We'll set the bone before we revive him."

Strong hands wrenched at his arm. Despite himself, he groaned. Opening his eyes, he saw himself reflected in eyes of dark blue. Miss Sophia ordered him to keep still, as her aunt would not be long. Claw-like hands held his upper arm and elbow. The pain was . . . ah! That was better. The capable hands of Miss Sophia passed linen round and round his body, binding his arm in. He was pressed back into the depths of a carved oak chair. The pain subsided. Someone held a pewter tankard to his mouth. The potion in the tankard tasted of herbs and was bitter. He refused it, requesting that a doctor be sent for.

"There's no doctor within miles," said a woman's voice

above his head. "Sophia and I are all the doctors you need, young man. Now drink up before I get cross with you."

Never before had he been treated so unceremoniously! His nose was nipped by thin fingers and the horrible drink tipped down his throat. His shoulder ached, and yet those intrusive hands would not let him alone, pulling at his free arm, twisting and pulling his legs....where had his boots gone? And his coat and waistcoat? A cool cloth was laid at the back of his head. It felt wonderful. But where had his wig gone? And his shirt? And did it matter? Did anything matter?

His head was tipped forward...water ran down his neck...he wriggled and was told to sit still. Cool hands slid round his forehead, holding a pad in place at the back of his head with a neat bandage...he was getting confoundedly sleepy.

He roused himself with a jerk.

"Prince. My horse. Also, I must send to the Manor to tell them what has happened."

"Your horse is being looked after. He's already in the stable, and has come to no harm, they say. We will send a message over to the Earl to say that you are safe and will return tomorrow when you have slept off the effects of your fall."

"That won't do." He tried to stand, but his limbs felt too heavy to move. "I must write." The firelight flickered before his eyes. Over the mantel was yet another of those ram's heads...damned ram's...he pointed to it. "Is that a rose behind its head? Is that the sign of the Ram and Rose?"

"He's feverish," said someone behind him. "Best get him to bed."

The girl in blue set his free arm across her shoulders and heaved him to his feet. "That's right," she said, humoring him. "That's the Tarrant crest, the Ram and Rose. This way...it's not far, you see...and when you've slept you'll feel better. You've nothing else broken, and only a slight touch of concussion."

"The Ram and Rose," he muttered. He must do something about it. These people must be Jacobites. They were his enemies. Who knew what harm they might do him, now he was drugged and helpless? Yet he suffered her to guide him out of the hall, up a shallow flight of steps, across a landing and into a wainscotted bedroom. Maids bustled about, laying a fire, and heating the bed with a copper warming pan. On

the wall opposite the bed hung a portrait of a lady in far-
thingale and ruff, stiff and unsmiling; her eyes were dark
blue and her hair thick and black under a cap of gauze.

"Another of you," he said. "Another Tarrant?"

"The original Rose of Tarrant Hall. There now, you'll feel
better once you've slept." She swung him around, his body
firm against hers from hip to shoulder, and laid him on the
bed as if he'd been a child. She began to remove his breeches.
He could not allow that. He had been brought up to believe
that the naked body was something to be revealed only within
the privacy of the bed-curtains, and even then, his wife had
not been too anxious to . . .

He pushed her hands away and began to remove his
breeches. He had assumed she would have the decency to
turn her back while he undressed, but she stood watching
him, her arms akimbo. She was shameless, utterly without
modesty. As soon as he had slept, he would give her a lecture
on conduct befitting gentlewomen.

"What's your name?" she asked. "I know you must be the
Earl's tutor, but I don't know your name."

"I am Rame."

"Yes, and I'm the Duchess of Marlborough. Come, now.
What do you take me for? Sir John Bladen has told us what
the Earl is like; he is uncommonly tall, elegant and black-
browed. It is plain that you are not he."

"I'm not?" He was very sleepy. It was an effort to follow
what she said. The Ram and the Rose . . . he had found them,
and the traitor must be here, too. This girl—was she the
traitor? He thought not. Her father, brother, husband . . . but
not her. When he'd slept, he could make enquiries. They
would not suspect anything of a man who had arrived in
their midst by accident. It was important that he should not
alarm them. If he insisted on his being Rame, there would
be a great fuss, he would be removed to the Manor just as
he wanted to sleep, doctors would be called in, and they'd
probably want to disturb the bandages which were holding
his broken bone in place. He didn't want any fuss, and he
didn't want any more doctors fussing around him when they'd
made such a mess of setting his arm after he'd been wounded
in Flanders. He wanted peace and quiet, and sleep.

He began to smile. He thought he was in for an amusing
adventure.

"That's right," said the girl, tucking the coverlet over him.

"You're beginning to feel better already, aren't you? My aunt's potions never fail. Now, tell me your name, and I'll leave you to sleep."

He opened his mouth to say that his name was Denbigh, and paused. Sir John Bladen had seen and talked with Mr. Denbigh and would remember him. Suppose Sir John were to call again on this family of traitors tomorrow—he was obviously on visiting terms with them, or the girl wouldn't have known what the Earl was supposed to look like. He fought sleep to reason the matter out. If Sir John called, he would learn of the accident to the stranger, would recognize him and unmask him. The name of Denbigh would not do. He must be someone else in the Earl's entourage, until he had discovered the traitor's name. Some family name....

"Rich," he said. "My name is Philip Rich. I am a kinsman of the Earl's, acting as his secretary. Came down with his baggage ahead of him. When you send to the Manor, will you tell Mr. Denbigh that I am at the sign of the Ram and Rose, that I'm quite all right, and don't want any fuss made. Tell him that I'm sure he will be able to manage the Earl."

The girl nodded, and drew the curtains round the bed. The curtains were of cream linen, embroidered with fantastic birds and flowers in blue wool. Restful....

Someone made up the fire, and the noise woke him. His shoulder ached, but the pain was endurable. He remembered what had happened, and opened his eyes. One of the bed-curtains had been drawn back, and a white-haired woman leaned over him. She had large, dark blue eyes, fringed with black lashes, exactly like those of the girl who had made him fall off his horse, but there the resemblance ended. This lady was tiny, a dainty little piece of femininity from coquettish cap to the tips of mittened hands. Moreover, when she moved he saw that she dragged one leg, and that her right shoulder was higher than her left. The Earl guessed that she would be about forty years of age. At first he thought her ugly, and then she smiled, and he revised his opinion. She was charming.

"You must be Aunt Nan."

She had the high, carefree laugh of a child. "Miss Tarrant

33

to you; but yes, I am Sophia's Aunt Nan. At the moment, I am also your nurse. You are feeling better?"

He raised himself on one elbow, and at once his shoulder protested. She pressed him back onto the pillows, and he was glad that she did so. He was not ready to sit up yet, it seemed.

"You have been a very good boy," the lady said. "You have slept the clock round and your fever has gone. Sophia will be pleased."

Had he been lying in bed for a whole day? What would Denbigh have done? Had his message gone to the Manor? What was it he had discovered just before he went to sleep...something about treason? He put a hand to his head and discovered he was wearing a nightcap, and yes...someone else's nightgown. How had that come about? Ah...he vaguely remembered being woken to take another of those nauseous draughts, and being pulled this way and that.

"Now, there's no need to frown," said Miss Tarrant. "My nephew Jasper took your message over to the Manor as soon as he got back from his cockfight, or whatever mischief it was he was up to in the village. He had hoped to see the Earl, but dear me, no! His High-and-Mightiness was still abed...at past two in the afternoon, if you please. Jasper spoke with your friend Mr. Denbigh, who was most upset about your accident, and insisted on riding back with Jasper to see you. I think he had some idea of whisking you back to the Manor, but we persuaded him to let you be. He talked wildly of doctors and bleeding and clysters and such-like, but Sophia and I soon dealt with that. We Tarrants haven't physicked the countryside for years without learning a trick or two. I told him that doctors cost money, and we've none to spare, and neither have you, to judge by the look of you. And if the Earl was so worried about you, he could have made the journey to see you himself. He didn't have any answer to that."

Philip began to laugh, silently at first, and then with the convulsions of near hysteria. He laughed until his cheeks were wet. He laughed until his nurse held a tankard to his lips.

"Now, not another sound out of you, my lad. Drink this; yes, it is the same mixture as before, only made with honey because Sophia said you might make less fuss if it was sweeter."

He tried to say that he didn't need it, but her fingers

lighted on the tip of his nose, and pinched it. "Come along, or you know what will happen."

Philip knew. He swallowed the draught, and almost at once his paroxysms ceased, and he felt languor creeping over his body.

"That's better," said his nurse. "We don't need doctors, Sophia and I. Broken bones, over-wrought nerves...it's all one to us."

"Over-wrought—?" Philip chuckled. "If you say so, ma'am. I was only laughing at myself."

"A sign of Grace." She nodded at him, smiling.

A sign of Grace. Wasn't that what Catholics believed? *"Êtes-vous catholique?"* he asked.

"Gracious, no. Whatever gave you that idea?"

Her laughter was the last thing he heard for a long time.

"Damn!" said someone, not loudly but with force.

Philip opened his eyes and looked around him. Had he slept the clock round again, or was it still the same night? One of the bedcurtains had been left open, and he could see Sophia Tarrant, seated at a table before the fire. Yet another stone ram gazed benevolently down on the room from over the fireplace, illuminated both by the fire and by a branch of candles on the table at which Sophia was working. Philip's eye wandered over the room. He was lying in a heavily carved four-poster bed. The coverlet on the bed matched the curtains. The ceiling was low, and had at one time been painted in bright colors. The room was warm, and he felt very much at home. He had no idea what day it was, or even whether it was morning or evening. It was probably evening, since candles had been brought into the room. How many times had he half-woken, and been attended to, and sunk back into sleep again? Miss Nan had been present twice, at least, and hadn't Denbigh been there, too?

He wriggled his shoulders. His collarbone protested, but not much. He was still strapped up, but comfortable.

Sophia had not noticed that he was awake. Underlip caught between her teeth, she was scratching out a blot she had made on the paper before her. Her every movement betrayed the vigor of perfect health, but her hair was not as tidy as it ought to have been under its lace cap, and her plain blue gown made no concession either to fashion or the fact that it was evening. It was, simply, a covering for her body, without panniers or even a knot of ribbon for decoration. Her complexion was good because winter had whitened her skin, but Philip guessed that in the summer she would be as brown as a berry and, moreover, that she would not care. Such lack of feminine grace, or any desire to please, ought to have made him view her with disgust. Her stride had been mannish. He remembered only too well the strength of the arm which had supported him, and the immodesty of her body pressing close....

He must have made a sound, for she looked up, saw that he was awake, and sprang to her feet.

"Properly awake at last? All alike, you London folk, racketing around till your health is gone, and then needing to recuperate in the country."

Before Philip could counter this unfair attack, she had her fingers on his pulse. For all her vitality, she knew how to control her movements to the slower pace of an invalid. She examined him thoroughly, but gently, her manner as impersonal as that of a doctor. Philip willed her to show some sign that she was aware of him as a man. The women he knew in London hung on his every word, flattering him, flirting.... the girl's color heightened under his scrutiny, but she retained her preoccupied manner.

Finally she said, "You will do very well, but in future you should confine yourself to riding horses which you can control. That is a valuable animal you were riding. You might easily have lamed him, and then what would the Earl have said?"

"Madam, I would have you know that I can ride anything that..."

"Before you injured your arm, maybe." She pointed to the scar on his forearm. "That is quite recent, isn't it?"

"A musket ball broke my arm at Dettingen. It did not set straight, and the doctors had to break it, and set it again." He was not averse to letting her know that he had been a soldier. Maybe that would make her look on him with respect.

"When will you men learn not to go dashing off to wars when you should be minding your own business at home? I daresay you left a perfectly good position to follow the fife and drum."

"It is true that some of my friends thought it foolish..."

"...and look what came of it! Men are all alike. My father and my elder brother were both soldiers, and now Jasper wants to go, too." The trim line of her figure slackened, and she leaned against the bedpost. There were dark lines under her eyes. Perhaps she had been sharp with him because she was tired.

This hint of weakness in her restored his self-confidence. He begged her to consider herself for a change, since he would do very well now. If he could but have some food sent him, she might safely leave him in the hands of servants.

"I can't go to bed till I've finished the accounts," she said. She pushed her hand through her hair, disarranging it even more. "Perhaps you are right, though. I confess I do feel tired tonight. I was up at five. There is so much to do, and Jasper will not help." She gathered her papers together and studied them. Evidently she did not like what she saw. She picked up her writing desk and made for the door. "You wanted some food? It would be safe for you to eat now. I will send you some, and perhaps my brother will sit with you for awhile, if I ask him nicely. I am afraid that the Earl has not called to enquire after you—he took a chill on the journey, and is confined to his chamber, they say—but that nice Mr. Denbigh came yesterday, and again today. He will bring you some clothes tomorrow. Your coat was torn; Aunt is trying to mend it, but she says it has been darned before, and is hardly worth repairing again."

"Tell her not to wear herself out trying to mend it. I have other coats."

"You do?" She looked relieved, but unconvinced. "Everything costs so much, nowadays...." She yawned, nodded at him, and vanished.

A maid brought Philip a bowl of gruel. He grimaced, but supped it up and asked for more. He felt surprisingly fit.

A thin, dark lad, poised somewhere between boy and manhood, entered the room. The maid curtseyed and left.

"Sir Jasper Tarrant," said the newcomer, proffering his hand. His eyes were even darker than his sister's, and restless. His mouth was mobile, and he had a nervously energetic manner. He wore his own hair, tied back with a ribbon, and a velvet coat which, though it would have been made by a country tailor, laid claim to being fashionable. He was a good deal younger than his sister and lacked her air of knowing precisely what she was doing. Philip thought: This is not the traitor—I must speak with the father and elder brother.

Jasper seated himself astride a chair, and smiled at his guest. "I didn't mind at all when Sophia asked me to sit with you, because I wanted a word with you. Oh, I suppose I ought to ask how you're going on first, but..."

"Very well, thank you," said Philip, trying not to laugh.

"That's what I thought. Sophia said I wasn't to bother you with business, because you wouldn't be up to it for a day or two, but I thought..."

"There is something I can do for you? I am greatly in your debt. If there is any way I can discharge my obligation, please tell me what it may be."

"The thing is, I wanted a word with the Earl, but he's not to be seen. I've ridden over to the Manor twice to report how you were, and I thought I might have the luck to see him today, if not yesterday, but he was still in bed. They say he has caught a chill and has to be careful of his health. He sounds a poor thing. I don't see how he could have shot a highwayman, if he's such a weakling, but...Oh, I forgot, he's some sort of cousin of yours, isn't he, and you won't want me calling him names. The thing is, no one except Sir John Bladen has seen the Earl as yet, although several of us have called on him. Mr. Denbigh told me that the Earl leaves the district again as soon as his cold is better, and I thought that when you got back, you might put in a word for me."

"I daresay I could. What is it you want with him?"

The lad looked over his shoulder to make sure that the door was shut, and inched his chair nearer the bed. "Sophia would be furious if she knew I had approached you about it, but I'd be a fool not to take advantage of this opportunity, wouldn't I? The thing is that I want to be a soldier. I've wanted to be a soldier ever since I was breeched. Sophia and Aunt Nan have tried to make me interested in the land, but I can't get up any enthusiasm for the rotations of crops and pigs and the like." He grinned. "It's no good pretending to be what you're not, is it? I'm like my father and brother—army-mad. The difficulty is that we've no money or influence at Court, and I want a commission. I could enlist as a common soldier, but I'd not make my fortune that way, and I daresay I wouldn't enjoy the life."

"I daresay you wouldn't," said the Earl, torn between amusement and annoyance. "You want me to ask the Earl to obtain a commission for you? Well, it is only fair to tell you, straight away, that your chances of success are small. The King makes all such appointments himself."

"Yes, I know that, but since the Earl is a Gentleman of the Bedchamber..."

"The Earl has never abused his position to solicit favors," said Philip, beginning to frown. "If you are so short of money, the Earl might make you a gift of a good horse, or your uniform, but...don't take it so hard, lad. Have you no relatives who can put in a word for you?"

"There is an uncle who lives in London. I wrote to him for help, but he has not replied."

"But with a father and a brother already in the Army..."

"They are both dead. Besides," the boy glanced away, reddening, "they didn't fight with the English Armies."

"Oh. Jacobites, were they?"

"My brother did it for money, because he didn't think he could get a commission in the English Army. The Tarrants have been poor ever since I can remember, and my brother John thought he could do well for himself abroad. He didn't, though. He was killed in a drunken brawl in Paris a couple of years ago. Someone wrote to tell my father about his death, and later they brought back his ring and his pistols. Everything else they sold to pay his debts. I would have liked to have had my brother's pistols, but my father said I was too young, and he sold them. He sold the other farm about that time, too, and Sophia said my father gave the money to the Frenchman to pay my brother's debts, and that it should be an example to me, that no one makes their fortune by going into the Army."

Philip wondered if the Frenchman who had brought Jasper's father news of his eldest son's death had been a Jacobite agent. It seemed possible. And if so, perhaps the money from the sale of the farm had gone, not to pay the Tarrant boy's debts, but into the coffers of Charles Edward Stuart, the Young Pretender.

"Your father also fought for Louis?"

"It was an open secret that he did. He would never talk about it, for fear that he would be fined for it. He was out in the '15, you know, and had to be careful afterwards. What a fool he was!" the boy cried. "Everyone knows the Stuart cause is dead!"

"And your father is dead, too?"

"He was never well after he heard of my brother's death. He

39

seemed to turn against me, after that, even more than...he
never liked me. He didn't like anyone much. He grew very
strange, towards the end. I don't think he knew what he was
doing half the time. He'd have left his affairs in better order, if
he had. Poor Sophia's had the devil of a time, trying to sort out
what we owe. Where the money's gone to, I don't know, but we
only have the home farm left, and debts everywhere. We can't
stay on here. Sophia and Aunt Nan will be provided for and our
debts paid if I sell the Hall, and that's what I mean to do. I can
sell as soon as I'm eighteen, next week."

"Won't you mind leaving this place?"

The boy drew himself up. Philip thought: he's going to lie.

"Of course not," said Jasper. "I've always wanted to go
into the Army, and this is my chance to do so. Only, I must
have a commission."

Philip was getting tired, but the boy hadn't noticed.

The boy said, "I was at my wits' end what to do, and then
you fell off your horse in the lane, and I thought that this
was Providence, taking a hand in my affairs."

"Maybe it is," said Philip. His head had begun to ache again.
He must think. Jacobites...commissions...letters from
France...the Ram and the Rose...

"Will you really help me?" Jasper leaped up, and his chair
went over with a crash. Philip winced. The boy seized his
hand and pumped it up and down. "I knew you'd see it my
way. I told Sophia that anyone who could jump our hedge on
that horse must be a right one."

"What did she say to that?"

"Oh, you don't want to take any notice of her. She's not
usually moody. I don't know what's come over her, lately. I
say—would you let me exercise Prince for you while you're
laid up? He's eating his head off in the stables, and not a sign
of trouble in his legs. I've been to see him twice a day, and
he knows me now."

Philip nodded. He could hardly keep his eyes open. At long
last the boy went away, and then there was silence.

It was Philip's last day at Tarrant Hall. Mr. Denbigh had
called early that morning to bring him some clothes and to
be promised an increase in salary for the discreet way in
which he had covered his master's absence. Philip was now
on Christian-name terms with Jasper, who hero-worshipped

him, and never tired of hearing his tales of war in Flanders. He was also on excellent terms with Miss Nan, but Sophia was as sharp with him as ever. He could tell from the attitude of everyone else at Tarrant Hall that Sophia did not usually behave so shrewishly; one after another they expressed surprise at her present behavior. Philip himself had witnessed an incident which proved she was not naturally cross-tempered; a stable lad had put the tine of his pitchfork through his foot, and no one could have been more tender or softervoiced than Sophia, as she gently cleansed the wound and reassured the boy. Philip could not help wondering how it would be if she were to act like that towards him, and how he would feel if she were to caress him as she had caressed that frightened boy.... Her refusal to flirt piqued him. Was he so deficient in graces that, without his title and fine clothes, he was unable to please a woman?

He strolled down to the stables to see Jasper ride off on Prince, "to prove he's fit again." He felt languid, but otherwise restored to health. He leaned against the front door, watching the servants bustle about. The Hall was well run, and everyone who worked there seemed cheerful. He could not make up his mind whether this was due to Sophia's energy or Miss Nan's wisdom.

He asked a passing maid where Miss Sophia might be.

"She's ridden out on the farm," sang out Miss Nan, perched on a window seat. "Come and talk to me, instead." She was mending linen with spidery stitches.

"Does she have to work so hard?" complained Philip. "She promised to rub my arm again."

"Someone has to do the work around here; Jasper won't, and I can't, and there's no one else."

"She looks tired."

Miss Nan sent him a shrewd, bright glance. "You are a good boy. Not many men would have noticed. I must also thank you for taking so much trouble with Jasper. It was kind of you to let him ride your horse, and to tell him what to expect in the Army. I hope—oh, I do hope that he can get a commission."

"I like the lad, and will do what I can for him, but what I don't like is that he has at least three suits of good clothes, whereas you and Miss Sophia wear the same dress, day after day."

"You are a kindly man, Mr. Rich, and thoughtful for those

less fortunate than yourself." Now what did she mean by that? thought Philip. Had she pierced his disguise? "Nevertheless," she continued, "I shall be glad when you are gone, even though I shall miss you. Heigho! We shall be so dull again when you and the Earl have gone, and there is nothing to talk about but the weather."

"There is Jasper's coming of age to look forward to."

"Which means the break-up of our family. He must sell, and we must prepare the Hall to receive its new master. But let us look on the bright side; perhaps Sir John will authorize the purchase of new linen to replace some of these torn sheets."

"Sir John? Sir John is to buy Tarrant Hall?"

"Did you not know? Now I wonder why Sophia did not tell you. What contrary creatures we women are, to be sure. Such a dear girl, so even-tempered in adversity, so affectionate and courteous...but recently so short-tempered, so curt, so impolite. I say to her: Sophia, what is the meaning of your behavior, and she slams the door in my face. You have noticed how badly she's been behaving, of course?"

Philip said, "I don't think so."

"That's strange, when you can hardly take your eyes off her. She lied to me last night, too. She said she had no idea what color your hair was, yet she spent hours gazing at you while you were in bed." Philip made an involuntary movement. "You were saying, sir?" Philip shook his head. "Dear me! Both of you dumb as oxen, yet both of you can use your tongues to good effect when you choose. You are not married, sir?"

Philip started. "I...no, I was; but she died. However, there are plans for me to remarry this summer."

"Just so," said Miss Nan. Her eyes appeared to be on her stitchery, but Philip had the impression that she was watching him carefully. "You are to marry soon, and so is Sophia. It will be a very suitable match for her, don't you think? Sir John's wife died two years ago, and he only has one daughter. He would dearly love to have a son, and Sophia is young and healthy enough to provide him with the heir he wants. Then Sir John's title is but a lately acquired affair, of no weight, and he understands the importance of allying himself with the Tarrants, who have lived here since before the Conquest. He will buy Tarrant Hall from Jasper, and this will enable us to pay our debts. I am to live with them. It is kind of him

42

to ask me, for who else would want to give a crippled woman a home? I should be afraid to live by myself. The villagers think of me as a witch, you see, because my body is crooked and I know how to cure warts. It is an excellent solution to our problem, isn't it, Mr. Rich?"

Philip tried to analyze his emotions. There was indignation at the thought of Sophia being handed over to that monster, Sir John, and a sense of loss... but what else? He met Miss Nan's gaze and thought: she knows. What it was that she knew, he did not attempt to define, but he rose from his seat and began to pace the room.

"Can you think of a better home for her?" asked Miss Nan.

He thought of his great house at Rame, and what Society would have to say if he were to attempt to take a rough country wench like Sophia for his wife, and for a moment he was exhilarated by the prospect. Then reason edged out emotion. What would Sophia do at Court? Why, the King himself had promised to find a bride for his favorite Gentleman in Waiting. Philip laughed.

"I am sure it will be a very suitable match," he said. He had a sudden urge to leave the room, and Tarrant Hall... to get away from this witch of a woman who saw too much.... What was he doing here, anyway? He fed indignation until it turned to anger.

"Miss Tarrant, I promised your nephew that I would speak to the Earl about a commission; the King reserves the right to make all such appointments himself, but the Earl has never asked a favor of His Majesty before, and I don't doubt that under normal circumstances he would be successful. However, there is something known against the Tarrants, some talk of treasonable activity, of their being Jacobites."

"We are not Jacobites," she said, but her color intensified. "I have brought up the children to honor King George and despise the Stuarts."

"Maybe so, but both your brother and your elder nephew were Jacobites, were they not?"

"Mr. Rich, your manner..."

"I have proof that someone in this house is or was a Jacobite. Letters have been intercepted which were intended for someone here. The King will not be inclined to grant Jasper a commission unless..."

"Unless... what? My brother and my nephew are dead. *Requiescat in pace.*"

43

"I need to know how far they were involved. I believe couriers came from France with letters for your brother, and went back with good English gold in their pockets. Isn't that so? Didn't the money from the sale of one of the farms go that way?"

"I..." She had her hand to her throat. "He did not confide in me. Sometimes I thought...but then, I would say to myself that he couldn't possibly be such a fool as to think the Stuarts...No, I never took him seriously. Mr. Rich, you did not know him. He was always thinking up schemes which came to nothing...saying that this year or next, we would be rich...borrowing money from his best friend and losing it when in his cups...he gambled, you know, and when I asked him where the money had gone to, he always said it was because he had bad luck with cards. It was all in his mind, that talk of plots and fortunes to be made...."

"Not quite all, I think. What about the letters which came from France? Did you see them? Did you read them? His Majesty will not give Jasper a commission unless I can convince him about those letters."

There was a long silence. Finally, she said, "I burned them. I found them in the secret drawer at the back of the cupboard in the parlor. You are right; the letters could have been described as treasonable, although I am sure my brother did not realize what he was doing when he...he was not well, Mr. Rich. I was afraid when I read them; afraid for my brother, and for all of us. So I burned them. There is no proof now that he ever was a Jacobite."

Later that night Philip met with another rebuff. He had spent an uncomfortable evening listening to Sophia attack the Earl's reputation. She seemed to know exactly how to wound him best. He defended himself with as much firmness as was commensurate with courtesy; he said that in his estimation the Earl was neither a fop nor a coward, and that although he wore Court dress when required, he was not milliner-mad. He denied that the Earl was supposed to be coldhearted, or that he had neglected his wife when she'd been alive. Only when Sophia attacked the Earl for being a bad landlord did his anger begin to mount.

Miss Nan intervened to say that she had first-hand information on the matter; Mr. Farrow had told her he had orders to wring as much as possible out of the Earl's tenants. She had remonstrated with him on several occasions about the need for repairs in the village, and on each occasion he had told her he was unable to do anything about it. "He is an unpleasant man, to be sure," said Miss Nan, "But he is only doing his job." She looked at Philip as she said this, as if she knew he could right the wrong done the villagers.

He said, conscious that his own color had risen, "I will ask the Earl to investigate Mr. Farrow's conduct of affairs. I know he is already worried about the condition of houses in the village, and I know that the Earl would never have given such orders as Mr. Farrow claims."

Jasper whooped with delight, and raised his tankard in a toast to his aunt.

"Here's damnation to Mr. Farrow!" he cried. "And victory to Aunt Nan! She told him she would bring him to book for his misdeeds, and sure enough, she has done so. You have no idea how much that creature Farrow hates and fears her, for wherever he goes, bullying and teasing, my aunt goes after him, with her wise words and her potions. He hates her because she organizes the villagers to protest against him. They love her... at least, they used to do. Only, lately they've begun to say.... stupid things! I believe he's at the bottom of the gossip about Aunt Nan. Do you know, he has the impudence to call her a witch?"

Sophia laughed, and threw her arms round her aunt's neck. "And a witch you are, indeed. The dearest, sweetest witch in Creation!"

But when Philip followed Sophia out into the corridor, she ceased to smile. He stood close to her, his hand on her arm to prevent her from departing. He wanted to put himself right with her, but did not know what words to use. He could see that her breath was coming short, and that her color had risen, and felt the same symptoms afflict him.

He bent to kiss her, and she slapped him.

"Oh, I wish you'd never come here!" she cried, and fled down the passage into the darkness.

Chapter Three

The cloth had been removed from the table, and the decanter set before the Earl and his guest, Mr. Carramine. Mr. Denbigh had already made an excuse to retire, and now the Earl signed to the servants to leave. It was the night after Philip's return to the Manor, and he had invited Mr. Carramine to keep him company. He moved his bad arm with care, but it did not trouble him unduly. He had resumed his fashionable clothes, periwig and paint, and instructed his servants to say that the Earl was now convalescent, but that his secretary Mr. Rich had been despatched to London on business.

It was the Earl who proposed the first toast, "His Majesty's health," and Mr. Carramine who proposed the second, "To your swift return to health."

"It was a bad cold," said the Earl, touching his nose with a monogrammed handkerchief.

"It was a bad fall," rejoined Mr. Carramine.

The Earl laughed. He was amused rather than annoyed at having his masquerade known to his guest. "When did you guess?" he asked.

"Jasper rode over—on your horse?—to see me yesterday. He wanted to tell me of his good fortune in making the acquaintance of the Earl's secretary. I had heard of 'Mr. Rich's' accident before, of course, and I had wondered...but it seemed no business of mine to speculate on such a subject. Jasper's artless confidences merely confirmed my suspicion

46

that the man I had met here, and the man who took a tumble at Miss Sophia's feet, were one and the same."

"I am glad you did not enlighten him. It would be very embarrassing for the Tarrants if their mistake were made known."

"It was a very natural mistake." Mr. Carramine considered his host, and thought that the man he had met the other day bore little outward resemblance to the black-browed aristocrat who sat opposite him, glittering with diamonds. Mr. Carramine, considering the Earl's firm jaw, wondered how Sophia had had the nerve to treat this man so discourteously, and he wondered even more why the Earl had allowed her to do so. Why, even Jasper, who usually discounted everything his sister did, had expressed surprise to Mr. Carramine at her bad manners.

"It was Sir John Bladen's description of me which misled them," said the Earl, carefully trimming a candle which had begun to gutter. "He must have been more impressed with my person than I was with his, for he reported that I was uncommonly tall, elegant, and black of brow. It was a superficial description. The loss of my hat and wig and the heel off my boot reduced me to normal size, and of course I was wearing old clothes." He refilled their glasses. "Victory for Cumberland, and Confusion to the French."

The Duke of Cumberland was not only the King's favorite son, but also Commander in Chief of the British Army in Flanders.

Mr. Carramine drank, and said, "I suppose that means 'Death to Smuggling,' too?"

"I must turn you from that pernicious business before I leave for Bath."

The two men had liked each other from the start, and found on further acquaintance that they had much in common. Although Mr. Carramine lacked the high rank of his host, he did not lack means, and in his youth had made the Grand Tour and had taken his place for a while in the fashionable world of London. Both men took an active interest in the running of their estates, both preferred riding to any other form of exercise, and both had well-stocked and -read libraries. While neither man had ever been involved in politics, both were interested in the subject, and held much the same points of view.

"So you go to Hanover with the King this summer," observed Mr. Carramine. "A pity. I had hoped we might see more of one another. I wonder the King thinks it wise to go this summer."

"It is his birthplace, and he feels at home there. The King finds it difficult to understand why he cannot rule Britain as he rules Hanover, through ministers of his own choosing."

"Like Lord Carteret?"

"My uncle still has access to the King at any time, day or night."

"Which cannot please Newcastle...."

The Earl hooded his eyes and did not reply. Mr. Carramine understood that the Earl considered they had discussed politics long enough, and sought for another subject of conversation. He lifted his glass to propose another toast.

"To the ladies who mended your broken bone—The Misses Tarrant."

The Earl also raised his glass. "To the Roses of Tarrant Hall."

Mr. Carramine's glass remained suspended in mid-air for a moment. Then he drank, and set his glass down. "You know, then?"

"I know that the sign of the Ram and the Rose is not a hostelry but the Tarrant family crest. I believe that the Tarrant women are often referred to as the Roses of Tarrant Hall. I know that treasonable correspondence has been carried on between the Young Pretender and the sign of the Ram and the Rose."

"I told you, the traitor—if he was one—is dead."

"It may be so." The Earl leaned back in his chair. "Tell me what you know of the family."

Mr. Carramine understood that this was why he had been invited to dine, but he was willing enough to talk. He had been brought up with Sir Richard Tarrant, the father of Sophia and Jasper. Both Richard and Mr. Carramine had loved the same woman, but she had chosen to marry Sir Richard, and lived to regret it. Mr. Carramine had married a cousin of his, and acted as godfather to Richard's firstborn, John. Sophia had been born the year after John, and Richard had then disappeared abroad for some years. Later, it was said that he had been fighting for French Louis, but even after his return Richard would neither confirm nor deny this. Jasper was born after Richard's return from the wars, and his mother had died giving him birth. He had been a sickly child,

48

and they had not thought to rear him at first, but Sophia and Nan between them had dragged and coaxed the boy through childhood. Richard had never been interested in farming, and neither was his eldest son, John. The family had always had Jacobite leanings, and had been heavily fined after the '15 uprising, so that they were always short of money. As soon as John was old enough, he had followed in his father's footsteps and gone abroad, never to return. In the meantime, matters had gone from bad to worse at Tarrant Hall. Richard left the running of the farms to Nan and Sophia, only demanding money periodically for his gambling debts. He lost most of his friends, but Mr. Carramine, who was very fond of Sophia and Jasper, stuck by him. In fact, Mr. Carramine was the family's chief creditor. After his eldest son's death, Richard had spent most of his days in a drunken stupor, only rousing himself to demand more and more money from the estate, or to beat his children. It was impossible to remonstrate with him, for he would merely make grandiose promises to repay his debts next month, or next year, if he were sober; and if he were drunk, he would fall into a rage, and lay about him.

"He would not give Sophia a dowry, so that she could marry, because she was too useful to him at home. She had several offers, but…" Mr. Carramine sighed. "I considered it myself, after my wife died, but Richard would not listen, even when I offered to take her without a dowry. She thanked me so sweetly… even though she said I would have been a fool to marry her… she said she liked me too much to marry me and make my life a misery. As for Jasper, I did what I could for the lad, taking him out with the guns, and mounting him… after Richard sold the lad's horse." Mr. Carramine's hand became a fist, and he breathed hard. "Richard was… very strange in the last year of his life. He could not seem to bear Jasper near him—I think because he'd preferred his elder son, and John was dead, and Jasper still alive. However it was, he used to lash out at the boy whenever he saw him. Jasper would have run away many a time if it hadn't been for leaving Sophia and Nan at his father's mercy… so I used to put the boy up here, and do what I could for him."

"Such as encouraging him to join the Free Traders? That explains where he got the money from, for his clothes and his cockfights."

Mr. Carramine winced, but did not deny the charge. The

Earl took out his snuffbox, and offered it to his guest. Mr. Carramine accepted the peace offering.

"My business is not with smugglers," said the Earl. "A treasonable letter came into my hands, to be delivered to the sign of the Ram and Rose. Miss Nan has admitted that Sir Richard had had some treasonable correspondence with the Pretender, but she says that she destroyed all his letters when he died. She says that Jasper has no sympathy with the Jacobites."

"No, he is not a traitor. He thinks his father and brothers were fools for fighting under the French flag. You can trust him, I am sure. As for his being out with the Free Traders, you may rest assured that it will not happen again...if it ever did happen. I'm admitting nothing, you understand?"

"I understand your position, but what I don't understand is how the boy intended to get himself a commission, before I came along so providentially."

"When he is eighteen he will sell the Hall to Sir John Bladen, in order to pay his debts. Sophia marries Sir John to give him an heir, and so that she may continue to live in her old home. Miss Nan will stay with them."

"I repeat, how did the boy expect to obtain a commission?"

"Through his uncle, Sir Gregory Midmain, who married his aunt Helen. He wrote to Sir Gregory as soon as his father died, and expects to hear from him any day now."

"Then why did he solicit my aid? Can it be that he doubts Sir Gregory's power to assist him? I believe I have met Sir Gregory...a man of limited understanding and income. He is a time-server, hanging on Newcastle's coattails in the hope that some sinecure will fall his way. I doubt if he will put himself out to help the son of a known Jacobite."

Mr. Carramine looked blank.

"Come now; you know that it is so."

"I greatly fear it. Nothing has gone right for the lad. He loves Marjorie Bladen, Sir John's only daughter, and I think she reciprocates his affection, but she is something of an heiress in her own right, and her father wishes to see her married into some noble family. He sees himself founding a dynasty at Tarrant Hall; Sophia is willing to marry him, to fulfill her part of the bargain, in order to help Jasper pay the debts Richard left. She won't marry me, because I am their chief creditor, and for the same reason Jasper won't accept any further loans from me. I am proud of them both, and grieve for them both. I wish I could help them, but they won't let me. It all depends on you, now. If you can get Jasper a commission..."

The Earl's chin was sunk into the lace at his throat, and he appeared deep in thought. At length he roused himself to pour them out some more wine.

"I, too, would like to do something for Jasper, yet the King will never grant him a commission if he were to learn what I know about the family. What should I do? Conceal the boy's background? Then again, I was entrusted with the task of finding out what I could about Jacobites in this area; I have done so. What I know about the Tarrants, if reported, would land them in the Tower, with their estates sequestered. They do not deserve such a fate. Yet is it not my duty to tell?"

"Uncle!" The Earl rose to greet Lord Carteret. "Are you very tired from your journey? We have had a bedchamber ready for you these three days."

"I came as soon as I could. No, no. I'm not tired. A trifle to eat and drink, and I shall be myself again. I can only stay the one night, so let us get to business."

Philip sent Mr. Denbigh to sit in the outer room, while he gave his uncle an account of everything that had happened since his arrival, only omitting to mention his clashes with Sophia Tarrant. His uncle listened in silence. Lord Carteret was a man of fifty-five, upright and soldierly. He suffered from gout, and his enemies said he was frequently the worse for drink of an evening, even though he had recently taken to himself a young and beautiful girl as his second wife. His manner was sharp, and his quick intelligence made him intolerant of fools. He had long been at the center of international diplomacy, and had won the confidence of the King; because of this, he found it difficult to accept his fall from power. He was fond of his nephew, but did not show it.

"Fate has taken a hand in my affairs," he observed, when Philip had finished. "You have stumbled across information which those fools at the Postmaster General's have been after for months, and moreover, gained a foothold in the Tarrant household which we can turn to advantage."

"As far as I am concerned," said Philip, a chill in his voice, "the matter is now at an end. The traitor is dead and his

51

papers burned. I leave for Bath very shortly, and do not intend to return. In fact, I may sell this place—it does not please me."

"You will do nothing of the kind." Philip raised his eyebrows, and Lord Carteret softened his tone. "My dear boy; you do not appreciate the gravity of the situation. For years France has nurtured the Pretender and his sons, not because Louis believes the time is ripe for the return of the Stuarts to his country, but because they are useful pawns in the game of European politics. The French do not have enough money or men to equip an invasion force, but they encourage the Young Pretender with promises for next year, or the year after. Next time we may not be so lucky, and we may find ourselves fighting not in Flanders, but in our own streets."

"Very true; but what has that to do with me?"

Lord Carteret limped to the fireplace, and took up a commanding attitude. "Philip, I have no son of my own, although Heaven may shortly bless my union with Lady Carteret. You have been my heir for some years now. I have even gone so far as to praise you to His Majesty, and to further your suit with my ward, Lady Millicent. It is not every man who deserves to wed an heiress who is also a reigning beauty. I have done more. The post of Ambassador to the Court of Sweden falls vacant at the end of this year, and I have suggested to His Majesty that you would fill it to admiration."

Philip tried and failed to conceal his surprise and gratification. "Why, uncle...this is something I had never thought...but I lack diplomatic experience."

"There would of course be a Resident in Stockholm to guide you in the petty day-to-day affairs. Now I do not say that you would get Stockholm; His Majesty is inclined to think it best to transfer a seasoned diplomat to Sweden, but this would create an opening elsewhere, and I think I may say that he is always open to suggestion from me. Of course, if you had been obviously unsuited for the post, I do not say that I could have arranged it, but you have the ability, the birth and the background for a position of this type; and, moreover, you are not tied to Newcastle's tail."

Philip bowed. "It seems that I am as corruptible as any other man in pursuit of office."

"'An incorruptible man is a dangerous man,'" quoted Lord Carteret. "No one can predict which way he will jump. Now I think I can say that I have studied human nature more closely than most. I knew you would want to be Ambassador, and I know what the Stuart boy wants, too. He is a rash, stupid youth, with all the Stuart failings—their belief in the Divine Right of kings, and their obstinacy—and very few of their virtues. He is nothing but a puppet, and I am the master puppeteer. I will pull the strings to bring him to ruin, and return myself to power."

Such a boast from a lesser man might have raised smiles, but Philip did not smile.

"You have a scheme?" Philip asked.

Lord Carteret put his chair close to that of his nephew. "I am going to provoke the Young Pretender into invading Britain at a time when France cannot back him with men or money. Then we shall have him." He clapped his hands and rubbed imaginary dirt from his palms as if to rid himself of a squashed fly. "And that will be the end of the Stuart menace."

"An imaginative scheme," said Philip, blinking. "But dangerous."

"Danger?" Carteret snapped his fingers. "You talk like a child. How many men did we lose at Dettingen? How much money do we lose every year by maintaining a standing Army, just to keep France out of Hanover? You cannot make an omelette..."

"Granted, but how do you propose to do this?"

"I have already begun. Do not look so surprised! Have I not been in politics all my life? Have I not spent hours in meditation on the subject? Do I not have the confidence of the British agent in Paris? The first steps were simple. Some months ago our man in Paris arranged for the Young Pretender to meet, as if by accident, with some Franco-Irish bankers. These men have long lived and worked in France, they are all wealthy, and most of them are descended from the Jacobites who aided the Old Pretender in the 1715 rebellion. They are not politicians, you understand. They are of the new middle-class, traders, unversed in diplomacy. They are flattered to be introduced to the Stuart boy, and he is flattered to have their attention, for he has made little impression on the Jacobites his father knows and trusts. This Charles Edward has some charm, but no stability. The older Jacobites mistrust him and refuse to help him in his wild schemes, but these new men, these moneyed men, offer him their all. They have chartered two ships from the French

Navy for the Young Pretender, and promised to fill them with a company of volunteers, arms, and appropriate supplies for a landing in Britain."

"I don't believe it. No private person would be allowed to charter a ship for such a purpose."

"Of course not. The French Minister for War has allowed the charters for the purpose of privateering—ostensibly. Of course he knows what they are really intended for; how could he not, when it is his business to know such things? But he also knows that the French will not be able to make any official attempt on these shores this year, and he thinks that the Stuart boy may draw some men from Flanders back to England if he lands."

"A landing here would certainly have the effect of weakening our forces in Flanders. Is that desirable?"

"Do not interrupt. Of course it is not desirable, but neither is it necessary. All that is required is a level head, a sense of timing, and poof! There is an end of Charles Edward. Of course, if the Young Pretender were to succeed in raising the country, the French would back him up, but that will not happen. Do you know of any responsible, well-to-do nobleman who would be mad enough to espouse the Stuart cause?"

"Surely he must be as aware of this as we are? How could he be fool enough to attempt an invasion, knowing that he will not be supported when he arrives?"

"You have put your finger on the point at issue. First I arrange for him to be put in touch with men who have funds to place at his disposal, then he charters ships—only two of them, but it should be enough—and finally, I induce him to set sail by sending him letters promising support from all over the British Isles."

Philip took snuff, as was his habit when he wanted a moment to think. His uncle appeared to be contradicting himself, but Philip knew that it was not wise to jump to conclusions where Lord Carteret was concerned. Lord Carteret had agreed that there were few men of note prepared to put their heads on the block for the Stuarts, and yet he talked of enticing the Young Pretender to invade with letters of invitation. He had talked, also, of suspected Jacobites being watched. Knowing something of the subtlety of his uncle's mind, Philip began to wonder whether these suspected Jacobites were not only being watched, but actively encouraged to invite the Stuart boy over. If so, it was no wonder that Lord Carteret had been so anxious to learn the identity of the Jacobite agent in Sussex.

"How many invitations have you managed to procure from Jacobite sympathizers so far?" he asked.

Lord Carteret smiled his approval. "Three or four. Three firm invitations from the North and Wales, and one more doubtful one from the Midlands. The poor fools little knew, when they entrusted their letters to the couriers, that they were putting their heads in a noose."

"But so far you have no invitation from the South of England?"

"Precisely. Your quick-wittedness gratifies me. I am pleased with you, Philip. The Stuart boy has written to the Tarrants, but this letter, as we know, was most unfortunately intercepted and has not yet been delivered. The Stuart boy must even now be pacing his chambers, wondering if it has miscarried, and his scheme betrayed. He must be put out of his misery. He must receive the kind of letter which will encourage him in his plans. It is regrettable that Sir Richard Tarrant should have seen fit to die at this juncture, but I daresay the boy will serve our purpose just as well. You must return to Tarrant Hall tomorrow, Philip. Go as Mr. Rich, or as yourself, whichever you prefer. Give the boy the letter from the Stuarts, and allow him to think that you sympathize with the Stuart cause. Encourage him to talk. If he was not in his father's confidence—which I find difficult to believe— you must get the woman to tell you what she knows. I don't believe that she burned that correspondence unread, and being a woman, she will have memorized all the important names. Then you will help the boy compose the sort of letter which we want, mentioning that he has firm promises of support from So-and-So, and Such-and-Such, and send the letter to me. I will see that it is forwarded to France without delay."

"I will not do it. The boy is no traitor, and you would have me make him into one. He will be perfectly happy, and remain a good servant of King George, if I can only get him a commission."

"A commission? Out of the question, with his background. I would block any attempt to persuade His Majesty to give him one. Is that understood? Oh, if you are so tender-hearted, I will guarantee the lad immunity from prosecution, always

55

provided that he does not come out in support of the Pretender in due course."

"I do not like your game, and I will not play it."

"It is a very little thing to ask of you, in return for future favors."

"If that is the price of my becoming Ambassador, then I regret I am not worthy of the position."

"Philip, you exasperate me!" Lord Carteret took a turn round the room. "Come, we will not quarrel. I will not disguise the fact that I am deeply disappointed in you, but I can easily find someone else to deliver that letter and obtain the sort of reply we need. You leave here this week, you say? I am surprised you go to Bath when Lady Millicent is still in London. How goes that affair? Do you wish me to make her an offer on your behalf?"

"I hardly know."

"This is no way to woo a young and spirited lady! First you flee to the country from her charms, then to Bath and thence to Hanover for the summer. What is she to make of it, eh? I tell you, this is a match I have had in mind for many months, but I have had other offers for the lady. Her estates are broad, and she has £15,000 in the Funds. Do you place any trust in that promise His Majesty made to find you another bride? The offer was made in the heat of the moment; I daresay he has forgotten he ever made it, by now."

"Yes, I know that. Forgive me, Uncle, but I am not yet ready to take another wife. I am very anxious about Thomas, and..." His eyes were on the fire, and perhaps he saw something there which made him sad. At any rate, he sighed. His uncle frowned.

"Are you not well, lad?"

"A little tired, perhaps. I expect you are right, and that I ought to remarry. Lady Millicent is charming. I will certainly call on her again when I return from Hanover, and perhaps her brown eyes will banish the memory of eyes of blue."

"Who has blue eyes, eh?"

But Philip would not tell.

The Earl of Rame might not have had first hand experience of raising pigs, or crop rotation, but he knew enough of human nature to understand that Mr. Farrow was in an excellent position to feather his own nest. Philip suspected that he himself had been partly to blame, for taking Mr. Farrow's reports at face value. Mr. Farrow's accounts and the amount of money he sent the Earl on Quarter Days had been adequate; it was the villagers who seemed to have suffered. Doubtless Mr. Farrow had never dreamed that the Earl would ever visit Hamberley, or that if he did, the condition of the manor house would ensure he did not stay long. Mr. Farrow had reckoned without Philip's sense of duty, which obliged him to investigate his bailiff's affairs not only for the sake of the villagers, but for the sake of his own reputation. Sophia's words had stung.

So one morning he ordered his coach, and drove down to the village with Mr. Farrow sitting at his side. It was the Earl's intention to make himself known to his tenants, and enquire if they had any complaints to make. He had expected to be met with a flood of grievances, but the villagers were oddly mute in his presence. He could hardly get a word out of them. They pulled their forelocks and made legs, bobbed curtseys, and muttered that it was very good of his lordship to enquire, but talk freely they would not. Philip turned sharply to catch Mr. Farrow in the act of pulling a threatening face at the innkeeper, which caused him to wonder if the villagers were afraid of his bailiff.

"They seem overawed by my person," he remarked to his bailiff, as he reseated himself in his coach. "Perhaps I made a mistake in coming down, dressed in a silk coat and periwig."

"Perhaps they have nothing to complain of," said Mr. Farrow.

"They seem very quiet to me. It is almost as if they were afraid of something—or someone."

"Ah, that'll be the witch, my lord. It makes them uneasy when she comes into the village. Mrs. Barnes's little one is dying, and they say the witch has cast the Evil Eye on him."

"What nonsense! I hope you don't encourage them in such foolishness."

"Not I, my lord. But these countryfolk will believe anything, if it suits them to do so. I wouldn't like to be in the witch's shoes if she comes into the village now...she'd get what's due to her...but I'd see to it that none of your property was harmed, my lord!"

Once back at the manor house, Philip dismissed Mr. Farrow and took out his bailiff's accounts. He had not been able to induce the villagers to talk to him, but he had a retentive memory and he had made a mental note of the properties which seemed to him most in need of repair...yes, he had been right. According to Mr. Farrow's accounts, most of those dilapidated cottages had been repaired during the preceding year at a total cost to the estate of—he totted up the amount and raised his eyebrows. It looked as if Mr. Farrow had pocketed the money which he said he had spent on repairs.

Philip's chin became prominent, and he sent for Chivers. Half an hour later, plain-suited and neatly-wigged, he rode down into the village on Prince. It was in his mind that the villagers might talk more freely to Mr. Rich, the Earl's secretary, especially if Mr. Farrow were not at his side to threaten reprisals.

At first the village seemed deserted. He could not understand it. There had been a fair number of people there earlier that day. Then he heard a murmur like a swarm of bees in flight, and equally threatening. Prince shifted uneasily between Philip's thighs. He tightened his grasp on his riding crop and remembered, with a prickle of fear, that Miss Nan Tarrant had been called a witch by Mr. Farrow. Could she be in trouble? He turned his horse in the direction of the buzzing sound. A girl ran stumbling down the street toward him, looking back over her shoulder. She leaned against a cottage, her hands pressed to her side. She was young but not a child, with flaxen hair and rounded chin. She saw Philip and made a run at him, clutching at Prince's bridle. She gestured to the road along which she had come, unable to speak clearly.

"Help! Oh, please...Miss Tarrant...they think... terrible...will you—?"

"Show me the way. Put your foot on mine." He pulled and she jumped up behind him, lithe country girl that she was. She was shorter than Sophia, but just as capable. She pointed over his shoulder, and took a firm grip round his waist as he set Prince to a canter. Through the village they went, across the triangle of grass before the smithy, past a stone cross set at a junction of roads, and then sharply right down a lane between dry-stone walls, twisting and turning.

"The mill," gasped the girl. "They are going to tie stones round her neck and throw her over the millrace to see if she's a witch or not. That awful man Farrow is there, egging them

58

on. I tried to stop them, but someone threw a stone at me, and so I ran back to the village, but no one would listen to me. They shut their doors in my face. So I was going to run to Tarrant Hall for Jasper...when I saw you."

The hum had grown louder. Individual voices could be heard, shouting. The end of the lane was blocked with the backs of men and women straining to see what was happening in front of them. The bulk of the mill towered to the sky as the walls fell away on either side of them. There was a sudden shout, and a splash. And then silence.

Philip raised his riding crop. "Back, you curs...back, I say! Make way! Make way, or I'll cut you down!" He forced Prince into the press. The horse reared and neighed in a panic. Philip mastered the horse and spurred him on, using him as a battering-ram to part the crowd. The girl had wound her arms tightly around him, and kept her head down. He was in among them...conscious of scowling faces on every side...of hands that tried to grasp Prince's bridle...of fists raised...of a stone grazing his cheek, and then he was through to the bank of the river, and the sullen splash of a great waterwheel turning close by. The wheel was large, capable of lifting many gallons of water at a time. The miller was being held flat against his own door, but he was struggling to free himself. He was held by two men, one of whom Philip recognized. Mr. Farrow's eyes narrowed. He had been shouting some obscenity. His mouth stayed open, and he turned a sickly color. He loosed his grip on the miller's arm, and that worthy individual wrenched himself free, and sent his other captor sprawling with a swing. With a shock of surprise, Philip recognized the second man as Greenwood, the footman he had recently dismissed. The man fell heavily, and did not resume the fight.

"You!" Philip pointed at Mr. Farrow with his riding crop. "Out of here! I'll deal with you later!" Mr. Farrow had seen the Earl unpainted, in his morning gown. He had certainly recognized Philip. His mouth worked. He might have said something, but the miller was not waiting for anybody. He picked Mr. Farrow up by his collarband and the seat of his britches, and swung him once, twice, and let him go, flying with a cry of terror over the path and into the deep, black waters of the mill-pool.

A sigh of horror—or was it satisfaction?—rose from the crowd. Philip turned on them. One or two women at the back

59

of the crowd ran away, up the lane. Another went. A man dropped the stone he had been holding, and took one step back, and then another. The crowd melted away, its cohesion gone.

The girl slipped to the ground from behind Philip, and ran to the side of the pool. She held back her hair as she peered into the water. Ripples spread as Mr. Farrow surfaced, spluttering.

The girl wrung her hands. "Oh, they've killed her!"

Chapter Four

There was hardly a trace left of the mob. Here and there stones lay on the path. Greenwood had vanished. Philip swung himself to the ground as Mr. Farrow painfully pulled himself out of the water, and slunk away.

The miller grasped Prince's bridle and pointed downstream to where some willows overhung the pool. "She'll be held over there...I thought I saw her surface a while back, but the roots will hold her. If you're quick, you'll save her. Hurry, Guv'nor. I can't swim."

Philip knew that this was quite likely to be true, as very few countrymen learned to swim. He slipped out of his coat and boots. Shedding his wig, he dived into the darkness of the pool. He could see nothing...feel nothing. The current was swift. He stayed under as long as he could, and fought his way to the surface. The current had carried him against the far bank, but he was a little way from the willows. He dived under the surface again, and let the current carry him where it would, groping with his hands as he went. Then he was being held by roots...he touched cloth. There was nothing for him to hold on to...his bad arm would never...he had brought his burden to the surface, but could not lift her out of the water, handicapped as he was. The water was freezing. Miss Nan was surely dead. There was a livid mark around her neck, but the rope which had been tied around it was gone. Her hands floated against him, bound in front of her. Perhaps she had managed to free herself of the stone

61

tied round her neck while she was under water...but what now?"

The miller and the fair-haired girl were watching him from the far bank. The girl had been on her knees, peering anxiously downstream. Now she was up and running along the bank, crying to him to hold on. Had she gone for help? The little fool! Who was there who would help them? What was the miller doing? Tying Prince to a ring set in the wall of the mill? That made sense, but...how long could he keep afloat? The bank above him sloped steeply, and the trees thereabouts overhung the water. He pushed and paddled himself along until he could grasp at the gnarled root of a willow, but the strain of holding Miss Nan up was beginning to tell on his weakened arm and shoulder. If he had had the use of both his arms, he could have climbed up, but as it was....

The whips of willow branches above him parted to let the fair-haired girl through. She scrambled down the slope above him. Bracing herself against the roots of the tree, she leaned over and grasped one of Miss Nan's arms. She was a strong, well-made girl, and determined. She pulled. Philip exerted all his remaining strength to push, and the body of the old woman slowly left the water. Philip could now reach up with both arms and hang onto a convenient root. He rested his head against his arms and felt the pain gradually recede from his shoulder, leaving it aching...he could endure that.

"Hurry up," said the girl. "Or you'll catch your death of cold. She's still alive. Job's gone to fetch his men, who hid in the mill when the mob came. We'll have to carry her round by the bridge, which is a little way downstream. It's not far, but I can't do it by myself. You'll have to help me."

Philip began to laugh. There must be something in the air of Hamberley which produced strong-minded, capable women, who always knew what to do in an emergency. Wearily he pulled himself out of the water, favoring his bad arm.

"Tck!" said the girl, annoyed. "Have you hurt your arm again? How clumsy you men are! Still, I suppose that at your age such things take time to heal."

"At my age—!" gasped the Earl.

"I told Jasper that he ought to make allowances for older people. Oh, by the way, I'm Marjorie Bladen."

"So I had supposed," said the Earl. Then up ran Job the miller, with two men, all swearing vengeance on Mr. Farrow and only too willing to carry Miss Nan to the mill. The Earl walked behind them, listening appreciatively as Miss Bladen scolded the men for walking too fast, not supporting Miss Nan properly, and having failed to bring blankets in which to wrap her. What was it Philip had heard about Marjorie Bladen? Oh, yes. She was an heiress whom Sir John wished to marry into the nobility. Poor Marjorie; Philip did not think she would find much to amuse her in Town life. She was a born housewife, young though she was. He could see her, married to Jasper, scolding and running about telling everyone their business from morning to night, with a brood of children at her skirts, as happy as the day was long. He could not see her adapting to Town life and fashions, any more than Sophia....

He sighed, and Miss Bladen turned on him to demand why he had not had the sense to run ahead to the mill. She must rub him down herself, she supposed, and retrieve his clothes, and send messages to Tarrant Hall and her own home....

The Earl said meekly but firmly that if she would deal with Miss Nan, he would attend to himself, and no doubt Job would be able to find someone to run errands for them.

"Suttenly, guv'nor," said Job, grinning as he handed the Earl a tankard half full of brandy. "This'll put you right."

The Earl sipped, frowned, and smiled. Then drank deeply. He supposed it was the first time that he had ever knowingly drunk smuggled brandy, but he didn't suppose it would be the last, in the company he was forced to keep at Hamberley. He toweled himself dry, resumed his clothes, and after satisfying himself that Miss Nan was recovering under the ministrations of Miss Bladen, strolled out to have words with Job. That worthy was only too willing to talk to the "gennelman" who had saved Miss Nan. He was a tenant, not of the Earl, but of the Tarrants, which explained why he had been willing to risk being hurt for her sake. He was also a mine of information about the misdeeds of Mr. Farrow, and very willing to give the Earl particulars of rents extorted and excuses and threats made by the bailiff. Twice he referred to Mr. Carramine, and it became clear to the Earl that the miller formed an important link in the chain of distribution of contraband in that part of the country. But, as he had said to Carramine, Philip was not in the least interested in apprehending smugglers. In fact, glowing with so much brandy, he was very far from wishing to do so.

The gig had not arrived from Tarrant Hall by the time dusk fell, although the miller had sent messages telling of the riot and its aftermath to the Hall, to Mr. Carramine, and to Sir John Bladen. A servant arrived to fetch Miss Marjorie, and although she was loath to go, the Earl persuaded her to do so. It would not be wise for her to walk unattended through the village in the dark that night. Miss Nan had made an excellent recovery, to which the brandy had contributed. She insisted she was well enough to walk home, but the Earl would not hear of it. Finally, it was settled that she would ride on his horse, perched like a child before him, and it was in this manner that they traversed the still silent village and made their way towards the Hall. Miss Nan sat huddled in blankets, the Earl's riding crop in her tiny hands.

Just beyond the village Jasper met them, with the gig. He had only just returned to the Hall from an outing...Sophia had been out all day, too...he was beside himself with horror and rage. He wanted to go down into the village and horse-whip every able-bodied man, there and then. The Earl persuaded him that his duty lay in getting his aunt to bed...it was not far...Mr. Carramine and Sir John, as magistrates, would deal with the matter....

Miss Nan was laid in the gig, and then trundled up the lane to the Hall. Sophia met them in the yard. She had just been told of the riot, and was setting out to meet them. With loving cries she bore her aunt off to bed, and Jasper remembered his manners long enough to order refreshments for Philip.

"Yes," said Philip, "I would like a word with you in private, if I may. I want to tell you about an adventure I had on the way down to Hamberley. I was given a letter to deliver to you. I think you were expecting it?"

The boy's bewilderment set Philip's last remaining doubts at rest. He knew now what he must do. He took the boy into the parlor and made sure that the door was shut and no servants within keyhole range before he spoke again.

The lamps were brought in, and the two men had finished a substantial meal before Sophia brought them the news that Aunt Nan was going to be all right.

"You are very quiet," she said, trying to smile. It looked as if she herself had been crying.

"We were wondering if it would be possible for your aunt to make a visit to one of her relations for a month or so," said the Earl. "I am sure that Mr. Farrow will be dismissed from his post after this, but I do not like to think of her being harassed by the villagers, now that they think of her as a witch."

"Aunt Nan go away? What nonsense!" cried Sophia. "Why, where would she go? To that fool of a cousin of hers in York, to look after his mad wife? He would make a drudge of her."

"I was thinking she might stay with her sister, Lady Midmain, in Town."

Both Jasper and Sophia shook their heads. "It would never do," said Sophia. "They never liked each other, even as children. Aunt Helen is very pretty but also very vain, and Aunt Nan used to tease her. Then Aunt Helen was supposed to have been responsible for the accident which crippled Aunt Nan. Aunt Nan forgave her, but Aunt Helen couldn't forget about it, and there were bitter things said before Aunt Helen married Sir Gregory and went away to London. Aunt Nan is in general the very sweetest of persons, but now and again the devil seems to get into her...."

"As it did when she came up against Mr. Farrow," said Jasper, nodding.

"Maybe time has softened Lady Midmain," suggested the Earl.

"I doubt it," said Sophia. "She's a jealous cat. When I was a child, she used to pet me, and give me presents, but as soon as she saw that I was growing up, she began to hate me because her gentlemen friends paid more attention to me than to her. Jasper, are you quite well?"

Her point was a good one, for the boy seemed to have aged several years that afternoon. The Earl stepped between brother and sister, giving Jasper time to make a recovery. "It grows late, and I must be on my way. I am glad to hear Miss Nan is doing well."

"She wants to see you before you go, to thank you. I will take you to her."

Miss Nan lay in a pleasant, tapestry-hung room. She looked like a child, lying neatly in her narrow bed, but her eyes were bright, and she held out his riding crop to the Earl as he entered the room.

"Thank you, my lord."

Philip turned, but Sophia had left them alone.

"How did you know?"

She indicated the silver crest on the knob of the riding

crop. "The sign of the Swan told me. I wondered, when I found a monogrammed handkerchief in the pocket of your coat when I was mending it. And then, your manners, your air...you puzzled me. When I saw the crest, I knew."

"You told Sophia?"

"No. You have your reasons for hiding your identity, no doubt, and I am already deep in your debt."

"I told her I was Rame, but she would not have it. She told me I was the tutor. I did not wish to embarrass her, and it did not seem to matter, for a day or so."

"It must have seemed like an adventure to you. I understand how it was. I saw that you were attracted to Sophia, and she to you. I watched your eyes, and I watched her, when she thought I wasn't looking. I was afraid for her, even before I guessed who you were. You have saved my life. I am deeply in your debt, but I urge you to leave without doing us any more harm."

"For Sophia's sake?"

"For all our sakes. I am no witch. I cast no spells. Only, sometimes I see things in the fire which come true. I have seen the Hall deserted, and heard Sophia weeping...and I saw the sign of the Swan replace the Ram and the Rose over the gatehouse...I am so afraid, so old and tired. I can feel evil all around me, and I do not know how to avert it."

"I am not evil. I mean you no harm."

But her eyelids were closing, and Sophia had returned to take him away.

Sophia drew him into the bedroom he had occupied during his stay at the Hall. She turned her head away from him, but not before he had noticed that she was still close to tears. She said that she wanted to add her thanks to those of her aunt. She said that she would like to check that he had not done his broken bone any injury. She took his riding crop out of his hands and laid it down. She began to push back his coat from his shoulders. He could not bear it. The desire to kiss her was so great that it was impossible for him to stand still while she examined him. He wanted her as he had never wanted a woman before; he had had women in plenty, before, during and after his marriage, but he had never wanted one as he wanted Sophia. The room seemed to darken. His arms went round her. Her mouth was slightly parted. She shook her head as he pulled her close, but the protest she was trying to make died away as he kissed her. This time she did not

66

repulse him. She sighed and closed her eyes, allowing herself to relax against him. As her arms went round his body, he, too, closed his eyes.

There was an exquisite pleasure in holding her like this. He had not thought she would give in so easily. He had wanted her from the moment he had seen her. Marriage was out of the question; she was as far beneath him as the village folk were beneath her. But a civilized period of flirtation, followed by seduction—discreetly carried out, as all his affairs had been—that was what he aimed for. If he had not been so tired, he would have taken his conquest a stage further....

She said, "I thought you had gone to London. I never thought to see you again."

"Nor I, to see you. Kiss me again."

She raised her lips willingly, and sighed his name, "Philip."

He thought: Better and better...she does know how to flirt, after all.

He said: "You say my name as if you had practiced it."

Her arms slackened. She was withdrawing from him, playing coy. Now she was blushing. That was good. She knew how the game ought to be played, in spite of her pretense of innocence.

He laughed, exhilarated by the joy of the chase.

Her eyes flashed, and she drew herself up. "I ought not to have forgotten myself. I was distressed about my aunt, and grateful to you for saving her. My conduct may have misled you into thinking that I wished you to...it is not so, of course. You must not forget that I am to marry Sir John Bladen."

He caught her hand and put it to his lips. "You do not view the marriage with pleasure, I am sure." He thought he was on safe ground. He was teasing her, willing her to play the game with him.

"What is it to you whether I wish it or no?"

She had him, there. His eyes narrowed. She was challenging him to state his interest in her, and he knew that he could have none.

"I understand you," she said. "You say nothing because you mean nothing honest by me. My aunt warned me."

"It is out of the question that I should marry you, but need that prevent our meeting, now and then?"

"I would not play my husband false."

"Husbands...wives...they understand these things. All will be well, provided only that we are discreet. The lady who has been selected for me to marry will turn a blind eye to..."

"Forgive me, sir." She swept him a curtsey which would not have disgraced a duchess. "My standards of morality differ from yours. I see that we have nothing in common."

She held the door open, and he had perforce to pick up his riding crop and leave. In the hall Jasper Tarrant was waiting; a servant with a lantern stood by, ready to light Philip back to the Manor. Philip had feared that Jasper might notice his confusion, but the lad had too much on his mind to be aware of other people's problems. Sophia, too, was preoccupied. The three of them exchanged formalities, and all the time Philip was wondering if Sophia would tell of his attempt to flirt with her. He hoped that she would not, because it might destroy the boy's trust in him. He believed she would not normally confide such a matter to a boy so much younger than herself. He had gambled, and lost. He cursed himself. He might have jeopardized everything for the sake of a passing desire for a pretty girl.

He said something to Jasper about not forgetting their intention to meet on the morrow, and Sophia interrupted to remind Jasper that he would be very busy then, with preparations for his coming-of-age party. Philip saw that she meant to deny him the opportunity of seeing her again, but Jasper took her intervention as a reminder to offer an invitation to the party to the man who had rescued their aunt. "Of course you must come," he said, "And bring Mr. Denbigh, too."

Sophia looked dismayed, but controlled herself sufficiently to second her brother's invitation. Her eyes sent Philip an explicit message—"Don't you dare to come!" they said.

"I shall be delighted," he said.

Chivers drew back the bedcurtains and announced that it was nine of the clock, and that the Earl had two visitors waiting for him downstairs. The valet seemed agitated; he swallowed hard and blinked. Philip stretched out his arms to be enveloped in his dressing-gown, and asked what was the matter.

"Nothing, my lord." Chivers swallowed again. "What do

you wish to wear today? One of the men is Mr. Farrow. The servants seem to be uneasy in his presence—that is, the local servants. He is waiting in the hall."

"Let him wait. It will do him good to reflect on his sins for a while. And the other?"

"The other person is in the kitchen, partaking of breakfast. It seems he has ridden down from London with letters for you, but he says he does not come from Lord Carteret. Indeed, I am sure that he does not. He says that he must speak with you urgently." Once more Chivers swallowed, and blinked. "My lord, I beg of you not to see the man. Let me ask him for his letters."

"My lord!" Mr. Denbigh burst into the room, his wig awry. "There is a man below who says he has letters for you from London, but I am sure he has come to kill you. I could not be certain at first, but when I looked again, I saw that it was the same man, the highwayman, the one who killed the French courier."

"Now this is very interesting," said Philip. "I will see him, as soon as I have dressed."

Mr. Denbigh and Chivers raised their voices in protest. It would be madness, the man would draw out a pistol and shoot the Earl at sight; they must send for Sir John Bladen, for Mr. Carramine, for everyone, and have the man taken into custody....

"Quietly," said the Earl, and they fell silent. He took his seat by the window, and signed to Chivers to begin shaving him. "If this is the man who killed the French courier, then I have nothing to fear from him. I believe he is a Government agent, sent here by my uncle."

Chivers' hands shook as he lifted the razor. "My lord, I implore you not to admit the man. For my sake, be reasonable."

"I am always reasonable. I think I had better shave myself today." The Earl took the razor from Chivers' hand and set about making himself presentable. The valet's head sank, and his hands fell lax at his sides. "What is the trouble, Chivers?" The valet shook his head, and would not say. Much against his will, Mr. Denbigh sent a servant for the newcomer, while the butler brought the Earl his hot chocolate. The fire was made up, and still Chivers stood, drooping, wordless.

The Earl told his valet to wait outside the door. Chivers

stared at his master, but went out of the room on unusually heavy feet.

A jovial-faced man was ushered in, and looked around him. He was neatly but quietly dressed, suggesting a well-to-do shopkeeper in his appearance. His build was bulky, but he was light on his feet, and his eyes were cold. He looked formidable.

He bowed to Philip. "Allow me to introduce myself—Dodge is the name, Jeremiah Dodge. We have met before, although you may not recall the occasion."

"I recall it very well."

"Ah. As I said to my mate at the time, I wouldn't mind meeting up again with a cove as handles his poppers as well as your lordship does."

"Indeed!" said Philip, waving his visitor to a seat. "I trust your—mate is recovering from the bullet wound I was forced to inflict on him?"

"Oh, that. That was nothing to a man of his stamp, I assure you. His missis was pleased to have him at home for a bit."

Philip began to enjoy himself. "And the man I was so unfortunate as to remove from this life? Does he leave a widow and children? I must admit that the possibility had not previously occurred to me, but perhaps..."

"Think nothing of it, your lordship. It's all in a day's work, and Mr. Stone has assured his wife of a pension."

"Ah," said Philip. Now he knew who was behind recent events! Mr. Andrew Stone was known to him primarily as private secretary to the Duke of Newcastle, but during his period of waiting at Court, Philip had learned that Mr. Stone was much more than he appeared to be. Those in the know said that Mr. Stone was the most powerful figure in the Government, although he chose to rule from the shadows behind the throne. What Mr. Stone decided on Monday, was preached by Newcastle on Tuesday, and endorsed by the King before the end of the week.

"We're on the payroll as Officers of the Watch," explained Mr. Dodge. "Sometimes it's the Postmaster General as wants something done, and sometimes it's Mr. Stone. But Mr. Stone generally has the more interesting jobs on offer, as you might say."

"So it is Mr. Stone who 'sees you right' if anything goes wrong? Such as in the affair of the French courier? So you rode back to Mr. Stone and told him what had happened. He

70

has now, I presume, given you instructions to obtain the letter from me, and to deliver it to the Tarrants. A pity you have had a wasted journey. I gave it to Sir Jasper yesterday." Mr. Dodge's eyes almost disappeared into his head. "Yes," said the Earl, "I gave the matter a lot of thought, and came to the conclusion that as I had given the courier my word that I would deliver the letter for him, I was morally obliged to do so."

"Ah," said the fat man. "And you got a reply?"

"I have arranged to meet Sir Jasper today at noon, at the mill. He was not *au fait* with his father's correspondence, and will have to apply to his aunt for the details we need to make his reply convincing. I shall be happy to give you Sir Jasper's letter, in exchange for a note from Mr. Stone granting him immunity from prosecution. I feel sure you have been provided with one."

"Together with a warrant for his arrest and committal to the Tower, yes. My instructions were to use whichever was found to be necessary."

Philip blinked. "Have you no pity for the boy? He is quite innocent, you know."

"The sins of the father..." intoned Mr. Dodge. "Besides, feelings is irrelevant in this job, my lord. You would do well to remember that, if you continue to play a deep game."

"What makes you think that I...?"

"I stayed the night at the inn in the village here, my lord. Very informative, I must say. They was all upset there last night, and nobody minds talking to Jeremiah Dodge. If I says so myself, I can add two and two better than most. You can't go rattling round the countryside rescuing ladies from drowning, and dispersing riotous assemblies without getting yourself talked about, my lord. Mr. Stone will be very interested to hear of your doings."

"What the devil have my recent actions to do with Mr. Stone?"

"Didn't you know, my lord? Mr. Stone has taken an interest in you for a long time, in spite of Lord Carteret's wishing to push you forward as his nephew. Mr. Stone is one as sleeps with one eye open, as the saying goes. By the way, my lord, before you dismiss me, perhaps I could give you a word of warning? Your bailiff, a man called Farrow, is a scoundrel as could do with watching; also, your man Chivers used to be a Gentleman of the High Toby; or, as you might say, a highwayman."

"Birds of a feather, were you?"

Mr. Dodge's face split into a grin, and for the first time his eyes lost their chill. "You might say so, my lord. You might, indeed. But reformed characters, both of us. I am sure you can trust him as you would trust me."

"And how far might that be, Mr. Dodge?"

Mr. Farrow was sweating, in spite of the chill of the morning. The Earl touched the corner of his right eye. Under the paint, the skin was discolored and slightly swollen. He thought it would be uncharitable of him to ask Mr. Farrow if he had thrown the stone which had caused the damage.

"No, Mr. Farrow, it will not do. Diverting money intended for repairs is one thing, and just possibly I can understand how it came about that you did it. A man in my position who does not trouble to look after his interests, almost deserves to be robbed."

"My lord, if I might explain..."

"But where a man has expressed certain opinions he has, I think, the right to loyalty on the part of his servants. You knew my views on witchhunts, did you not?" Mr. Farrow swallowed. "Precisely. Yet you left me only to lead one. A perfectly harmless gentlewoman, whose only crime was that she cared more for the village people than you did, was nearly drowned yesterday afternoon. What defense have you?"

"It is well known that the woman is a witch. The way she looks at you is enough to send shivers down your spine. She told old Garroway that he would die before the winter was out, and he did; and him as hale and hearty a man as you could meet. Now Mrs. Barnes' child is wasting away."

"I heard all about that from Job, the miller. The child is dying of consumption, brought about by a leaking roof and poor food. If anyone is to blame for the child's illness it is not Miss Tarrant, who has done what she could to ease the boy's cough, but you, who diverted money which ought to have repaired the roof. You persecuted Miss Tarrant because she dared to criticize you."

Mr. Farrow's mouth narrowed. "Everyone knows the Tarrant women are witches. Perhaps they've bewitched you, too."

The Earl opened his mouth to deliver a blistering rebuke, but Mr. Farrow hurried on. "Let me explain, first, why it was that I kept the money back. It was to further your interests. I thought you would be pleased if I could enlarge your property. You must know that I am very friendly with Sir John Bladen, and that he is to buy Tarrant Hall at a knock-down price. He's got those fools where he wants them; they're so deep in debt they'll take any price to settle their most pressing commitments. Sir John is very clever, and he's going to offer them about half of what the property is worth, and they'll take it, because he's going to give the Tarrant women a home when the place is sold." Mr. Farrow sniggered. "Sooner him than me, married to that termagant, but he says he knows how to break her in once they're wed. Now Sir John, being a friend of mine, is going to let me buy the mill off him, at a fair price. It's a fine investment."

"Thanks entirely to the Tarrant family, who have looked after their tenants better than you have looked after mine. No, Mr. Farrow, it will not do. I daresay you did intend to buy the mill, but the deeds would have been in your name, and not in mine."

"I swear by Almighty..."

"Pray, do not. I would not believe you, and if there is a God, He might hear you blaspheme. I will not prosecute you, if you compensate me for what you have stolen. I will have Mr. Denbigh go over the accounts with you, and decide what you must pay. Your tenancy of one of my cottages is hereby terminated; you have seven days to pack up and go."

"Not so fast." The man's voice grated. "You can't turn me out like that. I know too much. I've been watching you, I have, and there's things I could tell that you wouldn't like known. You're all alike, you stinking aristocrats, with your fine airs and your back-door intrigues. What if I were to tell the truth about Mr. Philip Rich, eh? What if I were to let it out that the Earl of Rame has been riding around the countryside in disguise, consorting with traitors and witches? That wouldn't go down well with your high and mighty friends in London, would it?"

The Earl touched the handbell at his side. The butler answered.

"Fetch the man Dodge, and two of your strongest men."

"What are you going to do?" asked Mr. Farrow, uneasiness taking the edge off his aggression.

The Earl did not deign to reply, but occupied himself with taking snuff. Mr. Dodge duly presented himself, backed by two large footmen. The Earl indicated his former agent.

"This reptile has had the temerity to threaten me. He is under notice to quit for fraud. I need him under my eye for a few days, until Mr. Denbigh has had a chance to go over the accounts with him. Would you be so good as to bestow him in some secure place about the Manor?"

"Now, look you here..." Mr. Farrow lunged forward, to be caught back by Mr. Dodge.

"Moreover," said the Earl, in the same gentle voice, "The man seems to have threatened some of the villagers with eviction and other unpleasantness unless they do his bidding. I would not wish any of the locally-recruited servants to be exposed to his malice. Would you place a trustworthy, and preferably deaf, guard on duty outside the room in which you propose to keep him? The same man should be present when Mr. Denbigh visits Mr. Farrow, to avoid violence."

Mr. Farrow spat. "You..."

Mr. Dodge laid a large hand over his captive's mouth. "There," he said soothingly. "You don't want to swear in the presence of your betters. Trust me, your lordship. He'll be kept on his tod, as the saying goes."

Mr. Farrow was hauled away.

Chivers glided into the room and hovered. He looked pale, but determined.

"Try smiling," said the Earl. "This is not the Day of Judgment, you know."

"My lord, I have served you for twelve years now, ever since you came back with Mr. Denbigh from abroad. You never asked me about my past, and..."

"But I knew, Chivers. Your previous master told me something of your history, and he also said that he could not have wished for a more loyal and discreet servant."

"You knew I had been in prison? And you never said anything?"

"I thought you preferred it that way."

"Yes, I did. But when I saw Jeremiah Dodge in that valley, standing over the Frenchman, I thought I'd seen him before. I didn't remember where until much later, and I've been living in dread ever since that he would turn up again and my secret would come out, and you'd dismiss me."

"Certainly not," said the Earl. "I wouldn't dream of doing

any such thing. Who else could make me presentable, when I've got a black eye? Smile, man: It's not a hanging matter."

"You don't plan to dismiss me?"

"Certainly not. Your presence will be of great assistance to me as a check on Mr. Dodge, who by the way is now a trusted agent working for the Government. If you had any notion that you might have seen him before, either in Newgate, or on a deserted road at night, I think you would do well to forget it. I am certain that he will be equally silent about your past."

Later that day Mr. Denbigh tried to persuade the Earl not to attend the party at Tarrant Hall.

"Philip, we have known each other a long time now, and you have been kind enough to call me your friend. As a friend I say to you: pause and reflect. I know you well; you have a reputation for good nature which is misleading. You are not tolerant, merely indifferent to most things that happen around you. Only now and again, perhaps once every five years or so, you become obsessed by some idea or person, and then you allow nothing to stand in your way. On occasion, I have applauded your ambition; for instance, I thought you wise to go into the Army. But at other times I have had to stand by and watch while you played havoc with other people's lives."

"You are thinking of the little sempstress who drowned herself? Was I to blame for her melancholia?"

"No, but you were to blame for pursuing her when you knew she was a respectable girl. You knew her parents would disown her."

"Am I any worse than any of my friends?"

"No, but you are more persistent when you really want something. Now I see you want Tarrant Hall. True, it is on the market, but consider that if you buy it, Miss Sophia and Miss Nan will lose their home. Had you thought of that?"

He shrugged. "Sir John will no doubt take his bride and her aunt into his own house. Tarrant Hall pleases me."

"What of the ideas you are putting into Sir Jasper's head? Can you send that lad into danger with a clear conscience?"

"I have warned him what to expect. Is it my fault that he is of an adventurous temperament?"

"And Miss Sophia? You cannot mean to marry her, and anything else is unthinkable—isn't it?"

The Earl held his smile until it became a grimace, and then stood up.

"I must go out. I have an appointment to meet Jasper at the mill."

Once more the great coach rumbled through the dusk, carrying the Earl, Mr. Denbigh and Chivers, but this time the Earl was dressed in a coat of dark blue cloth, without patches or paint. Only Chivers knew how much care the Earl had taken with his appearance for an unfashionable country party. Usually he went through the ritual of dressing for a function with the air of one grimly doing his duty, but this time he had shown an anxiety to appear at his best which merely reinforced the valet's forebodings.

The moon was up—no one would have contemplated attending such a party if the moon had not been available to light them to and fro,—and the lights of the village twinkled through the trees as they turned into the Tarrants' private road. The sky was cloudless; there was a drift of stars here, and yonder rose the moon, as fat and yellow as cheese.

"It's no wonder children cry to play with the moon," said Philip, breaking the silence which had reigned since they left the Manor. "I quite fancy the idea myself."

His companions regarded him in silence. Philip knew that they guessed what he intended to do that evening, and that they disapproved. He shot his ruffles and smiled to himself.

Seduction was an ugly word, which he had not had to consider before. Women of a certain class had always been willing, and he had not previously been tempted by a woman of his own class to have to think about it. Only, Sophia was not of his class. There was as big a gap between his rank and hers, as there was between his rank and that of the women of the opera whom he had patronized in the past. He wanted her, but marriage was out of the question. Tonight was his last chance to seduce her. A large party...long, boring hours at table...too much to drink...manners slipping away in the country-dances...he could arrange to whisk her into a sideroom and....

The consequences? She would not make a scene. If she were a virgin now, she had wit enough to fool Sir John that

76

she was still one when they married. He had a reputation for drinking heavily.

The coach drew up in the courtyard, amid a jumble of carts and carriages. The Earl descended and looked around him. He thought the situation of the Hall was delightful, and would be even better if a new approach road were to be made...a new roof...the ancient gateway was also in need of repairs...Like the moon, the Hall was his to grasp, if he wanted it badly enough. He was smiling as he passed through the doorway.

Chapter Five

The third course of dishes was being removed from the top table, and the wine glasses replenished. The food had already been removed from the lower tables, at which the tenants were seated; Philip acknowledged a wink from Job, the miller, who sat at the head of one of these tables. The gentry, seated at the top table, had been served with more courses of food, and had drunk French wine, instead of the beer which was being handed round to the tenants and their wives. Most faces were flushed with drink, and some bore traces of the food of which they had recently partaken. Here was an elderly gentleman with an ear trumpet who boasted to Philip that he had fought with Marlborough, and there a child in petticoats—sex unknown—who slept in its mother's lap. There were gaps at the tenants' tables, but the gentry seemed to have rallied to support Jasper, in spite of his aunt's reputation. Many had come considerable distances to be at the Hall that night and would in consequence be staying the night. Others, like the Bladens, would return to their own homes later.

Marjorie Bladen, all dimples and curves, sat next to Jasper. Sir John had been heard to disapprove of this arrangement in no uncertain terms, but Mr. Carramine had soothed him by saying that it would probably be the last time the two young people met. Marjorie was innocently proud of her new brocade dress which, she said, her father had bought her in anticipation of her making a visit to London. Yet her eyes were shadowed when she spoke of the metropolis, and eager when Jasper lifted her hand to his lips. Others beside Philip noticed the attention Jasper was paying Miss Bladen, and also concluded that the girl would be happier married to a local boy than packed off to London and the marriage market.

Miss Nan presided over the feast with an eye for everyone's plate but her own. She ate little, drank water, and her eyes seemed enormous beneath her lace cap. By tacit consent, no one referred to her recent experience, but Philip thought that it had aged her. She was resplendent in a black silk dress which had been turned twice, but to which she lent such grace that she made every other woman look overdressed.

Sophia sat at Sir John's side, playing the part of modest and gracious maidenhood. She bent her head, and smiled at him, whenever he chose to throw a word in her direction; this was not often, for it seemed that Sir John enjoyed his food as much as he enjoyed his wine. Sophia's hair was tidier than usual, but she had coaxed one long curl to lie along her neck and down over her bosom. This curl fascinated Philip, it was so round and dark and lustrous that he wanted to wind it round his fingers and kiss it. It would be soft and retain something of her fragrance.... She was dressed today in a rose-colored gown of old-fashioned cut, which might once have been her mother's. It suited her well enough, although it was cut lower in front than fashion decreed. Her bosom was whiter than ever by contrast with that swinging dark curl. He let go of his wineglass, lest he snap its stem.

He had been seated between a deaf old lady and a young girl who giggled whenever he spoke to her. Opposite, however, sat Mr. Carramine, whose conversation had made the banquet endurable.

"A very pleasant wine," observed Mr. Carramine, who had drunk as sparingly as Philip.

"Imported?"

Mr. Carramine laughed. "You dare not refuse it. Or the tobacco to follow. I know you—you could not be so impolite. Come, now; smile!"

"I was thinking that Jasper had become a man, almost overnight."

"Yes, the boy told me."

Philip took snuff, his eyes on Mr. Carramine's face. This was unexpected. Or was it? "What did he tell you?"

"Of your interest in his future. Of your suggestions as to what he might do." The Earl said nothing. "He asked my advice. I did not know what to say, and so I took the coward's part and said nothing. I will not influence him, one way or the other. I am reminded of what happened to our fishpond when someone introduced a pike into its waters; the fish disappeared almost overnight. I know when I'm outclassed." Mr. Carramine nodded to where Miss Nan sat, ignored by her neighbors. "She's worried, too. I told her nothing, because the secret was not mine to share, but she is so quick, so intuitive, that I would be careful what I said to her if I were you. She wanted to know if I were in your confidence, and what your plans were with regard to the Tarrants. I told her that you could be trusted to behave like a gentleman."

Philip hooded his eyes, and felt color rise in his cheeks, but still he said nothing.

"She wasn't talking about Jasper," said Mr. Carramine, driving the point home with a sledgehammer.

"Miss Tarrant ought to pay some of her relatives a visit," said Philip, speaking quickly to cover his discomfort. "Her position here must be most uncomfortable, with everyone declaring they don't believe in witches, but nevertheless managing to avoid speaking to her directly."

"I agree," said Mr. Carramine. "But where could she go? By the way, did you hear the latest? They say that the witch summoned up the devil to rescue her from drowning...."

The ladies rose and left the hall, with many adjurations to the men not to sit long over the port. Sophia passed behind Philip's back without a glance. He wondered if anyone else—apart from Miss Nan and Mr. Carramine—had noticed how much of an effort Sophia was making to avoid him.

Jasper proposed the loyal toast, to which Mr. Carramine replied with "Sir Jasper!" And then Sir John cried that they should all drink "To the Rose of Tarrant Hall!" There was much laughter, and some coarse comment about Sophia's marrying Sir John; laughter in which Jasper did not join. He moved round the table to sit next to Philip. He was as sober as Philip, and his eyes were everywhere.

"A man brought me a letter this afternoon," he said. "It is from my uncle, Sir Gregory Midmain. You remember that I asked him if he would help me get a commission? Well, he will not. It appears he wishes nothing further to do with me. He has been informed that I have had dealings with the

Jacobites, and that my father and brother fought for King Louis; he is pained and surprised that I should have applied to him under such circumstances. What do you think of that?"

Philip glanced around. Mr. Carramine's attention had been claimed by someone else. No one else was close enough to overhear them. "I think it might be interesting to know the identity of the man who brought the letter. It did not come by the common post, I take it?"

"No, a stranger brought it. He was fat and smiled a lot, but his eyes were..." Jasper shuddered.

"Ah. I think your uncle's letter was dictated by someone at Court. I know the knave who brought it to you, and he is in the employ of Newcastle. It seems someone has made sure your uncle does not help you."

The lad sighed. His shoulders slackened. Then he straightened in his chair and the lines of his face hardened. "Well, it is only what we expected, after all. It is quite clear what I must do. They leave me no alternative. Mr. Carramine said he couldn't decide whether to applaud my courage, or deplore my folly. You have been good friends to me, both of you."

"You have faced the fact that if you are caught your life will be forfeit?"

"Mr. Carramine pointed that out, too. So be it. I refuse to stay on here, in debt, with nothing to do except farm and get drunk. If I don't go this way, I'll likely be caught smuggling. I don't mind danger, but I do mind being bored. I am beginning to understand what drove my father and brother away. If I could only have got more money out of Sir John for the sale of the Hall, I'd be happy to go."

"Mr. Farrow told me that Sir John does not mean to deal fairly with you over the sale of Tarrant Hall."

"I hate that man Farrow; not only because of what he tried to do to Aunt Nan, but because he is capable of the filthiest trickery. A woman in the village committed suicide last year, and...but you won't want to hear about that. The truth of the matter is that Sir John knows no one else wants to buy the Hall, and that I must sell. He offered me a fair enough price at first, but he has dropped his price every time we discuss the matter, until it looks as if I shall be several hundred guineas out of pocket when I do get him to the point of signing. I don't mind so much for myself, but I did want to leave Aunt Nan and Sophia with something when I go."

"What is he offering at the moment?" Jasper told him. "I can double that, if you will sell to me."

The boy flushed. "I was not begging."

"I know you were not. It happens I have been looking for a place in this part of the country. You may ask Mr. Denbigh if that is not true. The Manor is hardly habitable, and I do not like its situation. The Hall would suit me very well."

"I could not take advantage of your generosity," began Jasper, only to be interrupted. The women had sent servants to clear the tables from the hall, in preparation for dancing. Chairs were moved to the sides, and the company staggered to its feet.

"Up and at 'em!" cried Sir John, being assisted to his feet by two equally drunken companions.

Jasper remembered his duties as host and hurried away. A group of musicians arrived and began to tune their instruments. Mr. Denbigh was happily arguing with a gentleman in a snuff-colored suit; his wig was awry and his face flushed.

Sir John caught Philip's arm, and held on to it in order to keep himself upright.

"Straordinary likeness," he said, squinting at Philip. "I know the Earl your kinsman well, you know. Poor relation, aren't you? Born on wrong side of the blanket?" His two friends, standing close by, sniggered.

"No more than you were," said Philip. He knew it was indiscreet of him to antagonize Sir John, but the words were out before he had time to think.

"Huh?" Sir John's cheeks became purple as he registered the insult. "You impudent young...What do you mean by insulting your betters? I'll thrash you till you..." One of his cronies whispered something in his ear about Miss Sophia. "What? Yes, there's that, too. You keep out of Miss Sophia's way, d'ye hear me? Seen you looking at her. Don't care for it."

"A cat may look at a queen."

"Not while the King's aroun'!" Sir John's cronies fell about with laughter at this witticism. Gradually Sir John's own face creased with mirth. He slapped his thigh, repeating the words. Philip walked away, lest he strike the man. Curious glances were being cast at him, but he ignored them. The reputation he had earned since his arrival would have made him a popular focus of attention, even among those who half believed that he was in league with the devil, but his manner forbade familiarity.

Miss Nan had ushered the women back into the hall, and was now seated between Mr. Denbigh and Mr. Carramine. The older women sat in clusters, the false curls on their foreheads nodding as they gossiped. The young men were making a lot of noise around Jasper, and the girls stood or sat by their mothers, waiting for the music to begin.

Sophia and Marjorie Bladen were in the group around Jasper. Sophia disengaged herself and glided across the room to Sir John. Philip was close enough to hear her ask him to partner her in the minuet which was to open the dancing. There was cream in her voice, and her manner was so uncharacteristically meek that a smile pulled at the corner of Philip's mouth. Was this exhibition of maidenly manners put on for his benefit?

"My brother wants to dance the minuet with Marjorie, but she is too shy to go on the floor alone with him, and no one else is familiar with the steps. You will come, won't you? To please me?" Her smile was sweetness itself. She had no word or glance for Philip, though she must have known he was nearby.

Sir John belched. "I'm not going to ape the French in those damned Court dances of yours. Get someone else to make a spectacle of himself with you, or better still, let's go straight on to the good old English country dances—'Strip the Willow,' 'Roger de Coverley'; I'll partner you in those."

Philip could see Sophia's smile fade. Jasper and Marjorie were standing hand in hand in the middle of the floor, waiting for her. Philip did not blame the young couple for not wishing to open the dancing by themselves. Here and there, and especially at the public subscription balls in Bath, it was de rigueur for a couple to open the evening's dancing together while everyone else looked on and criticized their performance. He had done it several times himself, and he knew what an ordeal it could be.

Two steps, and he was at Sophia's side, bowing. "May I solicit the honor, Miss Tarrant?" She shrank back. He smiled down at her, ignoring Sir John's grunt of rage. "Your brother and Miss Marjorie are waiting. See, everyone is looking at us."

Her hand was cold in his, but rather than allow an ugly

situation to develop into a brawl, she allowed Philip to lead her onto the floor.

"This will cause trouble," she said, low down. Jasper signed to the musicians to start playing.

"You should not have avoided me," he replied. "If I have to force an opportunity to speak to you...."

"I shall miss my step. I know I shall. I have never danced the minuet in public before." She faltered, he whispered a word of instruction, and she followed it. She was as graceful as a swan, the long curl over her bosom swinging as she pointed her toe this way and that, passed under his arm, around him, and curtseyed. He did not speak again. It was rare to have a partner who moved as one with him, her body an extension of his. It was extremely satisfying. He was sorry when the msuic stopped.

Jasper and Marjorie were flushed and laughing, each accusing the other of having forgotten the sequence of steps. Philip found he was still holding Sophia's hand. She was looking at him without animosity, with a question in her eyes.... Sir John's bulky figure interposed between them. He was holding a glass, half-full of wine. Did he intend to throw the contents of the glass in Philip's face? No sooner had the possibility crossed Philip's mind than Sophia acted, claiming Sir John as a partner in a country dance, and urging Marjorie to partner Philip. The Earl had to acknowledge that she had managed things adroitly. Marjorie was smiling up at him, confident of her welcome. He led her into the set which Jasper was arranging, and the music struck up again. Marjorie did not dance as gracefully as Sophia, but bounced around more or less in time with the music. He did not care. He had a fondess for her because she was courageous enough to show that she liked Jasper in the face of her father's disapproval. It amused Philip to pay her compliments, to make her laugh, and to know that everyone was watching them ... and watching Sophia. Poor Sophia! She had got her man on the floor, without his wineglass, but he was too far gone in drink to partner her properly. He slipped and fell amid laughter, not all of which was kindly. He was perspiring freely. Someone shouted to take care, as Sir John turned a bad color. At once a space was cleared around him. "Quick! He'll cast up his accounts on the floor!" "Take him out!" Mr. Carramine and Sophia bundled Sir John out of the room. The dance ended almost at once, and Philip slipped out after them. They had gone in the direction of the bedrooms, and he went that way, too. The staircase and landing were ill-lit. He heard footsteps, and slipped into the first bedroom. With his eyes to a crack in the door, he saw the bottle-green coat of Mr. Carramine pass by, returning to the ground floor.

On the landing once more, he heard Sophia ministering to Sir John, over unmistakable retching sounds. They were in the bedroom which the Earl had occupied during his stay at the Hall. Sophia came out of the room, saying that she would fetch Sir John a clean shirt, and that he might take a nap if he wished. She went across the landing into the room in which her brother slept. Philip went quietly along the landing behind her. He pulled the door shut of the room in which Sir John was recovering, and followed Sophia into her brother's room. She was bending over a chest, searching for a shirt. He closed the door behind him, and leaned against it. She had brought a candle with her, and its flame fluttered in the draft as he closed the door. She turned sharply, and her hand went to her side.

"This is not wise," she said.

"No one knows I am here. I closed the door of the room he is in." She turned back to her search. "Sophia, you cannot mean to marry that caricature of a man?"

"What other course is open to me? Who else would be willing to pay our debts?"

"Why should you be sacrificed to pay your father's debts? Surely you can find some other man willing to take you, even without a dowry?"

"I am a Tarrant, and I must keep faith with my family. Generation after generation, the Tarrant men go to the wars, while the women look after the land. I love this place, and I've no wish to leave it. By marrying Sir John, I help my brother, provide my aunt with a home, and remain mistress of Tarrant Hall. With God's blessing, I shall one day have children to care for..."

"I have a child," he said, "He is ten years of age, but not strong."

"Your wife—?"

"...is dead."

"But you are marrying someone—?"

"My uncle is arranging a good match for me. If only you..."

"...had had a dowry, or been born into some influential

family? I understand you very well, I believe." She showed her teeth. "I must go. They will be looking for me."

He continued to block the door. "No, don't go. Sophia, I love you." He had not meant to say that. He had not even known that he did love her until the words were out, but then he saw that it was so. She gave him one quick, uncertain glance, and turned her head away. She was breathing quickly. She put her hands over her cheeks as if to smooth away their sudden brilliance.

"I love you," he repeated. "I loved you the moment I saw you, kneeling above me in the field...your eyes, your hair, your courage...I can't let you go."

She clasped her hands together and set them to her lips. He held out his arms. She shook her head. He took a step towards her, and she swayed back, just out of reach. Her eyes were on his face now, but there was some shift of thought mirrored in her expression which he did not understand.

"Feeling as I do about you, how can I let you go without having made an arrangement to see you again? I will be in Hanover this summer, but we could meet when I return. Oh, it is true that I must marry someone else, but that should not—must not—be allowed to interfere with what I feel for you. If you decide against marrying Sir John, I am sure that some complaisant gentleman of mature years can be found who would be willing to go through the ceremony of marriage with you for a consideration...these things can always be arranged." His mind ranged over the possibilities; his retired steward was too old, but his lawyer had an elder brother who might be suitable. "You must arrange to visit Lady Midmain this summer. I will write to you there. Once you are married, I would make you an allowance, find you a house and servants, a carriage. I would be able to visit you several times a week, and..."

She made some sound from behind the shelter of her hands which he could not interpret. Turning her back, she walked to the window. He followed her, and put his hands on her shoulders. "Or, if you do decide to marry Sir John, I am sure you could so work on him that he would take you to London for the Season. Being an old man, he could not possibly object if his wife were to solace herself—discreetly—in the arms of another man..."

Again came that smothered sound. It was laughter, dry and cruel. She laughed until tears came, and still she shook

86

with laughter. His hands dropped from her shoulders as she sought for a handkerchief.

"Oh," she cried, blowing her nose. "I suppose it is better to laugh than to be angry. Such ardor! Such passion! Oh!" And she went off into another paroxysm of laughter. Philip shivered. Of such stuff were nightmares made.

"If only you could see yourself," she said, and giggled. "So ridiculously stiff! So businesslike!" She tittered, and shook her head at his folly. "Men are so stupid! Dear me, how Aunt Nan will laugh when I tell her...what a pity you did not get down on your knees, for I must tell you, as a connoisseur, that it improves a gentleman's performance out of reason if he goes down on his knees to a lady. Never mind; I daresay you did very well for a beginner, and if you take lessons you might make a conquest among the kitchenmaids next year. I really would not advise you to make the attempt with a lady's maid or a milliner; your style is not likely to recommend you to them. Oh, dear!" She dabbed at her eyes. "Now, should I tell Sir John, I wonder?"

He felt as if he would faint if he did not escape from her. He bowed, and moved towards the door.

"Oh, are you going? Perhaps to consult Mr. Denbigh, who knows exactly how to turn a compliment—?"

"Madam, I..."

"Go, then, but carry this thought with you. You despise Sir John because his manners lack polish, yet he has always treated me with respect, and I shall be honored to marry him. As for you, sir; you are no gentleman, and if you dare to show your face here again, I will have Sir John take his horsewhip to you."

Philip fled. He clung to the newel post at the head of the stairs, and let his head drop onto his hands. He heard the swift clop of her shoes as she crossed the landing behind him, and then her voice, comforting her betrothed. His brain began to work again. The numbness passed, to be succeeded by waves of pain as he remembered how she had looked...the words she had said...how could he ever have imagined he loved such a virago? Perhaps he had deserved to be rebuked for his offer, which could be construed as an insult to a virtuous woman, only need she have laughed at him, and said— what she had said? He had to admit that he had been clumsy in his approach. He had handled a dozen such affairs before and his proposals had always been gracefully phrased, and

as gracefully accepted or declined. Only, none of those affairs—with the possible exception of the little milliner who
had drowned herself—had gone deep with him, as this had
done.

He swore. Swearing helped to ease his pain. And damn
Sophia, and damn all the Tarrants!

Rage pushed back humiliation. How dare she speak to him
like that! If she had known who he really was...he would
be revenged on her. He would drop his disguise, so that she
should understand exactly whom it was she had insulted.
More, he would buy Tarrant Hall. He had always wanted it,
and the boy would not suffer, nor Miss Tarrant, for he would
pay a better price than Sir John. As for Sophia, perhaps she
would not be so cold to him, once she had had a taste of
marriage to Sir John. Perhaps she might even regret her
cruelty, seeing her home pass into the hands of a stranger.
When next he visited Tarrant Hall—and he intended to do
so frequently—he would call on her and...

The devil! He could wait, and in the meantime there was
much to be done. He sent a passing servant for Chivers, who
would be waiting below with a portmanteau containing all
that was necessary to transform his master once more into
a gentleman of fashion. He had told Chivers to bring his
things on the off chance, but now he was glad that he had
done so. Jasper appeared below. He wanted to know if Sir
John were all right. The Earl beckoned him to mount the
stairs.

"Jasper, my boy—a word with you?"

"The Earl is here!" The rumor seeped into the hall, no one
knew how. Miss Nan looked round for Mr. Denbigh, but he
had disappeared, as had Mr. Carramine. Sophia had been
hovering over a somewhat deflated Sir John, but now came
to sit with her aunt. Her color was high, and her manner
bright. Too bright, thought Miss Tarrant.

"What did you say to him, Sophia?"

Sophia's eyes changed direction. "I? To whom? To the Earl?
Oh, I have not been privileged to meet him. It seems Jasper
brought him in by the side door and took him straight to the
parlor. What should we do, Aunt? The food will be quite cold
by now."

"He has eaten already. Child, I saw him follow you from the room, and he has not been back since. What did you say to him?"

"You mean Mr. Rich? He insulted me, and I gave him a set-down." Miss Tarrant moaned. "Why, dearest—what is the matter? Do you feel faint?"

"It is all to come true, then. The tears, the Hall standing deserted..." She struggled to her feet, holding on to her niece's arm, as Jasper and Mr. Carramine entered the room. Behind them came a tall, shimmering figure, clad in cloth of silver. His peruke was snowy white, as was the fall of lace at his throat. The paint and patches on his face emphasized the aquiline nature of his good looks, and his height was enhanced by diamond-buckled, red-heeled shoes. The black-clad figures of Mr. Denbigh and Chivers followed.

"The Earl of Rame!"

The Tarrant ladies advanced to meet their guest, and sank into billowing curtseys. Sophia's eyes were on the Earl's face, and her expression was one of incredulity. "Why, he is as magnificent as a prince, or as..." Her whisper died away.

"As Philip Rich?" said her aunt.

The Earl bent and took Miss Tarrant's hand, raising her from the floor. "Do not look so alarmed, Miss Tarrant. I told you, I mean you no harm."

Miss Tarrant's hands clung to the Earl's. "Even now, it is not too late! I beg of you leave us in peace!"

"You cannot put the clock back," said Jasper, impatiently taking the Earl's arm. He swung him round to face the rest of the room. "The Earl wishes you all to be introduced to him later, but first I must tell you that he is to buy Tarrant Hall from me."

"No!" cried Sophia. The color had left her face. Her knees gave, and her head dropped. The Earl was near enough to grasp at her elbow and pull her upright. He was smiling down at her. Sophia opened her mouth to scream, and checked herself. She began to tremble. There was a tumult of voices in the hall. Her agitation passed unnoticed, except by her aunt and the Earl. She took one deep breath, and then another. She stepped away from the Earl, to her aunt's side, moving as if she were blind.

Jasper was saying that the Earl had made an offer for the whole of the Tarrant estate, an offer which was too good to refuse....

89

"You can't sell to him!" Sir John lumbered forward. "You agreed to sell to me!"

"If you had dealt fairly by me," said Jasper, "I would have done so. But week by week you have dropped the price until I could not cover my father's debts if I sold to you. The Earl has been more than generous; he will pay me enough to buy you, Aunt, an annuity. Sophia, there is to be a small dowry for you, too. Will you not thank him?"

"I will not thank him," said Sophia. "His action is despicable, and so is he!"

Few were near enough to hear her words, and none understood them, except for the Earl and Miss Tarrant. Philip bowed to Sophia, and turned to address the guests. He did not raise his voice, but it carried well. He said he had long wished for a residence in their part of the country, but that the Manor House had been too dilapidated to be suitable. He understood that his ex-bailiff, Mr. Farrow, had not discharged his duties properly, but a new man was to be appointed who would redress any grievances the villagers might have. He himself was obliged to go to Hanover with His Majesty that summer, but hoped to stay at the Hall in the autumn, when the workmen would have finished their repairs and alterations. His new bailiff would have orders to avail himself of local materials and labor wherever possible, in order to stimulate trade in the county.

"Three cheers for the Earl!" cried Job, the miller. Most of the guests followed Job's lead, and then crowded round the Earl to be introduced.

"Cleverly handled," said Mr. Carramine in Sophia's ear. "He'll be the most popular landlord the county's ever known."

"Mr. Carramine, can't you stop this sale? Can't you see he's buying the Hall to revenge himself on me, to deprive me of my home?"

"Gave him the brush-off, did you? Well, if you prefer Sir John...that's your affair. I must be off, my dear. There's a thousand things to be done if I'm to go to London with him. Yes, he's offered me a place in his coach when he goes. We have an appointment with someone in Whitehall, you know. I wouldn't have missed this for the world!"

"And I am off to...guess where!" cried Jasper.

"France?" said Miss Tarrant. Tears sparkled on her cheeks.

"If you say so, dearest Aunt." Jasper kissed her. "Come now; smile. You knew I had to go."

"But not like this!"

"Not so fast!" Sir John thrust his bulk between them. "What about the five hundred your father owed me?"

"He owed you nothing. You have often boasted that you were too fly to lend him anything."

"Maybe so. Maybe I didn't boast of it, but I did lend him five hundred last autumn. You have cheated me of the Hall; will you cheat me of my money, too?"

The Tarrants looked at each other. They found it difficult to believe in this newly-disclosed debt.

"You have his note of hand?" asked Jasper.

There was a moment of hesitation. "Not here," said Sir John. "The signature is almost illegible. He was drunk at the time. But I can bring an independent witness to the transaction, if you doubt my word."

"You shall be paid in full," said Jasper, "If it takes the money I would have given Sophia for her dowry."

"Well, as to that," said Sir John. "I fancied living here at the Hall, and didn't mind taking Nan along with Sophia— then. But if I'm not to have the Hall, I'll be damned if I'll take the witch to live with us. I'll take Sophia, as I said I would; a taste of my whip now and then will keep her in order and cure her temper, but..."

"I cannot leave Aunt Nan," said Sophia.

Miss Tarrant drew herself up. "My dear, you must think of your own future. If there is enough money, I will rent a cottage nearby. If not, I can always go to my cousin in York, who needs someone to help nurse his wife."

"No," said Sophia, "It will not do. It seems I have deceived myself not only about Philip, but about my reasons for wishing to marry Sir John. I have been foolish, and I shall pay for it, but I will not compound the injury by making Sir John pay for it, too." She swept him a curtsey. "You are right, sir— I would have made you a very bad wife. I wish you better luck elsewhere."

"What?" Sir John's cheeks became purple. "I would have you know, miss, that there is many a fine woman this side of Lewes who would be delighted to become Lady Bladen."

A sudden hubbub, and the Earl was bowing over their hands, saying everything that was correct in his light, unstressed voice. Jasper seized Sophia's arm and asked if he

91

might tell the Earl that her marriage with Sir John would not now be taking place.

"I forbid you to mention it," said Sophia, sinking into a curtsey, as Philip bowed above her. Her eyes glittered. He was saying something complimentary to Jasper about his sister's being a true Rose of Tarrant Hall. And then he was gone and the room was dark, and all was despair.

As the Earl drove under the ancient gateway and down the winding lane to the highway, he turned to Mr. Denbigh and asked him to take some notes on the work he wished done at Tarrant Hall.

"I want the Ram and the Rose on the stone gateway replaced with the crest of the Swan...."

Chapter Six

Sophia sighed, and then wished she hadn't, for her corsets hurt her. It was a hot day at the end of August, and she was sitting in the sewing-room at the top of her aunt Midmain's house in London, mending a lace tippet. There was barely a trace left of the careless girl who had scrambled over stiles and through hedges at Hamberley. Her skin was pale, she had lost weight, and she was dressed in the plain black gown and white apron of an upper servant—or poor relation.

Sir Richard's debts had been greater even than they had feared, and when all was settled, Aunt Nan had taken her leave of them to go to her cousin in York, and Sophia had sought refuge with her aunt in Town. Her youth and beauty, her untidiness and poverty, all irritated Lady Midmain, who did not like to admit to the existence of a niece of marriageable age. Sophia was trussed into a corset and given a cast-off dress of her ladyship's; she might stay, if she made herself useful and kept out of the way. But Sophia's height and manner did not aid her; and she was all too noticeable, especially to Lady Midmain's admirers. Then came the rumor that the Young Pretender had landed in Scotland, and that Jasper Tarrant had been seen with the Jacobite forces. Lady Midmain said she was sure she would not have taken Sophia in if she had known that Jasper was a traitor.

Sophia denied the charge, but could not say where Jasper was, for no one had heard of him since he left Tarrant Hall at the end of March. Lady Midmain brooded on the subject for some days, and then, after losing a particularly large sum at cards, announced her decision as to Sophia's future. The girl might stay, because Heaven knew it was not in her ladyship's nature to turn her brother's child onto the streets, but she was not to appear in company any longer, and would defray the expenses of her keep by assisting the housekeeper with the care of the linen. Thus Sophia donned black gown, cap and apron, and went to live in the attics.

If she raged, she did so in the solitude of her bare bedroom. She had no illusions about her aunt; Lady Midmain would turn her onto the streets, if Sophia gave her sufficient cause by behaving badly. She did not complain of her lot to her Aunt Nan, who was being very brave about her post in her cousin's house, but who could not disguise the fact that her health had not been good that summer, for her handwriting quavered all over the paper, like that of an old woman. Sophia wrote to Mr. Carramine, but did not receive any reply. At first she was indignant that he should have neglected her, but then, as the weeks wore on, and her own once splendid health became undermined by the low diet served to the servants at Lady Midmain's, she grew to accept the fact that she was no longer of consequence to anyone. As if to underline this, Marjorie Bladen wrote to say that Sophia would hardly know Tarrant Hall now that the outbuildings had been cleared away, and a new drive made. Marjorie was to spend the autumn in Town with her father, who was still looking for a bride. The letter had concluded with a request for news from Jasper—which Sophia could not provide—and the hope that the writer might meet her old friend often during her visit to London. Sophia did not ask Lady Midmain if she would be permitted to receive a visit from Marjorie, for she knew that it would be forbidden.

Often she thought of the Earl, and how he was faring in Hanover with the King. Often she wondered—especially when she went to bed—what her fate might have been if she had accepted his offer. He would never know how nearly she had accepted it...how much she had wanted to do so...how many times the memory of his face had come between her and her work....

She hated him. It was he, and he alone, who had been responsible for their present plight. Jasper, out with the rebels; her aunt, slaving away at a task too great for her physical strength; and herself in tears in a hot room on a lovely summer's day. Down below in the pretty garden, the guests wandered among the orange trees which had been set out in green-painted tubs. It was one of her aunt's At Homes, which were always well attended. Her uncle would be bustling about, trying to appear more important than he was, hanging on the words of anyone who might help him to a sinecure, and worrying about the bills. He had been timidly kind to Sophia at first, but had learned to ignore her, under his wife's tuition. Today he would be busier than ever, for the King had returned from Hanover and there would be fresh scandal to glean from those who had been with him. Sophia wondered if the Earl were married again by this time. She wondered why she continued to think of him.

The door opened to reveal the butler, looking flustered. Someone had called to see Miss Tarrant. The butler was set aside. A tall, elegant man entered: He was wearing a watered brown-silk suit and a shining white wig; he was powdered and patched and carried a lace handkerchief, which he was using as a fan. Not a stranger, but Philip Rich. No, not Philip Rich; but the Earl of Rame.

She sat with her needle poised and her mouth open, staring.

He produced a quizzing glass and surveyed the room, her work and her attire. His fingernails were polished pink. "Deplorable," he said flatly.

She had forgotten that he never raised his voice and rarely exhibited emotion. She stumbled to her feet, her work slipping to the floor. She put a hand to her collar and felt the rough stuff of the unbecoming gown. She remembered the frightful cap she wore. She knew she could never have looked more plain.

She curtseyed. Her hands were trembling, so she clasped them in front of her. Would he notice? Yes, of course he would. He noticed everything. He did not smile, but then, he did not smile readily. He looked well, she thought; better than he had done in the spring. There was an air of competence about him which surely had not been there before?

"I see that Miss Tarrant is not dressed for company today, so I will take a dish of tea with her before joining Lady Midmain downstairs." A coin was dropped into the butler's hand, and disappeared. "I assume we will not be disturbed, in this out of the way place?"

"Certainly not, my lord." The butler bowed and withdrew.

The Earl inspected a rickety chair. "Will it bear my weight?" he wondered.

In confusion, she begged him to sit. Then she was angry that he was so much in command of the situation. He waited for her to sit. She did so, feeling helpless.

"You must not scold your butler. I enquired if you were at home, and his answer was evasive, not to say incoherent. The only word I could make out clearly was 'sewing-room,' so I asked him to show me the way to the sewing-room. I daresay I would not have done so if I had realized it was up three flights of stairs, but there you are."

"Why are you here? To gloat?"

"How ungenerous of you to question the motives of one who comes to relieve the monotony of the sick-...I mean, the sewing-room...for you. Yet, perhaps you are right. I must admit to a certain sense of satisfaction, a sense that justice had perhaps been done, when I read your letter. I beg your pardon; the letter you wrote to Mr. Carramine. He has been abroad much of the summer, and only received your letter last week. He could not come to Town to see you himself, so he sent your letter on to me to deal with. He was surprised and shocked—as I was—to hear that you had not married Sir John Bladen. We had pictured you deep in wedded bliss these many months. What was your brother thinking of to allow this to happen to you?"

"I have not heard from him for months. He is out with the rebels. Didn't you know?"

"Some such rumor had reached my ears, but I had disregarded it."

"It is not wise to claim acquaintance with me or my brother nowadays. You will find few people bold enough to do so."

He raised black-pencilled eyebrows. "Attendance at Court would be thin if everyone who had a brother or cousin or friend with Jacobite sympathies were to be excluded. Half the nobility of Scotland have sent their wives, relations or friends to protest that while such and such a person may be a rebel, they themselves are loyal. Has Lady Midmain made a servant of you because your brother is a suspected Jacobite?"

"That is what she says."

"I suspect her ladyship has allowed her vanity to overrule her common sense. Her raddled complexion and thinning hair would not show to advantage beside the looks which you once possessed." He put up his glass again. "My admiration for your aunt increases; I would not have thought it possible to reduce you to insignificance."

"Put that glass down," she snapped. "You are not so short-sighted that you cannot see me at a distance of two paces."

"How well I remember those shrewish tones. Your spirit is not quite broken, I see."

The door opened, and the butler and a footman brought in the paraphernalia for making tea. The Earl proceeded to make polite conversation.

"Did you know I am to be congratulated on the birth of a new cousin? A boy, too. My uncle is beside himself with delight, only tempered with the reflection that he must go into mourning for his wife, who died as the child was born. I truly believe that Lord Lincoln mourns more sincerely for her than my uncle."

"Why should that be?"

"Did you not know that she was Lincoln's first love? They could not marry, because he had many debts and she had nothing but her looks. So he married his first cousin, to please his uncle Newcastle, and my uncle Carteret married her. The cream of the joke was that Lincoln, being a Gentleman of the Bedchamber, had to present the new Lady Carteret to the King on the occasion of her marriage. The King was much amused."

"How heartless of you all to laugh at what must have been a painful situation!"

The Earl signed to the servants to leave.

"No," he said quietly. "You misunderstand, as usual. Lincoln made the right decision; he gave up a romantic interest in a lady who would have brought him nothing but a life of worry over money, and instead he married a girl he has known from childhood, who has much affection for him, and who brings him the certainty of a political career and wealth. The lady kept her pose as Romantic Love until the very end, and my uncle got himself an heir. There is a sense of fitness about it, don't you see that? You understood it yourself once, when you decided to marry Sir John Bladen. You refused what I offered you, for a life of security, and you were right to do so. I had a decision to make then, and I made the wrong one; it was a moment of madness on my part, but it is over. I am glad you rejected my offer. You had more sense on that occasion than I did."

"Is that meant to be an apology?"

97

"N-no. For if I insulted you, you returned the compliment, did you not?"

"And in revenge, you ruined me."

"Come, now; I had no idea you would refuse to marry Sir John. All I wished to do was..."

"...to deprive me of everything in the world that I loved."

"Do sticks and stones mean more to you than your family and friends?"

"No, or I would have married Sir John, would I not?"

"I do not know. Your motives, like mine, appear to be very mixed."

The kettle emitted steam, and she tipped the boiling water into the teapot. The fragrance of China tea filled the room. She thought that Lady Midmain would soon know her niece had had a visitor, for the butler would have had to apply to the housekeeper for access to the China tea, which was kept locked in a chest, and only doled out on special occasions. Servants—and Miss Tarrant—were not normally allowed to drink China tea.

He accepted a cup of tea, and observed that her cap put fifteen years on her age. She took it off, and shook her hair around her shoulders; curling one or two long locks round her fingers, she brought the longest forward to lie over her breast. She watched his eyes, and saw them widen before he turned his head away. He was not as unaffected by her presence as he pretended. There was an uneasy silence. Twice she opened her mouth to make some comment and desisted. He was studying the fingernails of his right hand, his tea forgotten. She wished she knew what he was thinking.

He said, "What do you think of the fashionable world, now that you have had a chance of observing it at close quarters?"

"I? I have seen nothing, done nothing, and been nowhere. No, I lie. I went to one rout party when I first came to London, and knocked over a china ornament. I also went with my aunt to a card party, but as I do not play cards, I sat in a corner all evening and no one spoke to me. I do not blame them," said Sophia grimly. "My hair was unfashionably dressed, I wore a dress of my aunt's which was far too short for me, and I broke the fan she gave me to carry. Oh yes, and I scandalized my hostess by discussing farming methods with her son, and trying to talk politics to her uncle. My aunt was ashamed of me, and swore she would never take me out again."

"She is a very foolish woman. Granted, your path would have been easier if you had been fair and petite and known how to flirt, but..." He moved to the window and surveyed the company below. Laughter and the clatter of cups delighted the ear. "Do you want a taste of that?" He indicated the party below. "Suppose your hair was properly done, and your dress suitable, do you think you could hold your own down there?"

"According to my aunt, it would be more a question of holding my tongue."

"Not everyone who moves in Society is a fool, but I grant you might do better if you used your eyes rather than your tongue at first. What would you settle for? A ball, a rout party, a visit to the opera, an evening at Ranelagh, and a presentation at Court? I daresay I could arrange it for you."

"In return for...what?"

"That lovelock." He indicated the curl of hair over her breast.

"You would do all that for one lock of my hair?"

"And for the pleasure of putting you in my debt." Her face reflected uncertainty. Was she to take his offer seriously? He made his leisurely way to the door. "By the way, what have you told your aunt about our previous meetings?"

"Only that you came to visit my brother several times prior to purchasing Tarrant Hall. Nothing else."

"Very wise of you. I do not think you have seen me today, either. I must remember to tell the butler about that. A guinea should do the trick."

"I don't understand. What do you mean to do?"

He gestured to the open window. "Listen, and you will learn." He was gone. She hurried to the window and crouched down beside it. The sun was high and warm on her bare head. She played with her lovelock, and then set it between her teeth. Had he meant it? He had enjoyed her discomfiture, but by inviting her to laugh at it, too, he had made it seem that they were almost friends, instead of enemies. She would like to take him apart, to see what he was made of.

There was a swirl of movement in the garden below, and a tall figure in brown silk made his way among the guests, stopping here and there for a word, a compliment, to kiss a lady's hand. Lady Midmain sat on cushions on a stone seat in an arbor, with her cronies around her. The Earl made his way to her, and apologized for being late. The arbor was covered with roses, but their first bloom was over, and Sophia could see him well enough. He was bending over Lady Midmain's hand, and then looking around, as if searching the company for some face that he had expected to see. "So where have you hidden her, Lady Midmain?" He had raised his voice slightly. Sophia could hear every word.

"Who?" asked Lady Midmain. She smiled up at him. Evidently he was a favorite with her.

"Why, the latest rose from Tarrant Hall. The Tarrant ladies are known as the Roses of Tarrant Hall, are they not?" He bowed to Lady Midmain once more. "Have we not all sat at your feet since your husband plucked you from the rosebed in Sussex? All these months that I have been at Hanover I have wondered how your niece was faring with you. She was not in the same class as yourself, not a tea rose, but...a wild rose, shall we say? A rustic Venus, tall and stately, and with such eyes and hair..." He kissed the tips of his fingers and threw the kiss in the air. "I must confess to curiosity. With your knowledge of the world you must have been happy to tutor the girl, for though she may have been the toast of the county, yet she lacked polish, and would not have known how to comport herself as your ladyship does, in Society. Well, madam, what have you done with her?"

"Why...I..." Lady Midmain was vexed.

"Is she ill? But no; Miss Sophia was never ill." He looked around at the company, gathering their attention. "She has told you the story of our first meeting, I suppose? Was it not amusing? I was telling my friend Lincoln about it the other day, and he said it was just the sort of tale His Majesty would find diverting. Yet I hesitated. I thought it had probably been told a dozen times this summer in England. Stale jokes, you know, are..."

"What is this story?" enquired a stout matron.

"Why, surely you must have heard it from her own lips! My foolishness on that occasion was..."

"My lord, you intrigue me."

"Tell us!"

"Oh, but this is absurd. Of course you must know. Well, if you must hear it again, know that it was all my own fault. When I am in the country, and not expecting company, I like to wear old clothes; clothes which, according to my valet, are a disgrace and ought to be burned. Now you must know that I had never visited my Manor at Hamberley near Tarrant Hall before this spring, and I was not known there except to one of the magistrates. He, poor fellow, was so over-awed by my appearance in formal attire, that he gave it out I was six-foot-six high. The following day I rode out unattended, wearing one of my comfortable old coats. I was riding a spirited horse, which had been some time without exercise. I let him have his head, on a private road. Miss Tarrant appeared under my horse's hooves, and I fell off my horse at her feet...." A buzz of appreciative laughter. The Earl shook his head, mock-tragic. "Ah, but you must not laugh. When I recovered consciousness, I thought I had died and been transported to another world, for there was this beautiful girl bending over me, all solicitude...her eyes...her hair...her complexion...What beauty! What tenderness! I was slightly hurt...no more than I deserved to be, for I had nearly ridden her down. She took me back to Tarrant Hall and—now you may laugh, if you will—she mistook me, in my old coat, for my own secretary! Yes, it is quite true. There was I, without hat or wig, wearing a coat with a patch on it, and I could not convince her that I was really the Earl of Rame. Yes, I had to laugh, myself. Her mistake was very understandable."

"I daresay it made her blush when she found out the truth," said the stout matron. "Poor thing!"

"Over that we will draw a veil," said the Earl. "She treated me better than I deserved, and nursed me back to health. When I heard that the Tarrants would be forced to sell the Hall, I made them an offer for it. It will prove an admirable hunting box, when various alterations have been carried out. So now you understand why I ask—where is Miss Sophia?"

"Oh, clever!" whispered Sophia. There was a spattering of applause in the garden below, where everyone had crowded round to hear the Earl's tale. "Very romantic!" said one. "Is she so very pretty?" asked another. "I don't remember the girl, egad!"

Lady Midmain had her answer ready. "My niece has been suffering from a summer fever, a lowness of spirits which made her avoid company."

"Not fatal, I hope?" said the Earl. "Perhaps I should ask my doctor to call?"

"That will not be necessary," said Lady Midmain, smiling widely. "The girl will be perfectly well soon."

"Tomorrow, perhaps?" said the Earl. "I am at St. James' tonight, and if Lincoln has not already told the King the story, then I will. Only, if Miss Sophia is really sick, and the

King wishes to have her presented to him, as he surely will when he hears that she is your niece..." And he bowed gracefully to Lady Midmain.

"She will be well tomorrow," promised Lady Midmain.

"Ah. Then perhaps we may all meet at Ranelagh tomorrow night? I hear the latest divina to sing there is something out of the ordinary."

Certainly Lady Midmain intended to go, as did most of the company there. And most certainly Sophia would be urged to join them.

"Then I am satisfied," said the Earl. He bowed to the company, and making the excuse that he had some tiresome business to attend to, left.

Sophia should have been exulting in her change of status from poor relation to debutante. Instead, all she could think of was that her corsets hurt. Gone was the black stuff dress and hated cap; she wore one of her ladyship's newest gowns, a confection of white silk embroidered with pink flowers and trimmed with lace. The skirt had been let down to a reasonable length. There was a posy of pink flowers in the knot of lace pinned on her fashionable coiffure, and the lovelock along her neck had been polished with silk till it shone. There were thin slippers of pink silk on her feet, and a gauze scarf had been draped around her shoulders by her ladyship's own maid.

Many carriages were making their way to Ranelagh that night, to hear the latest Italian singer perform. Lights shone in the trees and were reflected in the waters of the pool in front of the rotunda. Sophia marveled, and was dumb.

"Hold your head up," said Lady Midmain, who had not stopped admonishing Sophia from the moment she had been called down from her attic to assume her new position in the household. "And keep your elbows in. Don't drop that scarf, whatever you do."

The paths round the pool were filled with the fashionable crowd as they slowly made their way into the rotunda, where the concert was to take place. The wide skirts of the ladies, the brocaded coats of the gentlemen, were mirrored in the pool. Sophia wanted to say that she had never seen anything so beautiful before, but her aunt was still talking.

"...and remember never, never contradict a gentleman as I heard you contradict Sir Gregory this morning. You know

102

nothing of politics. No woman can ever know anything of politics. Or farming. Remember that!"

She widened her lips into a false smile, bowing to an acquaintance. "What a dreadful man that is! A tongue like an asp, but it would never do to cut him. A connection of the Walpoles, you know. For heavens' sake, child! Don't stand there, gaping like a fish! Smile! Look as if you were enjoying yourself!"

She exchanged curtseys with a passing belle. "What a fearful shade of green...it makes her look fifty! Now, remember that you cannot expect to engage the Earl in conversation for long, but even a few minutes may establish you in the eyes of the world. He will certainly make a point of speaking with you, if he intends to present you; although, with the Pretender in Scotland, I don't really know what the world is coming to, and a thousand things may happen to divert him.—Lady Lincoln, your servant. Yes, this is my niece, Sophia. Truly, a rose, as you say. How kind of your ladyship, we most certainly will be there. A pleasure.... And remember, Sophia, that is just a sample of the kind of invitation you may expect, if you can interest the Earl for more than a minute or two. A rout party at Lady Lincoln's! True, it will be a dull affair, for she is not one of the smartest of hostesses, but her influence—her uncle, you see, is..."

"The Duke of Newcastle, I know. She married her first cousin, Lord Lincoln, and he is also a nephew of Newcastle's. She seems very pleasant."

Lady Midmain uttered a genteel scream of anguish. "Don't! My dear child, don't ever let me hear you speak of anyone as 'pleasant'!" She shuddered. "What would the Earl say if he heard you! Lord Lincoln is one of his most constant companions. If you mention the invitation to the Earl, you must do so in terms of gratitude."

"Just had a thought!" said Sir Gregory, stopping in the middle of the path. "The Earl—why he should pick out Sophia? Mystery, really. Heard something this morning which might explain it. They said he was to marry Lady Millicent Fairweather, did they not? Arranged by Lord Carteret; good match, well-connected, wealthy. But it hangs fire. For some reason the Earl can't be brought up to scratch, and goes off to Hanover for the summer instead of marrying the lady. Heard this morning that Newcastle's put forward his own candidate for the Earl's hand. Miss Paget; distant cousin of

Newcastle's, very wealthy. Nothing against her, that I know of. Interesting, isn't it?"

"Sir Gregory," said his lady, pulling him from the path. "We are in the way. People are being prevented from passing. Why should the Earl's marriage cause him to take an interest in Sophia?"

"Politics," said Sir Greogry, tapping the side of his nose. "The Earl's a coming man, they say. Always at the King's elbow this summer. Very close with that secretary of Newcastle's, the man Stone. Looks like Newcastle wants to lure the Earl into his camp, by offering the Paget girl. Carteret wouldn't like that, having arranged for the Earl to marry Lady Millicent. The Earl wouldn't wish to offend his uncle, but if he wants to make his way in politics, he mustn't offend Newcastle, either. Cleft stick. Plays for time. Doesn't take either of the girls till he's seen which party has most to offer him. Pays court to Sophia to throw dust in their eyes. Subtle man, the Earl of Rame."

Sophia felt very tired. She had been in the hands of dressmakers and perruquiers since dawn that day, and her aunt had decreed that she must eat less, to reduce her figure to acceptable proportions. She did not know quite what she had hoped for from the Earl, but Sir Gregory's words had stripped her of illusion. His explanation felt right. She was no more than a pawn in the game the Earl was playing.

"If that is so," said Lady Midmain, "then we should order a couple of new gowns for Sophia. If he launches her into Society, she may take...even without a dowry, it might not be impossible for her to catch a husband. It all depends on the Earl."

Sophia caressed her lovelock, and said, under her breath, "Damn him, damn him, damn him!"

Lady Midmain hissed, "Hold your shoulders back, girl; and don't mutter!"

The great rotunda was divided into three sections; there was a platform in the center, on which the orchestra were at present tuning their instruments, there was a wide floor space around the platform on which the company would promenade in the interval, and lining the fabric of the building were the privately hired boxes, to one of which Sir Gregory now led the way. A footman was already laying out a choice supper for the Midmains and their guests. Sophia was very hungry, and felt she might enjoy the evening, after all.

104

Life was very odd, she thought; yesterday she had been wondering how many dreary years of service she would have to put in before death put an end to life; yesterday she would have imagined herself in seventh heaven if she had received an invitation to spend an evening at Ranelagh. Now she was there, and all she could think about was the pressure of her corsets on her ribs, and whether she could manage to filch some chicken off the table before her aunt could stop her from eating anything. Then there were people to whom she had to be polite, and smile and say yes, it was very romantic meeting the Earl of Rame like that, and yes, didn't he have the most beautiful manners, and yes, she did think he was one of the most handsome men she had ever met. . . . How well he had done his work!

Damn his eyes!

A heavyset young man plumped down beside her and panted out a greeting. He said he had been wondering where she had been all summer. She did remember talking to him at his mother's card party in the spring, didn't she? He had often thought of her, and her theory about Jethro Tull's new seed drill. Now she remembered him. Of course! She had got into trouble with her aunt through talking farming to him, but it appeared that this strange young man thought none the worse of her for her interest in that direction. In the course of conversation it emerged that he had not heard the gossip about the Earl of Rame and Miss Tarrant. Sophia was amused. Had she made a conquest, all by herself, without help from the Earl?

Young Mr. Dalby—for that was his name—disappeared when the divina arrived to sing, but he promised to return in the interval. Lady Midmain told Sophia that she had behaved very prettily so far, but must discourage Mr. Dalby from monopolizing her. The divina sang at length, and with many trills. Her "shake" was much admired, according to the Midmains. Sophia formed the impression that neither the orchestra nor the singer knew precisely which note the latter was aiming for, but kept her opinion to herself.

The divina retired amid applause. Sophia turned, and found the Earl was seated directly behind her. She had not heard him enter. She felt color rise to her cheeks. He looked amused. He bowed over her hand and said that he was charmed to renew their acquaintance. He complimented Lady Midmain on her protegée. He said all that was right and proper, and then turned from the ladies to speak to Sir Gregory.

Lady Midmain signalled to Sophia to speak to the Earl, but she could think of nothing to say. Her aunt was not to be denied, however. She said that Sophia must be tired of sitting still for so long, and suggested that the Earl might care to promenade with her during the interval. The Earl hesitated—a masterly stroke, thought Sophia—and then offered her his arm.

"You blushed quite charmingly," he said, once they were out of the box. "How was it managed?"

"When you are tightly laced," said Sophia grimly, "Any sudden movement is likely to produce an undesired physical effect, such as blushing, or fainting. You do not have any food on you, do you? I am starving, and my aunt says I must diet."

He actually unbent enough to laugh. "Must I come courting you with food, in future?"

"You are not courting me at all. You do not fool me. You are using me as a screen, while you decide whether you marry Lady Millicent or Miss Paget. Sir Gregory told me all about it. I assume that one—or both—of them is here tonight, and that that is why you hesitated to be seen walking around with me. Am I right?"

"Miss Paget is not yet sixteen, and is in a ladies' seminary at Bath. Lady Millicent is here, certainly."

"I expect someone will be bound to tell her about you and me. How will you explain your latest escapade to her?"

"She is too well-bred to make a scene. She will take my story at its face value, or pretend to do so."

"What if I were to tell her that you offered me carte blanche?"

"She wouldn't believe that," he assured her. "It would be out of character, you see."

"But it happened!"

"Did it? Who says so? Did anyone overhear us? Can you bring a witness?" He pinched her arm, just enough to hurt. "Don't make mischief unnecessarily, Sophia."

"Oh!" she cried, and broke away from him.

"Gently," he said, and catching her hand, tucked it back within his arm. "Everyone is looking at you. You cannot afford to be seen quarreling in public with me until you are established in society. Did Lady Lincoln invite you to her

106

party? Ah, good. I won't be there, but she will look after you."
He took out his watch, and frowned at it. "I must go."

"To pay your respects to Lady Millicent, I suppose?"

"Certainly, but I did not mean that. I have another engagement later this evening, and I leave Town early tomorrow morning."

"Ah, you travel to Bath, to inspect Miss Paget, no doubt. I hope she will be suitably impressed by the honor you do her."

"She is very prettily behaved, I believe, and an accomplished needlewoman."

"She sounds dull."

"Perhaps, but one does not marry for such considerations, although I own it would be pleasant to have a quiet, well-ordered home, and to be welcomed to the supper table by a woman who could be trusted not to make a scene whenever she saw you."

That hurt her, as it was intended to do. She bit her lip. Could she never defeat him? He was taking out a pocketbook, and asking for the address of her aunt in York. He said he had business in the north, and could easily detour to pay Miss Nan a visit. She hesitated to ask what his business might be; she did not like to risk another snub.

He chose, however, to enlighten her. He said he had long been concerned about the harm which Free Traders were doing to the economy, and that he had been asked to prepare a detailed memorandum on the subject, with a view to presenting a bill to increase the penalties for smuggling. His journey to the north was for the purpose of investigating the strength of the Free Traders there.

Sophia was astounded. "I don't believe it."

His eyes flickered. "Why not? Everyone else does."

"Because... I don't know why, exactly. If you had said you were interested in prison reform, or education for the lower classes, I would have been able to believe you; but not in this."

"Every man should have a hobby, don't you think? Mr. Dalby thinks and talks of nothing but seed drills, and I think about smugglers."

They were near the Midmain's box once more. Sophia saw that Mr. Dalby was already there, waiting for her, and that her aunt had turned her shoulder on him.

"Well," he said, "we have made two complete circuits of

the rotunda without scratching each other's eyes out. Your aunt should be pleased with you. I shall tell Miss Nan of your success, and if I hear any news of Jasper while I am in the north—through my smuggler contacts—I will let you have it when we meet at Lady Rochester's ball next week." He indicated a lady sitting next Lady Midmain. "Trust me; it is all arranged that you will receive an invitation."

He was going. She clung to his arm. "Please; don't go like that. I ought to thank you. My aunt will be sure to ask me if I have shown my gratitude to you, and... What was that about Jasper? Do you really think you could learn something about...? Oh, Sir Gregory is coming! How vexing! Could you...do you think you could pretend to be very gallant, and kiss my hand, or something? To convince them that I have been very, very good?"

It was a moment of triumph for her. He laughed as he bent over her hand. "Sophia, you are a baggage! I think I should press your hand, and gaze lovingly into your eyes as well, don't you? Do you think you can keep your temper and remain well-behaved until I return? Otherwise my lovelock will be lost to me for ever." He kissed her hand, pressed it to his heart, and only released it with a well-timed sigh as Sir Gregory came up, beaming.

"Bravo, my dear," whispered Lady Midmain, as she welcomed Sophia back to the box. "May I introduce my niece to you, Lady Rochester?"

Lord Carteret had been annoyed but not deflected by Philip's initial refusal to aid him. He had gone from Philip direct to Mr. Stone and demanded that worthy's assistance in bringing the Tarrant boy to heel.

Mr. Stone's first reaction—as he told Philip later—was to have Lord Carteret confined in a straitjacket because he had clearly tipped over the edge of sanity into megalomania. But Mr. Stone soon saw that such action would serve no good purpose; the Pretender now had financial backing and would be arriving on these shores, whether Lord Carteret was at large or in Bethelhem Hospital. Besides, the King would object most violently if his favorite were to be forcibly removed from his side especially if the removal were accomplished by a member of the hated Newcastle's staff.

Mr. Stone was in a quandary. The Pretender's invasion would not evaporate if ignored, but to combat it meant that Government forces must be engaged in support of a scheme of Lord Carteret's. Newcastle was a nervous man, prone to tears and lacking in self-confidence at the best of times. Mr. Stone's power lay in his ability to handle the Duke, but on this occasion it took all his time to prevent Newcastle either from resigning, or denouncing Carteret as a traitor.

Philip's *volte-face* could not have been more timely. The plan which he and his friend Mr. Carramine had unfolded to Mr. Stone was at once daring, simple, and comparatively easy to execute. Newcastle authorized its adoption, and told Mr. Stone to offer Rame his own terms, if he would but join the ministry. Somewhat to Mr. Stone's surprise, Philip agreed to take an active part in his counter-invasion plan, and named as his price that he should be appointed Ambassador to Stockholm, when the present man relinquished office. Newcastle accepted these terms with glee, only to find that Lord Carteret had taken all the credit to himself for Philip's interest in politics. Mr. Stone admired Philip's adroit handling of the situation, which had left Newcastle and Carteret equally convinced of the Earl's allegiance. Mr. Stone had often pondered how to interest the Earl in politics, but had despaired of breaking the ties which bound him to his uncle. Newcastle's secretary now set himself to gain Philip's confidence.

The Town house of the Earls of Rame had been little used since the death of the Countess. Most of the rooms had been shut up and the furniture put under holland covers. Thomas lived in Norfolk, although this summer he was to spend at Bath. Mr. Stone had an office in Whitehall, but this was too public a place for discussions and meetings connected with Philip's plan. Since the Earl was to be in Hanover that summer, he offered Mr. Stone the use of the great library in his Town house, and suggested that Mr. Carramine should be his guest, and thus be in a perfect position to act as link-man for the very private and important correspondence which was to pass between the Earl and Whitehall that summer. Mr. Stone accepted with alacrity.

So it was that the Earl's library gradually became transformed with maps and records. Two clerks—officially termed "secretaries" to Mr. Carramine—worked there during the day, and two runners—of whom Mr. Dodge was usually one—

killed time in the hall behind the Earl's sedan chair. Servants were excluded from the library, and care taken to screen the tall windows from the eyes of passersby. It was the duty of one of the clerks to burn every scrap of wastepaper in the fire, and only Philip, Mr. Carramine and Mr. Stone had keys to the room.

Here, then, were the maps of the English Channel over which Mr. Stone and Mr. Carramine had pored so anxiously at the end of June. On the 21st of that month the Pretender, accompanied by two of his banker friends, two elderly noblemen who had more imagination than common sense, and three adventurers who made large and unjustifiable claims to being experienced soldiers, slipped out of France in disguise.

The worthy but naive Lord President of Scotland sent Mr. Stone assurances that never before had Scotland been so satisfied with Hanoverian rule. Within a week he had changed his tune. The Pretender had landed on Eriskay and sought help of the Macdonald clan. The British General Cope was sitting roughly in the middle of Scotland, waiting for news, but what news he received was unhelpful. The country was wild, the natives reluctant to tell what they knew, and his troops were subject to acts of sabotage which damaged their morale. Mr. Stone wrote to Philip, urging that the King be advised to return to Britain at once. Philip did his best, but His Majesty was enjoying himself and, on the advice of Lord Carteret, treated the Pretender's arrival in his domains as a joke. As head of the ministry, Newcastle ought to have been at the King's elbow when he went to Hanover, but the Duke suffered from seasickness, and almost invariably sent a substitute. The void created by his absence was more than filled by Lord Carteret, busily feeding the King's dislike of Newcastle and furthering his own plans.

The Pretender marched towards Fort Augustus in order to give battle to Cope. Being short of trained men, Cope withdrew a little way up the road, to be nearer his base. The Pretender hesitated. He could pursue Cope northwards, or bypass him and descend on Perth, which was now unprotected. He chose Perth. In military terms, it was the wrong decision to take, because it left an unbeaten force behind him, but it looked to many people as if the rebels had cleverly given Cope the slip. It was another psychological victory for the Pretender, and for the first time alarm was felt in England. Newcastle's brother summed up the situation, when he said that he did not fear the strength of the enemy so much as the apathy of his friends. "Nothing can go right," said Pelham, "until the Government has a head once more."

At long last the King sailed home, to be greeted with the news that the Pretender had entered Perth in a tartan outfit trimmed with gold. The rebels had met with no resistance and had been joined by Lord George Murray, the Duke of Perth and several other noblemen. This last piece of news was another blow to the Government, for Lord George Murray was not only an experienced soldier but a man of conscience. His example must influence others to declare for the Pretender.

His Majesty took up residence at Kensington and proceeded to show his ministry how little he trusted them by being rude to the members of his cabinet, and consulting Carteret on matters of policy every day. Philip moved back into his Town house, but pressed Mr. Stone to continue using the library. Mr. Denbigh brought Thomas up from Bath to install him in the newly-decorated nurseries at the top of the house, but Mr. Carramine moved out into lodgings near St. James', while continuing to work for Mr. Stone. It was not long before Mr. Denbigh, too, was drawn into the library, for there was much to be done, and few people who could be trusted to do it. At Mr. Stone's suggestion, Philip resigned his post as Gentleman of the Bedchamber, and gave out that he was preparing a memorandum on smuggling with the help of Mr. Carramine. This enabled them to make contact without remark with men of varied backgrounds, and served as an excuse for their frequent and sudden journeys into the country. The fashionable world was amused that the Earl of Rame should devote himself to stamping out what after all was a socially acceptable crime, and thought no more of it.

Philip and Mr. Carramine did actually prepare a bill to increase the penalties for smuggling, but this was only a cover for their real work, which was to set up and correlate the activities of a network of agents spying on the Jacobites. Provision was made at posting-houses for horses to be kept ready at all times so that their agents could speed information on its way to London. Mr. Stone's existing force—men such as Mr. Dodge—were insufficient for this purpose, so Philip and Mr. Carramine recruited new agents from the network of smugglers with whom the latter had contacts.

111

While Philip had been in Hanover, it had been Mr. Carramine's task to sound out his smuggler friends by letter, pointing out the advantages to them of abandoning their illegal activities and being paid for information. Mr. Carramine now had a confidential file on men who might be prepared to cooperate with the Government, if the terms were right and they could be granted indemnity for past misdeeds. Mr. Stone was perfectly prepared to grant such letters of indemnity, for everything except the crimes of murder and forgery, and now it was up to Philip and Mr. Carramine to consolidate these contacts with visits to the areas most at risk from the Pretender's invasion.

The day after Philip's return, Mr. Carramine left Town for Sussex. He was to meet there with several of his smuggler friends, but this was not the whole reason for his journey. He had not been back home since March, and since it did not seem likely he would be able to leave London again while the Pretender stalked the north, he felt he must put his domestic affairs in order. His eldest son must take control of the estate, and his second son be settled with a farm of his own. Then, too, he had promised Philip to oversee the improvements under way at Tarrant Hall.

The Earl himself was to travel with Mr. Dodge but without his valet, and dressed in his shabbiest clothes, to Scotland. There, under the name of Mr. Rich, he was to confer with existing agents and recruit new ones. At Ranelagh he had told Sophia that he had an engagement for later on that evening; it was not with Lady Millicent, as she had supposed.

Mr. Stone was seated in the Earl's favorite chair in his library when the clock on the mantelpiece chimed twelve. He put down the newspaper he had been reading—it was the Opposition newspaper, *The Craftsman*—and took out his watch to check the time.

"The Earl is never late," rebuked Mr. Denbigh, who was bending over a map at a table nearby.

As he spoke, the double doors were opened, and the Earl entered, still in the clothes he had worn to Ranelagh. He closed and locked the doors behind him before greeting his guests.

"Is there any news?"

"None. The ladies speculate about the Pretender's great height, the men as to whether General Wade is not too old to carry out the job which Cope has failed to do. I did hear

112

the Pretender has vowed not to change his linen until he reaches London; perhaps he is careless in his personal habits? Also someone said the French had ten thousand men ready to embark at Dunkirk; he was laughed at. No one believes it."

"No, there is nothing in it yet. My agents in Paris and Normandy will let me know the moment there is any movement of troops in the area. By the by, we miss that protegé of yours, David Vere, in France. He was most helpful there this summer. Has he turned up again anywhere?"

"I expect to see him when I get to Edinburgh. He always wants to be in the thick of things. I told you ex-smugglers would make good recruits. I wish you would take on the Tarrant boy; he would be excellent material."

"Out of the question, with his background. I'm sorry to disoblige you, but the answer is still...no."

Philip sighed. Mr. Denbigh offered him a glass of hot toddy. Mr. Stone also accepted a glass. The three fell into the relaxed attitudes of men who are used to being in each other's company, and had long dispensed with ceremony. Philip threw his wig onto the nearest table and dropped his coat on the floor in order to don a worn and comfortable morning gown. Mr. Denbigh picked up his master's coat, laid it on a chair and lit a pipe without asking permission. Mr. Stone rubbed his nose. He was a spare man in his late forties with a keen eye, but otherwise undistinguished features. His manner was self-effacing. He was not a man whose face would be easy to remember.

"We are in for several months of anxiety."

"I will do what I can. I did hear a rumor that the Duke of Cumberland is being brought back to Britain to act as Commander in Chief. I remember him in Flanders. An uninspired commander, but thorough."

"The King wants him back. He's over-young—twenty-five, isn't he?—but the knowledge that it's his father's throne at stake should provide him with enough impetus to sweep his Stuart cousin into the sea."

"I believe my uncle suggested it," said Philip.

Mr. Stone gave the impression of pointing to attention, without actually having moved.

Philip nodded. "You are right to be worried. I dined with him today. He takes all the credit to himself for this treaty we are about to conclude with 'Antimac.' His international reputation did help; but not of course to the extent that he believes it did. However, taken together with the success of his plan to get the Pretender over without foreign troops at his back, this treaty plays into my uncle's hands. It has added greatly to his credit with the King. I fear that His Majesty may attempt to dismiss Newcastle and reinstate my uncle."

"You are his favorite nephew. He has asked that you should receive the post of Ambassador to Stockholm when it becomes vacant. Why should you fear your uncle's return to power?"

"A change of ministers now would divide the country politically, and this could only be of advantage to the Pretender."

"You remind me of a man walking a tightrope," observed Mr. Stone. "Which way will you jump off? Toward Newcastle, or toward your uncle?"

Chapter Seven

A week later, tired, hungry and thirsty, the Earl reined in his horse outside an unpretentious half-timbered house on the outskirts of York. A dirty, half-grown lad offered to walk the beast up and down while the gentleman was visiting.

"Is this Mr. John Tarrant's house?"

The lad affirmed that it was, and added that the gentleman needn't look for no proper grooms at Mr. Tarrant's.

"Very well," said Philip. He dismounted, gave his horse into the lad's care, and rapped on the front door. A pretty young maidservant told him that Miss Tarrant was at home, but didn't receive visitors. Philip might be dusty and tired, but his manner still carried authority. The maid went to fetch Mr. Tarrant. Without being asked to do so, Philip stepped over the threshold and entered the hall of the house. There was evidence of neglect everywhere; the ashes of a fire left in the grate, dust, a careless clutter of riding crops and guns on the floor. What was Miss Nan doing in a place like this?

A stout, fussy gentleman arrived, adjusting clothing which had most probably been disarranged by the hands of his maid, who hovered, primping, in the doorway behind him.

"You want Miss Tarrant? She's not here as family, you know. She's here to nurse my wife."

Philip bowed. "May I introduce myself? Philip Rich, in the service of the Earl of Rame. I have letters from my master to Miss Tarrant. The Earl feels he is under considerable obligation to Miss Tarrant. I trust she will be willing to leave

115

her patient long enough for me to speak with her."

"I suppose I could get someone else to sit with my wife for a while. The Earl of Rame, you say? Nan never spoke of him."

"She is too modest. She is a very dear friend of his. You have met the Earl, of course?"

Philip guessed that Mr. Tarrant would be flattered by this, and he was.

"I . . . well, we haven't, actually. Oh, come into the parlor. No sense standing in this drafty place. Have some wine . . . some cold meat? I think there was something left of a side of ham." The bell in the parlor did not work, so the master of the house lifted his voice in a stentorian bellow for someone called Bess.

"You know she's as deaf as a post," said the serving wench, sulkily.

"Fetch her yourself, and then sit with my wife for a while." The girl pulled a face, but left.

"Might I have a dish of tea?" asked Philip.

"I have some capital Burgundy that never passed through the hands of the King's men before it reached York." Mr. Tarrant tapped the side of his nose meaningly. Oh no, thought Philip; not another smuggler! but this man would not have the intelligence to organize. He would merely be a receiver of smuggled goods.

"No, thank you," said Philip. Mr. Tarrant went to the door and bellowed out a demand for tea, while the Earl surveyed the parlor with distaste. It was very nearly as cheerless as the hall.

A light, halting footstep, and Miss Nan appeared in the doorway. She appeared unsure of her welcome. Philip went to her, kissed both her hands, and smiled down into her troubled face.

"Life is full of surprises," she said. "I had been thinking of you a lot, lately, but I never expected to see you here. It's not bad news?"

"No, no. On the contrary." He glared at Mr. Tarrant, trying to make the man understand that he wished to speak to Miss Tarrant in private.

"Ah, well," said Mr. Tarrant, nodding and winking. "I'll leave you to your gossip. If I'm off before you leave, Mr. Rich, pray give my compliments to the Earl."

He was gone. The room felt damp and unused, in contrast to the bright tones of the summer's day outside. A small fire burned in the hearth. Philip set Miss Nan in a chair by the

116

fire and chafed her hands. "What is it?" he asked. "You are cold. You are not well. Have you seen a doctor?"

"I had a fall which upset me for a while, and then I contracted a chill. It is nothing. A chapter of accidents ...stupid...nothing to concern you...." A tear sparkled on her cheek.

"I know exactly what it is. They do not know your value here, and so you are unhappy, and when you are unhappy, you suffer in health."

"It is my own fault. Foolishly I criticized Bess, the housekeeper here, before I realized that she was mother to that girl. Words passed between my cousin and me, and I allowed myself to say things that were better left unsaid about his neglect of his poor, bedridden wife, and his taking that girl into....But, indeed, I don't think she meant to push me down the stairs...it was an accident."

"Gracious heavens! What is Jasper thinking of! When you told him, he should have taken you away at once!"

"Hush! They will hear you. Nothing can be done. It was all my own fault. If I had only held my tongue...bided my time...besides, I do not know where Jasper may be. We have not heard from him since he went to France in March. And you must not worry Sophia by telling her that I am miserable here. I am well enough, and lucky to have a roof over my head, as my cousin says even though I have nothing to do here but keep his wife away. She is not really ill, you see, only fat and lazy."

"This is all my fault."

"Indeed it is not. It is no one's fault; or, if it is anyone's fault, it is my brother's fault for getting into debt."

"It is my fault. I ought to have known better than to have trusted Jasper. I knew he was thoughtless. I ought to have made absolutely sure that there was enough money, after paying the debts, for provision to be made for you. I suspect Sir John Bladen cheated you out of a good deal of money, once I was gone."

"I don't like to think ill of anyone—except Mr. Farrow and that girl out there—but I'm afraid I have to agree with you. I expect he regarded it as compensation for the double loss of Tarrant Hall and Sophia. Tell me: have you seen her? Her letters give no hint of what she is doing, or whom she meets. Has she some new dresses? Is she much admired?"

Philip thought of Lady Midmain's sewing-room, and of

Jasper's fury at being refused a commission once again, and of the miserable existence which Miss Nan was leading, and shivered.

"You asked me to leave you all alone. I wish, now, that I had done so. Even if Jasper had gone to fight for Louis, at least you and Sophia would have been safe."

"I don't think there was any likelihood that Sophia would go through with the match, once she had met you."

A slatternly servant, breathing heavily, clumped into the room and threw a tray of cold meats onto the table. There was no tea, but some ale had been provided. The woman retired without speaking, and Miss Nan busied herself setting a place for Philip at the table.

"All is not well with Sophia, then?" she asked. "I was afraid of it. Every time I think of her, I feel waves of misery and anger beating at me. Come and sit down. Eat. You look tired, and I daresay you are up to no good, dressed like that, and going around without a servant. You needn't deny it; I haven't lived through forty-five summers without learning a thing or two about men, and one of the things I have learned is that you must feed them before they are capable of telling you what you want to know. So eat! You have been here ten minutes and I still do not know why you came, or how Sophia is, or..."

"I will tell you. Sophia is well, and in a fair way to becoming the toast of the Town. I have seen Jasper, and he is well and enjoying himself mightily. He has given me a letter to deliver to you, which I will do when I have eaten. I also have letters for you from your old friend Mr. Carramine, and from my old friend Mr. Denbigh."

"Oh!" she cried, and her face broke into a child's grin of delight.

"Moreover, I did not come here just to pass the time of day, but to take you away from here. I have a far better job for you to do, in London, so that you may see Sophia often. I want you to come and look after my son Thomas, who is delicate and in need of a woman's care."

"Oh!" she cried again. "How I wish that I could! But it is impossible."

"Nonsense. Your particular talent for homemaking is wasted here, and I am prepared to pay well for it. My house in Town is large, but comfortless since my wife died. My boy has nurses and doctors, but no one to love him as a motherless

118

boy should be loved. There is Mr. Denbigh, too; ever since I have known him, he has been trying to complete a book on Latin poetry, and failing to do so because he is quite incapable of settling down to work at a certain time every day. He worries about this and that, and goes to see if Thomas is all right, and I am not missing a meal. He speaks of you often, and like me, he compares the cheerlessness of our house with the comfort of Tarrant Hall. Then there is Chivers, my valet. He believes it his duty to sleep in an airless cubbyhole because it is the room nearest mine, in case I should want him, early or late. I never do, but he believes that he ought to be there, in case I did. If only he could be found a better room...but I cannot discover one. I have no talent for arranging a household."

"I should think not, indeed! But indeed, my lord, you must not ask me..." Once more tears began to sparkle on her cheeks. "I wish...oh, I do wish that it were possible...to be wanted...to feel that I was not a burden to everyone."

"Mr. Carramine thinks you should come, too. I believe he says as much in his letter."

"No. My dear boy, no. It cannot be. You see...I told you I was not a witch. I perform no spells, I go to church and believe in God, but every now and then I see some scene in the fire, some picture of an event which is to happen in the future. If that is being a witch, then I am a witch, and I deserved to be ducked in the millpond. I watched Mrs. Barnes's child sicken, and I saw this picture of the boy's grave, and I warned her that if she did not feed him better, he would die. She thought I had ill-wished him, but I had not. I told you that I had been thinking of you lately. Last night I was looking into the fire and thinking of you, and I saw a coffin, covered with holly and Christmas roses. I felt that you were moving through dangerous places, and I feel it still, now that you are beside me. I think I saw your coffin, and because of that, I cannot—dare not—do what you ask of me."

Philip chewed steadily on a mouthful of ham that had suddenly become tasteless. Then he pushed his plate away. He had lost his appetite.

"Come now!" he said. "I don't believe in such stuff. You are overwrought. You have been under a strain for a long time. I do not—will not—believe that you foresaw my death. It is merely that you are intuitive. You collect a hint here and a guess there, and your imagination does the rest. Anyone with an eye to the political situation at present might be forgiven for having thoughts of death, but my arm is too weak for me to rejoin the Army, and my future place in events is to be round the council table. I am in no physical danger, I assure you. I see you are going to point out that your prediction about the Swan replacing the Ram and Rose came true. Well, that is so; but it did not take much intelligence to see that I coveted the Hall, and as soon as I bought it, I remembered what you had said about the crest being replaced, and gave orders that it should be done. You brought about your own prediction, if you like."

"Yes, but..."

"As for Sophia; of course she is angry. She is furious with me."

"What...still? Tell me...she would never speak freely of what happened the night of Jasper's party. That you two quarreled is obvious, but..."

"I did not behave well."

"And she boxed your ears for it?"

The Earl attempted to laugh. "I wish she had. I insulted her, and she retaliated in kind. She was justified in what she said, but...I have no excuse. Then I lost my temper, and told Jasper I would buy the Hall, to hurt her. I had no idea that the consequences would be so disastrous for you and for Sophia, and I want to make amends. I am doing what I can to establish her in Society, but she cannot be happy while you are miserable; and neither can I. For both our sakes, you must come to me."

"But if you are to marry again..."

"I understand you well enough," said the Earl shortly, "But it will not do. I want a quiet life. I cannot face the prospect of war at home and abroad. There is a certain Miss Paget, young, well-mannered and quietly spoken...she would respect your privileged position in my household. But in any event, I intend to make legal provision for you by way of a pension, so that you may never again be forced to drudge for a living. I will give you an hour to pack whatever you need, and we will be off. There is a tolerably good inn here, I trust? We will stay the night, and I will engage the services of a respectable abigail, who will look after you on the journey south. And a courier, too, if you so wish. I shall have to travel fast, ahead of you, but I will leave you sufficient money to hire a chaise, or whatever you will. Take three or four days over the journey. More, if you prefer. Your rooms will be ready by the time you reach London."

"I cannot leave my cousin like that, without giving him notice."

"If he had treated you with consideration, I would agree. Luckily for me, he has not done so. Come to think of it, I will wait down here while you pack. He dare not shout at you if I am here. Hurry! Off with you!"

"If I come with you, will you try to make allowances for Sophia?"

"I have paid my debt to Sophia. I made a bargain with her, and when it is concluded, I shall see no more of her. I am asking you to come to me for your own sweet sake."

She hesitated, then turned to the door. "I feel as if I were eloping," she said, and left him. Philip pulled the cold ham towards him, and began to carve.

Rumor traveled fast in London Society. Although the Earl of Rame was out of Town, the news that he had taken up the Tarrant girl and dubbed her his "wild rose" was repeated everywhere. Enquiries were made; the girl's breeding was acceptable, even though there was a Jacobite brother in the background and she had no dowry. Those mothers whose sons were on the lookout for a wife with money decided she was of no interest to them, but many others followed the lead supplied by Lady Lincoln and Lady Rochester. The mantel-piece of Lady Midmain's boudoir became crowded with in-vitations, all of which included Sophia. The front door knocker was rarely still, as Society hostesses called on Lady Midmain to inspect Miss Tarrant. For the most part, they went away satisfied that the girl would pass muster, for So-phia had borne in mind the Earl of Rame's admonition to use her eyes and not her tongue. For the first few days, excite-ment possessed her to the exclusion of all other feelings. She was being made welcome at houses which had only been names to her a week ago. Everything was wonderful; the spacious rooms, the polished manners, the dances, the music, the exotic flowers in rooms lit by hundreds of wax candles, the rare dishes in unfamiliar sauces. She might well have lost her head, but as the Earl had said, Lady Midmain knew exactly how a girl ought to be steered through Society.

That night at Ranelagh...like a fairyland. The rout at Lady Lincoln's...witty conversation and delicious food, all in good taste. A card party at Mrs. Faulcon's....Mr. Dalby helped Sophia with her cards and made an appointment to walk with her in the Park. Everyone who was anyone went to the service at St. James' on Sunday morning, and walked in the Park afterwards.

Lady Midmain ordered two new dresses for Sophia. The girl had lost weight, and if she dieted for a while, would soon acquire a trim figure—or so said Perkins, Lady Midmain's personal maid.

Lady Midmain herself gave a rout party to launch Sophia officially into Society, and it was a great success. There was hardly room for everyone to stand, the food ran out, and a lady fainted. Sophia's admirer, Mr. Dalby, had an argument with a middle-aged gentleman on the merits of crop rotation and asked her to adjudicate.

Lady Midmain was not amused. "Have some sense!" she said. "It will be all over Town that you can talk of nothing but farming, and then where will you be? Gentlemen do not expect ladies to express an opinion on such matters, and they do not care to be contradicted. Please confine yourself in future to talk of the weather, or the latest fashion in dress. What would the Earl of Rame have said, if he heard you?"

"He knows that I managed my brother's estate, and that I have a tongue in my head. I daresay he would not care what I said. Mr. Dalby doesn't. Mr. Dalby likes me because I am able to talk to him about the things in which he is interested. Mr. Dalby doesn't care what the Earl might think; in fact, Mr. Dalby didn't even know that the Earl of Rame was interested in me."

"Mr. Dalby is a very good sort of man, but not the marrying kind. His poor mother has been trying to get him to offer for a suitable girl for years. I doubt if he even knows that you are a female. He cannot advance your prospects in any way; the Earl can. If Lady Millicent heard you, or has had your foolishness repeated to her—and depend on it, there were a number of women who did hear you and are jealous enough of you to tittle-tattle—then the King may hear, and you may whistle for the honor of being presented at Court."

"I don't care," said Sophia.

Lady Midmain slapped her.

Sophia began to think, which was a function she had abandoned for the last week. The Earl had bargained that she should go to a ball, to Ranelagh, to the opera, a card game, a rout, and be presented at Court in exchange for her lovelock. When she had made the bargain she had thought these things unobtainable, and when she saw that they might come within her reach, she had thought it would take months to work through that list. Yet Philip had been gone just over a week, and with the invitation to Lady Rochester's ball on her aunt's mantel, there was only the presentation at Court still to be arranged. How had she managed to pack so much into such a short space of time? Could she not have made some excuse to avoid going to the opera last night? But Lady Midmain would not have allowed it, and Mr. Dalby had sat beside her for the last act....

Was she to have only ten days of this new life, and then be banished to the sewing-room again? Ah, but the presentation at Court might not take place for some time. The King was at Kensington, it was true, but the news from Scotland might put festivities out of the question. She might have as much as a month, before he held another Drawing-Room.

Sophia resolved to extract the utmost from her glittering new life, while it lasted. Each time she stepped into a sedan chair, or into the Midmain's carriage, or took her place on the dance floor, she reminded herself that it might be her last.

An elderly gentleman composed a poem on her eyebrows. He was a foolish creature and normally Sophia would have despised his offering; but this might be the one and only poem she ever received, and she valued it accordingly. One of her new dresses was to be a ballgown, suitable to wear at Court later on. It was to be of white silk, worn over a pale pink petticoat, and trimmed with pink ribbons.

"I prefer blue ribbons," said Sophia.

"You are known as the Tarrant Rose, and the Earl of Rame will undoubtedly send you a posy of pink roses to carry at the ball, so pink ribbons it must be."

"And what am I to do with Mr. Dalby's roses?"

"If he sends any—and I'm sure I shall be very surprised if he does anything so gallant—then you will give them to Perkins. A posy from a man with a small country estate cannot compare with flowers from the Earl of Rame."

"I think you assume too much," said Sophia. "It is ten days since we heard from him. The ball is tonight. I daresay he has forgotten about it."

"Not at all," said Sir Gregory, who had just come in. "He is back, and asking after you. I saw him at the Duke's this morning. He engaged me in conversation in a most pointed manner...quite ten minutes. Sent you his apologies for not calling this morning, but only arrived back in Town last night. Enquired if you were to wear pink...said I thought so. Told me to tell you that your presentation is to take place on Sunday at the Princesses' Drawing-Room at St. James'. Some trouble, apparently, about it...something about pigs...couldn't understand it, myself. Agreed with him that we'd never heard you talk about pigs. Lord Lincoln said so, too. Wanted to know who'd spread the story, because the King was in two minds whether to have you presented...but all is well. Lincoln arranged it, or the Earl did...one or the other."

"I knew it!" screeched Lady Midmain. "The little fool has ruined herself with her talk of the farmyard!"

"No, no. Assure you, not ruined. Don't know how or why, but you're to take the girl to St. James' on Sunday. Ten to one, the King is curious. This person says she talks of nothing but pigs, and the Earl says she's a delightful linguist, with a fair command of the German language. Don't know how he knew, but he told Newcastle in front of us all...very significant!"

"Do you speak German, girl?" Lady Midmain shook Sophia. "Do you? A little? Why didn't you say so? Don't you understand what an asset this might be, socially, when it is His Majesty's native tongue? Oh, heaven grant me patience! What a fool you are!"

"Very significant," said Sir Gregory, raising his voice to attract his wife's attention. "The Earl told Newcastle that Miss Tarrant was proficient in several European languages."

"Well?" demanded his wife, staring. "What of it? I assume Nan taught her from books, or..."

"I learned partly from books, and partly from Aunt Nan, in order to teach Jasper. My father wanted Jasper to speak French and German, in case he had to go abroad to seek his fortune. I don't know how the Earl learned of it."

"What is it, Sir Gregory? You have heard something?"

Sir Gregory chuckled, rising on his toes and then falling

back on his heels. "Very significant," he repeated. "The Duke told me later...private conversation...just a hint. Not a firm promise, mind, but...a post in the Treasury for me, at last! All due to Rame, of course. Wouldn't be getting it, otherwise."

"Speak more clearly, Sir Gregory!" shrieked Lady Midmain. "I am on tenterhooks."

"Rame is spoken of as the next Ambassador to Stockholm, or if not Stockholm, to The Hague. The Duke told me...in confidence, of course!"

Sophia sat down abruptly. It seemed as if her heart had stopped beating for a moment, and then restarted at a faster rate.

"No," she said, and hardly recognized her own voice. "You are mistaken. The Earl is not serious in his attentions to me. He made a wager with me, that is all. I am to give him my lovelock, in exchange for a certain number of invitations into Society life."

"Better and better," cried Lady Midmain. "The man must be besotted with the girl to risk so much for a lock of her hair! What a tale this will make. It will wipe out the story of the pigs, entirely! I see it all, now. He met you under romantic circumstances, tried and failed to forget you during those months in Hanover, and in spite of the marriages which the Duke and Lord Carteret are trying to arrange for him..."

"Perhaps because of them," said Sir Gregory. "Caught between two parties, he chooses to marry neither of the ladies concerned. By taking Sophia, he offends no one, because he can pass it off as a romantic affair. Fact that Sophia has no dowry is unimportant...because no dowry, no obligations, except to me, of course. Hence the post in the Treasury."

"I am sure you are wrong," said Sophia, near to tears. "He does not like me, nor I like him. You have no idea of what has passed between us...the very idea of marriage is out of the question."

"Then why did he make such a point of your being able to speak French and German this morning...in public...when it is known he is to go abroad as Ambassador? It can only be because he envisages you as his wife, being able to converse with diplomats."

Sophia tried to stand, but the pressure of her corsets was unbearable, and the room was so stuffy....

She came to herself, lying on the sofa with her laces cut. She was able to breathe properly for the first time for weeks, and her aunt was coaxing her to drink some wine. She felt better. She sat up. Then she saw the posy of pink roses in a silver filigree holder, on the table beside her.

Lady Midmain's eyes glistened with anticipation of the triumph she and her niece were to enjoy. "As you see," she said, indicating the flowers, "The Earl did not forget."

What was she to do? What could she do, but say she was feeling better, and submit to being laced up again, and dressed, and inserted into the coach, while Lady Midmain talked and talked....

"...and if that cat Millicent Fairweather should be at the ball—and of course she will—you must hold up your flowers and smile. No need for you to say anything. Trust me to put it around that the Earl sent you the roses. She is so jealous of you, they say, that she is telling everyone you are more of an Amazon than a Rose. Of course, she is small, and the contrast with your height.... If she speaks to you, you may find it best to sit down, so that the difference in your heights is minimized. Be sure she will find some way to discredit you if she can. Your dancing, now...are you happy with the steps of the quadrille?"

Sophia had been having lessons with a dancing-master. She shook her head. The sequence of steps in the quadrille was hard to remember.

"Then make some excuse not to dance it. You have twisted your foot...wish for a drink...must speak to me. I have it! Put Sir Gregory's name down on your dance card against the quadrilles. He will not dance, of course; he will be busy in the card-room. That will provide you with an excuse for refusing to stand up with anyone else. I will explain it to him. Dear child!" Lady Midmain brought her cheek to within an inch of Sophia's. "You are almost as pretty as I was when I first took the Town by storm!"

"Dear aunt," said Sophia, with an equally false smile, "I owe you so much."

The coach took an age to thread its way through the traffic to Lady Rochester's. Sophia kept telling herself that she must enjoy this evening. It was her first ball...the music, the dancing...her beautiful dress...yet all the while she was close to panic. She must see the Earl and tell him what his thoughtless words to Sir Gregory had done. The Earl did not wish to marry her. He would be horrified to hear the rumor...would have to make some public statement. Of course,

126

if he disavowed her, Society would send no more invitations to Lady Midmain's niece, but she would not go to these great houses under false pretences. She did not know what would become of her...back to the sewing-room?

"You are never crying, child?" asked Lady Midmain. "Here, take my hartshorn. Your nerves are overtaxed with all this excitement."

The ballroom at Lady Rochester's was on the first floor. Sophia climbed the stairs behind Sir Gregory and Lady Midmain, together with a hundred other members of the fashionable world. She curtseyed to her hostess, and made polite conversation and felt her face tighten into a smile for this acquaintance and that. She admired the painted ceiling, and the enormous candelabra with their hundred of wax candles, and dutifully exclaimed how large the room seemed to be because it was lined down one side with enormous mirrors. She accepted compliments and returned them. She danced, although she could not have said with whom. She admired a flower arrangement, someone's plumed headdress, a new fan, a waistcoat encrusted with brilliants....

Mr. Dalby was talking. What a very large mouth he had, to be sure! And yet he was a worthy young man, a man who would eventually have two thousand a year, and a man who was familiar with all the things she knew about. He complimented her on her looks—who had told him to do so? His mother?—and made sure that his name was down on her program for another dance later than evening. Perhaps she might be tired enough by then to sit on one of the settees, and listen to a very particular question?

What could he mean? From any other man, that might mean he intended to propose, but coming from Mr. Dalby, it probably meant he wanted to consult her about pigs. She sighed. She had never been particularly fond of pigs, and it was vexatious that her name had become associated with them.

He was gone, and another man took his place. She did not know him. Yes, she did. It was Lord Lincoln, looking worried, as usual. They talked. She must have said something amusing, for he laughed, and he was not over-ready to laugh. Her aunt said she was doing very well, and moved away to talk to a severe-faced woman. Her next partner was Sir Gregory— well, he would not appear, and she could find herself a seat and think!

"Ah, the Amazon!" drawled a female voice. Lady Millicent Fairweather dipped a curtsey. "I have been longing to make your acquaintance, but this is positively the first moment I have been able to spare all evening." Remembering her aunt's warning about Lady Millicent, Sophia sank onto a nearby settee. The girl who was reported to be her rival for the Earl's affections was well-formed but small. She had ash-blond, feathery ringlets and a most expensive complexion. Sophia was sure that Lady Millicent must darken her eye-brows and eyelashes.

"How kind of you," she murmured.

Lady Millicent seated herself at Sophia's side, with feigned impulsiveness. At once Sophia felt gauche and as if her hands were too large. Lady Millicent laughed, a pretty, practiced sound.

"Dear me, how very tall you are beside me! But then, you are extremely tall for a woman, are you not?"

Sophia smiled until her face hurt. "I believe so."

"You must find all this..." Lady Millicent indicated the seething crowd in the ballroom with a flirt of her fan, "...so very different from your pig farm."

"You must be confusing me with someone else. We have never kept pigs. I come from Tarrant Hall in Sussex. There have been Tarrants at the Hall since the Norman Conquest. And you?"

For a moment the doll-like face lost its composure. "Oh, we have a place in Kent, but of course we are always in Town for the Season."

"This is not your first Season, then? I thought ladies were only allowed one Season on the Marriage Market?"

"Perhaps two, if their families can afford it. This is my third Season. I have had many offers, of course, but my guardian says that only the best is good enough for me." Honors were even. They sought for fresh holds, like wrestlers.

"The tale goes," said Lady Millicent, "That you picked my poor Philip out of a ditch, after he had fallen off his horse. Did you carry him yourself? I am sure you are strong enough."

"Oh, no. He was not that badly hurt. He walked to the house. People exaggerate."

Lady Millicent understood that this was meant for her. "I must say I found it hard to believe. Philip is such a notable horseman. Many's the ride we have together early in the

128

morning in Rotten Row. I have not seen you there, Miss Tarrant. Do you, perhaps, ride astride? One can expect anything of an Amazon such as yourself."

Sophia stifled a pang of regret for the horses she had been used to ride in the country. They had been sold, with Tarrant Hall, and she had not ridden since. She started to sigh, and checked herself. It would never do to let Lady Millicent see that she had scored a point.

"I would find riding in the Park very tame, after my gallops in the country. But why are you not dancing, Lady Millicent?"

"I turned my ankle," said Lady Millicent, with a terseness of tone which forbade further enquiry. "It is only a quadrille. I shall be quite all right for the next dance."

Sophia smiled. Was Lady Millicent unhappy about the steps of the quadrille, too? "Oh, I am so sorry," she said. "Are you sure you are wise to dance again, this evening? Such injuries may seem slight at first, but..."

"It is quite all right," said Lady Millicent. "It doesn't ache at all, now. But why are you sitting this dance out?"

"I was engaged to dance with my uncle, but I fear he has forsaken me for the card-room."

"Poor you!" sympathized Lady Millicent. "If you had known, perhaps you could have got another partner."

"And you?"

"I sent mine for a glass of lemonade."

They smiled at each other, and even their smiles were weapons. Sophia showed better teeth, but Lady Millicent contrived a dimple.

"Your lemonade, Lady Millicent." It was the Earl, elegant in dark green satin with a silver-embroidered waistcoat. He was wearing a new tie wig, which suited him well. He handed Lady Millicent her glass, and bowed to Sophia. "Your servant, Miss Tarrant."

"Oh!" cried Lady Millicent, squeaking deliciously. "How you startled me! Come and sit down, beside me." She patted the seat beside her, on the opposite side to Sophia.

"I could not enjoy the sight of the most beautiful women in London sitting together, if I were to join you. Let me feast my eyes at a respectful distance."

"You flatterer," cried Lady Millicent, using her fan to good effect. "You know I cannot compare with the beautiful Miss Gunning."

"True, she is beautiful; perhaps equally beautiful. But it is quite impossible to converse with her. You heard what she said to the King the other day? She told him she was greatly enjoying the sights of London, but that what she really wanted to see was a Coronation."

Sophia said she hoped she would not make such a silly mistake, out of sheer nervousness, when she was presented.

"It is not likely that you will," said the Earl. "You seem to have acquired a reputation for good sense, as well as for beauty."

"And for a knowledge of pigs," said Lady Millicent, laughing merrily. "I believe she is fond of entertaining the company with dissertations on the subject of pigs."

"I mentioned crop rotation, once," said Sophia, shortly.

"I am happy to say I know nothing of pigs," said Lady Millicent.

"I don't know as much about pigs as I do about crop rotation," said Sophia, "But then, my acquaintance with them has been slight—until now."

The Earl put a hand to his mouth to cover a smile. Lady Millicent frowned, remembered that frowning produced wrinkles, and treated them to one of her dimpled smiles. She rose, laid her hand on the Earl's sleeve, and suggested that they finish their dance in some place not quite so warm.

"Delighted," said the Earl, not moving. "But I see your next partner hastening across the floor to claim you."

Lady Millicent bit her lip, slapped her fan shut, and went to meet her partner. The Earl took the seat she had vacated at Sophia's side, and picked up her dance card.

"I must speak with you," said Sophia, "But I see my own partner approaching."

"Yes, yes. You have not given me any dances, but I see that Mr. Dalby has two. Hm! Sir Gregory has the other quadrille? How unlike him."

"I am not too happy with the sequence of steps in the quadrille," muttered Sophia.

"Neither is Lady Millicent. She would not, however, admit it. She does not dance as well as you do." He crossed through Sir Gregory's name, and wrote his own against the next quadrille. "I doubt if you will make a mistake, but if you do, I will prompt you."

"But..."

"I have news of your brother and your aunt; good news.

130

Ah, here is your partner? Mr. Dalby, is it not? I believe we have met somewhere before. You are the young man who is so interested in pigs?" His tone was kindly, but his quizzing glass was brought into play.

"Crop rotation," said Sophia, between her teeth.

"That's so, my lord," said Mr. Dalby, eager to please. "We have a considerable acreage which is not producing as well as it ought; Miss Tarrant is an encyclopedia of information on the subject. You must understand..."

"We must have a long talk about it, some other time. Miss Tarrant, as you can see, is waiting to dance."

Mr. Dalby apologized. Sophia gave the Earl a speaking glance, and took the floor. Mr. Dalby whispered he wished they might sit the dance out. She shook her head. She saw that it would be indiscreet of her to leave the dance floor. She was being watched not only by the Earl and Lady Millicent, but also by her aunt, and all the dowagers who were not playing cards. Mr. Dalby, undiscouraged, said he would call at Lady Midmain's the following morning. Sophia smiled and lowered her eyelids, and began to wonder if it would be possible to bring Mr. Dalby to the point of making her an offer, and if so, whether Lady Midmain would still wish to present her at Court; Sophia rather thought that Lady Midmain would be so incensed that she would not. And if so...there were a number of imponderables in this line of reasoning which occupied Sophia until the next quadrille.

The Earl's hand was cool in hers. She felt warm, in spite of her low-cut dress. At first he did not attempt to talk. His eyes were watchful to see that she did not make any error. Twice she faltered, and he whispered an instruction. She did not think anyone would have noticed that he was guiding her through the dance.

There was a moment of leisure in the dance.

"You have done well," he said, in a low voice. "I am amazed. Your aunt said that you learned quickly, but I did not think that you could appear at ease so soon in Society."

"I must speak to you. Something terrible has happened. Sir Gregory has mistaken the reason for your interest in me. It is very embarrassing. The sooner this farce is over, the better."

"But not till Sunday, when I may claim my lock of hair."

"You may have it now, if you wish. You have paid for it."

"I will call on you tomorrow morning."

She thought of Mr. Dalby. "I have another engagement. Could you not make it some other time?"

"No, I am otherwise engaged, tomorrow. I have a letter for you from your brother, and I also have news of your aunt."

They must move again. This time she did not make any mistakes. Another pause in the music.

"My aunt is well?"

"She is traveling down to London, at this very minute. She has accepted a position in my household. I need someone to look after my son."

She put a hand to her heart. Once more the constriction of her stays made her feel faint. Then the moment of panic passed, and anger took its place.

"You move us about like pawns in a game of chess. Beware! Pawns can be dangerous to handle. The worst possible construction will be put on your bringing my aunt down to London. Do you not see how you are compromising yourself by championing me, and telling the Duke of Newcastle that I speak French and German? How did you know, anyway? You must be more careful."

"True. But I was in a quandary. I returned to find the Town ringing with the tale of you and the pigs. His Majesty demanded why I wished to present an ill-bred Amazon to him. I could see my lock of hair receding into the distance. I said that perhaps Lady Millicent might have been jealous of an innocent but well-educated country girl who had attracted so much notice. I spoke of your knowledge of languages and of European history; luckily, Miss Tarrant had been singing your praises, so I knew I was on safe ground. The King has a soft spot for anyone who speaks German and has studied the doings of his forebears. He smiled again, and said I might still bring you to him, so that he could judge whether you were Amazon or Rose."

"That is all very well, but how am I to disabuse my uncle's mind? He is certain that you intend to offer for me."

"Gracious heavens! The idea never occurred to me."

He was laughing at her. She did not know what to make of him.

The music ended. She curtseyed, he bowed.

He led her back to her aunt. "Till tomorrow."

Chapter Eight

"Any news?" It was the Earl's invariable greeting nowadays when he entered his library.

Mr. Stone abandoned his frowning study of the map of Scotland. "We are expecting the courier any minute. What is the latest gossip?"

The Earl was still in his ball dress. He yawned, and leaned against the mantel, studying the fire.

"The men criticize the Government for inaction. One or two talk of raising a company of volunteers to fight the Pretender, but it is all rather as one talks of the prospects of hunting next season. Academic, rather than immediate. They grumble because the King has prorogued Parliament, but that is more because it cuts off their vent for hot air than because they want to plunge into action. There is a general feeling that happenings north of the Border are no concern of theirs."

Mr. Stone grunted. "Your uncle's to blame, as usual. He doesn't want Parliament to meet on the 19th, because he wants to keep Newcastle out of touch with his supporters in the Commons. I believe you are right, and Lord Carteret is working for a coup d'état. Cabinet discussions have been heated, shall we say? The King puts forward your uncle's ideas at every point. No wonder the business of the nation is at a standstill."

"Many of my uncle's ideas are good, and his knowledge

of European affairs is second to none. The treaty with 'Antimac' goes through?"

"My apologies," said Mr. Stone, after a short pause. "I have allowed myself to lose sight of the larger issues. You need not remind me that your uncle is a master of strategy. I only wish that he were not plunging us into civil war to gratify his ambition. No, I apologize again. I agree with you; he did not intend the Pretender to have any success at all. He forgot that Wade and Cope are only human, and make mistakes like the rest of us. Sometimes I think he sees politics as some giant game of chess."

The Earl started, but Mr. Stone did not notice, for Mr. Denbigh hurried into the room, holding a letter in an oilskin pouch. "From David Vere, Edinburgh."

The dispatch was opened and spread on the table, so that all three men could read it at once.

"So Edinburgh is lost!" said the Earl. "This will create a stir."

"Cope will stop him. With fresh troops..."

"Troops newly embarked from sea transports are never at their best. Besides, these are recruits, as raw as the rebels. What does David Vere say about the strength of the Highlanders? Ah...here it is. 'Reports say they have two thousand men who are well-armed and well-shod, and upwards of one thousand more who are indifferently armed and clad, and whom the local people call Walidragles. They are billeted outside Edinburgh, and I will ride out to see them at first light tomorrow.'"

"Two thousand well-armed, and another thousand badly-armed. Undisciplined troops, without horses, and with little ammunition." Mr. Stone began to look happier. "Well, that is good news, if it can be trusted. This is the first report we have received from Edinburgh."

"Others will follow," said the Earl. "Trust me. I am sure of five men, who will be with us heart and soul in this business. Three others have promised to gather information and send it to us, but will not actively spy for us. We should have ample information coming in, from now on."

"You have done well," said Mr. Stone. "And now that you are back, will you not see what can be done to moderate your uncle's influence in the cabinet? We must have Lords Lieutenant named for all the northern counties, but the King delays, which means that the militia are not being raised..."

The Earl nodded. "I will see what I can do. Perhaps my uncle can be persuaded to look on himself as proxy Commander in Chief? I can do nothing with the King direct. I am too young and untried a politician."

"And don't forget that Newcastle expects you to present your bill on smuggling this session."

"What? Are you serious? To prepare it is one thing, but I had not expected to have to present it. It stands no chance at present. No, I should be laughed out of court."

"Does that matter? We have to manufacture some reason for advancing you in the ministry, or giving you our confidence if you go abroad as Ambassador. We cannot trumpet your work with our agents for obvious reasons. Let it be the bill, if you please."

Sophia put her hands on her hips and glared at her reflection in the mirror. She was wearing a blue saque gown of her ladyship's, which was very becoming, but she did not look pleased with herself. She swung round, the sacque swinging from her shoulders, strode across the room, and drummed on the windowpane. Lady Midmain closed her eyes. She was not feeling strong that morning....perhaps the champagne last night, or the battered oysters—?

"Sophia, do sit down and keep still! My head will split!"

Sophia sat down, but she did not sit still. She tugged at her lovelock, curling it round her fingers. Her eyes went from side to side of the room, considering possibilities. The Earl could not possibly mean to make her his wife...it was not to be thought of...she would not think of it. It was merely that he had seen an opportunity to turn the tables on her, and had done so. It amused him to laugh at her, as she had once laughed at him. Once Sunday was past, and he had claimed her lovelock, she would see no more of him. What, then, were her prospects?

The Midmains had invested a certain sum of money in her, buying her new gowns, giving her tutors, taking her everywhere. It was not to be thought of that they would throw good money after bad by continuing to treat her as their favorite niece. No, once it was made clear to Lady Midmain that the Earl was not going to marry Sophia, she could hope for little in the way of further aid. The invitations would cease to arrive. Perhaps Mr. Dalby might call once or twice more...a pity that he was not a marrying man....Mr. Carramine had written to say he would be in Town again next week, with Sir John and Marjorie Bladen. It would be pleasant to see old friends again, although she hardly knew what she would have to say to them. So much had happened....

The doorknocker resounded. Sophia flew to the window. A footman was leaving; perhaps he had brought a note from the Earl of Rame, apologizing for not being able to come.

The butler entered, bearing a posy on a silver salver. "For Miss Tarrant, my lady. From Mr. Dalby."

Lady Midmain started and sat upright. Almost, she had dozed off. "From whom? Dalby? Great heavens above! What next?"

Sophia was looking for a note, but there was none. "He said he would call on me this morning. He has a particular question he means to ask."

"What? This morning? Child, where are your brains!" To the butler, "Deny him; we are not in this morning. Except to the Earl of Rame, of course. He is expected any minute, that may be him, now!"

Once more the doorknocker fell. The butler left. Sophia caressed the posy, measuring the strength of the hope that it brought her. She said, "Mr. Dalby will propose, I think. It will be a very suitable match. Don't you agree, Aunt?"

"I do not agree. You must not see him until the Earl has proposed to you, and everything is settled. You were foolish to encourage Mr. Dalby by giving him two dances last night. I thought at the time that..."

The butler threw open the doors. "The Earl of Rame."

He bowed over Lady Midmain's hand. "How kind of you to receive me when others are turned from your door. Mr. Dalby is making quite a commotion out there in the street."

"Yes, I had to refuse him. My head aches sadly this morning, and I could not...but such an old friend of the family as yourself....Sophia? Make your curtsey, child!"

Sophia swept the Earl a curtsey, but continued to hold Mr. Dalby's posy. He levelled his glass at it, but made no comment. No doubt he had guessed its provenance. His bow had been perfunctory. He turned back to Lady Midmain.

"I would not for the world overstay my welcome if you are unwell. I came merely to bring some letters to Miss Tarrant from her brother and aunt. I was up in the north recently, you know, and happened to come across young Jasper. He is quite well, in decent lodgings. We cracked a bottle together and exchanged news. Did you know he was corresponding with little Miss Bladen? His news of Hamberley was more recent than mine."

Sophia said that she doubted if Sir John approved of his daughter's writing to her brother.

"Where is he?" asked Lady Midmain, holding out her hand for Jasper's letter. "Edinburgh? What might he be doing there?"

"Then he is not with the rebels," said Sophia, thankfully.

"People will jump to conclusions," said the Earl. "I daresay he went to Edinburgh just to have a look at them."

"But the rebels are not in Edinburgh, are they?"

"I'm afraid so. The news will be all over Town by now. You have not seen the papers this morning?"

"I only read the gossip columns," said Lady Midmain. She pressed her fingers to her forehead carefully, so as not to disturb her maquillage.

Sophia sat still, absorbing the blow. It was cruel of Fate to destroy her chance of a good marriage like this. And what foolishness, to follow the Pretender...she did not need her aunt's second sight to know that this escapade of Jasper's was bound to end badly.

"He said nothing to me about joining the rebels," said the Earl. "I do not think one should condemn him unheard."

"He gives no reason for being in the north," said Lady Midmain, scanning Jasper's letter. She held it out to Sophia. "Here, take it. It is addressed to you. Nothing but assurances that he is well, and that we are not to worry about him. When anyone tells me that I am not to worry, I feel strongly inclined to have hysterics. Nothing is more certain to produce feelings of anxiety than to be told that you are not to worry."

"Perhaps my other piece of news will please you better," said the Earl. "Your sister, Miss Tarrant, is at present on her way down to London to take over the administration of my household, and in particular to look after my son."

"Nan? Coming here? Why...she could not possibly...you have not considered...her back, you know. And although she may be able to give the impression of being an agreeable person on short acquaintance, her temper is not...in short, I cannot feel that..."

"I have always had a particular fondness for the Tarrant

ladies," said the Earl, seating himself beside Lady Midmain and pressing her hand. "They are so sprightly, so accomplished, and such a pleasure to look at. If I may make so bold, they adorn company, wherever they go." He raised Lady Midmain's hand to his lips. "You are such modest creatures, you Tarrant ladies, that you underestimate your effect on other people."

Sophia began to shred the posy in her lap.

"But her back...she is not strong," said Lady Midmain.

"She must not be asked to overtax her strength in any way. I agree with you entirely. Once I have her safely under my roof, we shall have to see what the doctors can do for her, although I fear it is too late for us to be able to achieve any great improvement in her condition."

"But...I do not see the necessity...she was happy enough in our cousin's house in York. At her age, and with that white hair, she cannot expect to move in the best Society."

"'Age cannot wither her, nor custom stale her infinite variety,'" quoted the Earl. "She was most unhappy at her cousin's house. Her opinions were of no consequence, and she had nothing to do but sit and listen to the grumbles of a foolish, lazy woman. You would have wished to remove her, as I did, if you had known the truth. As for moving in Society, she will do as much or as little of that as she chooses. I believe Jasper managed the disposition of his affairs badly, but once I looked into the matter, I found that with a little judicious management, enough could be set aside to provide a pension for your aunt. It is she who honors my house by accepting a post with me, not the other way round."

"But..." Here Lady Midmain's gaze alighted on Sophia, and she stopped. Sophia met her eyes, and accurately translated the expressions which flitted over her ladyship's face. There was speculation, followed by hope, followed by excitement. Lady Midmain had come to the conclusion that the Earl had invited Miss Tarrant into his household in order to please Sophia.

"Niece, you say nothing. Why do you not thank the Earl? Stupid girl, look what you have done! You have pulled Mr. Dalby's posy to pieces. But that is no matter."

Sophia rose and fled to the window, laying her forehead against the cool glass. She did not know why the Earl had done this thing, but she was almost certain that he had not been influenced to do so by the thought of pleasing her. Was it all a trick? Did he mean to bring Aunt Nan down to London, and then to dismiss her as capriciously as he had engaged her? He would then have deprived her of all means of livelihood. But then, what about the pension of which he had spoken? Jasper had certainly not supplied the money for that. Lady Midmain might believe it, but Sophia knew better.

Down in the street someone waved to her. It was Mr. Dalby. She stared back at him, and then waved. She wished she had not destroyed his posy, or she could have held it up to show that she appreciated the gift.

The Earl was at her elbow, glass to his eye. "Ah, Mr. Dalby. A very pleasant young man. He waves to us. How friendly of him. We must wave back, must we not? I wonder if he is intending to walk my way. I have a book which may interest him, by his hero, Jethro Tull. Of course, he may already have read it."

Having managed to give the impression that he and Sophia had together saluted Mr. Dalby, the Earl wandered back to Lady Midmain, and resumed his seat beside her. Sophia heard him say something about having met Mrs. Dalby, who was cock-a-hoop that her son should at last be thinking of matrimony.

Their voices sank. Sophia guessed they were speaking of her. She did not move from the window, but tears filled her eyes, and began to spill onto her cheeks. She saw it all now; the Earl had raised her high in Society, so that he could watch her fall. He had given her the opportunity to meet eligible gentlemen, and now he was instructing Lady Midmain to deny Mr. Dalby access to her niece. Everything he did, was to one end; that she should be humiliated.

She heard the name of Sir John Bladen mentioned. She wiped her cheeks dry and moved closer to her aunt.

The Earl was saying that he had had a letter from Mr. Carramine, who should be back in Town that week. He was to travel up with Sir John and Marjorie Bladen, who were to stay with some relatives in the city. It appeared that Sir John was come to seek another wife, having been refused by two matrons in Sussex.

"It is not clear," said the Earl, "Whether Sir John wants wealth or health most in his future bride, but in either case, Miss Marjorie is in the way. No stepmother wants a pretty girl like that around...so capable, too. They wager ten to one that Miss Marjorie will not return to Sussex unwed, and five to one that Sir John will take back a bride. It is said that he is become desperate, after having been rejected so often. He beat his first wife to death, I believe? Or is that a slander? And my friend Mr. Carramine reports that Sir John talks of renewing his acquaintance with Sophia."

"Over my dead body!" promised Lady Midmain. "I assure you the man shall not set foot in my household."

"I do not see how you can prevent him," said the Earl. "His manners are not precisely...what is the word I am looking for...elegant? But he is a man of some substance...in every sense of the word."

"You never liked him," said Sophia, turning her shoulder on the Earl.

"True. But he did not precisely take me to his ample bosom, either. A coarse creature."

"His daughter is one of my dearest friends."

"A delightful girl. I remember her with pleasure."

"And will you arrange for her to be presented at Court, too?"

"I doubt it. A most fatiguing business, arranging for the entry of a young girl into Society, especially when she cannot keep a still tongue in her head. Lady Midmain, your servant. I fear I must leave you." He made a slight inclination of the head in Sophia's direction and left.

"Hussy!" screamed Lady Midmain. "How could you be so wicked! You destroy all the chances he gives you! Have you gone mad to speak to him so rudely?"

Sophia flushed, but did not answer. It was all too true; she had behaved badly. She moved to the window to watch the Earl leave. He had not brought his sedan chair, but a large man whose features were vaguely familiar, attended him. Mr. Dalby was still there, lounging against the railings. The Earl crossed the road to speak with Mr. Dalby, but evidently did not persuade him to abandon his vigil. The Earl left, walking rapidly.

Sophia waited for a pause in her aunt's diatribe, said she was sorry if she had seemed rude, and might Mr. Dalby come up now?

"Mr. Dalby? Are you out of your mind? Do you want it spread all over the town that you receive Mr. Dalby as soon as the Earl's back is turned? You must be more circumspect, my girl. When the Earl has declared himself, you may see whom you will, for it will be no concern of mine what you do then. But from now on, we will keep a close watch on you; no more tête-à-têtes, or giving Mr. Dalby two dances at a ball."

"I believe Mr. Dalby to be serious in his intentions."

"It may be so. The Earl has said that it is possible, and he should know. All the more reason for you not to be seen in his company—at least until after Sunday. As the Earl says, it would not do for you to contract some ineligible alliance before you are presented to the King."

"And how are you to prevent my seeing Mr. Dalby, or Sir John Bladen, for that matter?"

"Very easily," said her ladyship. "If you choose to act like a disobedient child, then you shall be treated like one. Up to your room!" She advanced on Sophia and grasped her arm.

"What?" Sophia did not know whether to laugh or be angry.

"Up to your room, miss! And if you do not go of your own accord, I shall ring for the footmen to carry you up. That would not please your High-and-Mightiness, would it? To be carried struggling up the stairs, with all the servants looking on! Ah, I thought you would see it my way. Up, up, girl!"

Sophia marched up the stairs and into her room, her cheeks blazing. Perkins, Lady Midmain's maid, came tripping up to enquire if miss were ill, that she should retire to her room so early in the day.

"She is about to be extremely ill," said Lady Midmain. "Draw the curtains closely, Perkins, and assist Miss Tarrant out of her clothes. She has a low fever and must stay in bed for a few days. We will see what three days on a diet of bread and water will do for her. Meanwhile, you will tell the servants, Perkins, that Miss Tarrant is suffering from nerves and must be kept quiet. Positively no visitors, Perkins. You understand?"

"Perfectly, my lady. Three days on bread and water may refine her figure. We are still too thickset, in my opinion."

Sophia put her head under the pillow. She was in a trap. There was no way out. The Earl had played the piper, and she must dance to his tune.

The Town seethed with rumors. The Jacobites ate babies...Captain Sweetenham had been set free on his word

141

of honor not to bear arms against the rebels again ... the King was at Kensington; no, he was at St. James' ... Lord Carteret had declared he would not marry again, but remain a widower like the King ... his nephew's bill to increase penalties against smuggling was to be heard at the next session of Parliament ... a new style of wig had been introduced from Paris; smuggled, of course....

Sophia heard none of this, locked away in her room with little to drink and less to eat. On Sunday she was laced into her ballgown, her hair was dressed, and her face painted. As Perkins said, miss had lost all her country color but gained a fashionable figure. Sophia did not reply. Lady Midmain asked her whether she were well enough to go to the Drawing Room, and she replied listlessly that she supposed she was.

Sir Gregory accompanied them, in the family carriage, talking all the way about what the Duke of Newcastle had said to him, and what he planned to say to the Duke next time they met. Sophia turned her eyes on the busy streets and saw nothing. She had not been to St. James' Palace before, but she felt no curiosity as she followed her aunt and uncle across the courtyard and through low-ceilinged passages into the reception room, which was a long, low gallery. The room was uncomfortably crowded, hot and stuffy. All the world and his wife seemed to be there. Sophia managed to find a place against a wall and leaned there. Lady Midmain was all vivacity, talking, talking ... everyone talking, except herself. The women were wearing their widest skirts, the men their brightest suits. The gentlemen all wore long, curled periwigs, which were de rigeur at Court; these wigs were powdered, some in gray, some in pastel shades, but most in white. All the men, and most of the women were painted, scented and patched.

Suddenly he was at her elbow. He bowed over her aunt's hand, but his yes were on her face.

"Miss Tarrant is unwell?"

Trust him to notice. She had a strong desire to sink to her knees and implore him to be merciful to her.

"The silly child overstrained her nerves, and I have had to keep her confined to her room these last few days. Of course, we could not restrain her from coming tonight." Lady Midmain unfurled her fan, and used it with vigor.

The Earl bent over Sophia. "What is it? You wish to retire? The heat is too much for you, I can see that."

"It is not the heat." Her lips barely moved, because she could see that her aunt was trying to overhear their conversation. "If I am pale, it is because I have paint on my face for the first time in my life. If I am not in spirits, it is because I have been imprisoned in my room for the last few days. If I should faint, it will be because I have been deprived of food and drink. But you should know all this, having authorized it."

He took snuff in leisurely fashion. His fingernails were painted pink. He looked around the room, his height making it easy for him to see over the heads of those nearest them.

"Lady Midmain, I see my old friend Lincoln beckoning me to bring Miss Tarrant to him. You will excuse us?" He put his hand under Sophia's arm, and steered her through the throng. Heads turned at their passing, mouths stretched into smiles, tongues worked. She could feel her head going round, but his arm was strong under hers, and she knew he would not allow her to fall. He was saying something about not buying a horse broken in by Lady Midmain, for her methods would ruin any filly's mouth.

"You did not tell her to lock me up?"

"Of course not. I merely suggested that she might be wise not to allow you a series of private meetings with Mr. Dalby, before you were presented to His Majesty."

"Why? To make sure of your lovelock? I told you that I would let you have it."

"I prefer to carry my part of the contract through, first."

"So be it. But tomorrow morning, you will make it clear to Lady Midmain that you have no further interest in me."

"If I do that, you will be returned to the sewing-room."

"I do have other matrimonial prospects. Mr. Dalby..."

"...is not man enough to master you. You would go mad from boredom six months after you had married him, plunge into excess after excess, and finally ruin your health and reputation."

"I disagree. There is also Sir John Bladen, who is coming to Town."

"Ah, yes. My favorite magistrate. Mr. Carramine has told me something of his reputation. He beat his first wife to death, did he not? At least I will not beat you."

"But you do not wish to marry me!"

"Do I not?" he said, more to himself than to her. "I am not

143

sure. I have never been sure. I rather think I do wish it, and it is the logical way out of your difficulty."

She could not help herself. Tears began to tumble down her cheeks.

"Be generous," she said. "I admit you have me in your power. I will admit I was wrong to laugh at you. Now for pity's sake, let me go! You have pursued me only out of hurt pride, and a desire for revenge."

He did not reply, but guided her through the throng more rapidly than before. She turned her face to his shoulder in an effort to disguise the fact that she was crying.

"My dear!" It was Lady Lincoln, all concern.

"Miss Tarrant is feeling faint. She has been unwell and unable to eat anything today. Would you find her something to eat and drink, and let her rest in your room for a few minutes?"

Once more his lordship had pulled the strings, and the puppets danced to his tune. Sophia was borne off through a huddle of rooms into the apartment occupied by Lord Lincoln, in his capacity as Gentleman in Waiting to the King. She was given food and wine, and clucked over. She continued to cry until Lady Lincoln told her she was making her nose swell, and then she laughed, and washed her face, and admitted to feeling better.

"I know how these things are," said Lady Lincoln. "I was scared to death the first time I came to Court, and couldn't eat for two whole days beforehand for excitement."

"It was not that," said Sophia. The wine had acted fast on her empty stomach, making her reckless. "It is the Earl's attentions which distress me. My aunt has kept me locked up and starved me, on the off chance that he may offer for me, and to prevent my seeing other suitors. I have no friends, and no money. What can I do? I wish I were dead."

"But don't you wish to marry Philip? I thought it was all arranged. I am sure I would have been delighted if my father and uncle had decided that such a match... although he was still married, then. And in short, although my dear Henry is the most delightful... but once you are married, you know, such fancies commonly disappear, and you can have no idea how pleasant it is to have your own household."

"That's just the trouble. I did have my own household, and a loving family. He has ruined all that for me. He is so cruel, and hard, and unforgiving."

144

"Who? Philip?" Lady Lincoln tried not to laugh, because she realized that Sophia was deeply distressed. "My dear, you have a very strange idea of him."

"Did he not neglect his first wife? Is he not proud and cold? Are his children strong and healthy? No, they are sickly, or dead. I doubt he is capable of siring healthy children."

"Barbara was a foolish, frippery creature. I daresay they did not spend much time together, but that is not surprising since they had no interests in common. She only cared for dress and cards, and to be flattered. They say that her last child was not his, though I think that a lie myself. As for the children being weakly, I am sure it is no wonder, for she would insist on tight lacing when she was breeding, even though he implored her not to do so. Three of the babes were born with dislocated limbs and the births were all so protracted that . . . in short, she brought about her own death and the death of her children through vanity. I am now in the same position," here Lady Lincoln blushed, "And I assure you that I have already obeyed my lord's wish not to lace myself tightly. I do not care if my waist is large, so long as my baby is healthy."

"I have heard that your marriage was arranged, and yet you seem happy."

Lady Lincoln smiled. "We are cousins, and have always known that our parents wished us to marry. My lord has no money of his own, and I have plenty. If he had not been good and kind, my parents would not have pressed me to marry him, but I consider I have been very lucky. Of course I knew that he had a fancy to marry another lady, who was much more beautiful than I, and learned, and musical and a better dancer." Here Lady Lincoln sighed a little. "But it could not be, for she had no fortune and was happy to accept Lord Carteret when he offered for her. Poor lady; you know she died in childbirth? My dear lord was much cast down. I confess I was a little jealous of her once, as you will be of . . ." She stopped herself, glanced at the clock, and rose. "My dear, you must hurry! His Majesty hates anyone to be ill, because he is of such a robust constitution himself, and as for unpunctuality!" She raised hands and eyebrows. "It will condemn you utterly if you are late, and he must be in the Gallery by now."

She seized Sophia by the hand and rushed her back through the palace. The noise and heat were as great as ever

145

in the Gallery, but Sophia, fortified by food and wine, could now separate the medley into its component parts. There was Mr. Dalby, looking around...for her? His mother, talking to Lady Rochester. Sir Gregory, bending close to overhear something a stout gentleman was saying to another man. And was that...surely it was Mr. Carramine? Yes, he had seen her, and raised his hand in greeting. Lady Lincoln pulled her through the crowd. A smile here...a word there...a group of Lady Midmain's cronies, whispering together as they looked her way...Lady Millicent Fairweather, biting on her fan...Lord Lincoln, cleaving a way through...

"Only just in time," he said. "Philip has been asked for you. 'Someone'—they call His Majesty 'Someone'—has evidently remembered that you are to be here, and being of an impatient disposition...you know how to curtsey to him? And what to say?"

"Yes...no...what am I to say?"

"Let him do the talking. He likes to talk to pretty girls, but he doesn't expect them to be capable of rational conversation."

The Earl joined them, looking slightly less calm than usual. "Devilish nuisance. Mr. Stone wants me at once."

"Does he, now!" said Lord Lincoln. "Do you think that means there is news from the north?"

"Probably. But if Cope had trounced the rebels, you'd have thought we'd all have heard about it. I've been looking around. My uncle's not here, and neither is yours."

"You think it's bad news? You'd better go then, hadn't you?"

"No. Bad news or good, it will wait five minutes; Miss Tarrant's presentation cannot wait."

"I will undertake it for you, if you wish," said Lord Lincoln.

"This is something I must do for myself."

There was a commotion in the group of people standing nearby. The women curtseyed to the ground, the men bowed. Sophia caught a glimpse of a stout man with a red face surmounted by a large white wig, and then the women rose, and her view was obstructed. The Earl bent over her.

"I will go to Mr. Stone as soon as you have been presented, but I may not be able to return. I will call on you tomorrow morning, to claim my lovelock."

"I will cut it off tonight, and wrap it in a screw of paper for you. You need not ask to see me, then."

146

"No, I must see you cut it off, or better still, do it myself. You might cheat me otherwise, by passing off some of your maid's hair as your own, or even by buying a tress from some poor girl."

"How dare you!" gasped Sophia. "As if I would!"

"Ah, you look better now. You were altogether too pale before."

Before Sophia could favor him with her opinion of his morals, the ranks of people in front of them parted, a red coat advanced into view, and she sank to the floor in a profound curtsey. Lady Midmain was there, beside her—she could see the purple of her skirts. The Earl was murmuring an introduction, and the King was telling her to rise. She did so, but kept her eyes down.

"So this is the Tarrant Rose?" A heavily accented voice. "Delightful, my dear Rame. Not an Amazon at all. Who was it slandered the girl so? I remember . . . the fair girl who smiles too much . . . not enough of her to satisfy a man's requirements . . . not like this one, eh? What, what? Hey, miss . . . What's her name? Sophia? Good name, Sophia. Like that sort of name. Caroline, Sophia. Good sort of names. Well, Miss Sophia, and how do you like my capital, eh? I hear you speak German. That's good. Very good."

She raised her eyes. He was not alarming at all, she thought. He was a genial man, old enough to be her father and very ready to be pleased. "An it please you, sire, I like London very much indeed."

"It does please me. We shall see more of you in future. Sit a while together and talk in German. Very pretty, Rame. Pretty eyes . . . hair . . . teeth . . . and what have you. Yes. How old are you, girl? Twenty-four? Why, what are our gallants thinking of! You ought to have been married and presented some happy man with a family long before now."

"Do not be too hard on us, sire," said Philip. "I only met the lady in February, and then what must you do but sweep me off to Hanover for the summer?"

There was laughter around them, and the King moved on, leaving Sophia to blush, and Lady Midmain to congratulate her. "Tantamount to a declaration, and in public! Oh, I am so happy, I swear I could cry if it did not disturb my face! My dear, you are made! His Majesty approves! You will be Countess of Rame before the year is out."

Chapter Nine

Sophia sat by the fire in her aunt's drawing-room, listlessly opening and shutting her fan. Once more she wore the blue saque, and once more she was waiting on the Earl of Rame's pleasure. Her aunt stood by the door, listening for an indication that he was coming, for he had been closeted with Sir Gregory in the study for nearly half an hour.

On the table at Sophia's side lay a posy of pink roses, and a note from the Earl. *"There has been a sharp encounter between Government troops and the rebels, near Edinburgh. It appears the rebels won the day, but your brother was not in arms, and was seen shortly afterwards riding back to Edinburgh, unharmed."*

She thought: Could I have prevented this happening to me? If I had not laughed at him that night...but indeed, if I had not laughed at him, he would have taken me as his mistress, and what would have become of me, then? Well, if I must marry him, I shall make him pay for it. I may be trapped, but even trapped animals can bite.

Her aunt shot away from the door, flapping her hands. "They are coming! Oh, my dear, how happy I am! What a splendid match! Sit up, Sophia! No, stand! A smile! Let me pinch some color into your cheeks. Is there time for us to rouge your cheeks? You look so pale."

"I am well enough." She sank into a curtsey as the Earl entered, with Sir Gregory beaming and bobbing at his side.

"Miss Tarrant. Sophia." He bent and kissed her hand,

raising her from her curtsey. "Your uncle has given me permission to pay my addresses to you. May I hope you look with favor on my suit?"

What a farce this was! She said something about being very happy. He released her hand. Lady Midmain produced a few tears and invited the Earl to kiss her on the cheek, since they would soon be related. Sir Gregory hopped from one foot to the other, making faces at his wife, and saying something about drafting a notice of the engagement to be sent to the papers.

"Of course!" said Lady Midmain, understanding that Sir Gregory wished the newly-engaged pair to be left alone. "I will come and help you do it."

The Midmains left, and Sophia sank back onto her chair. She felt numb.

"So you have gained your point," she said. "You know that I dislike, even despise you. You know that I could have married someone else if you had not interfered. You know that I would never have come to you willingly. If you are happy to marry me, knowing these things..." She shrugged.

"You protest too much. If you had really disliked the marriage, you would have run away rather than marry me. You could have climbed out of the window, even if the door had been locked."

"And where would I have gone, friendless and without a penny in the world?"

"To Mr. Carramine."

"I do not know his direction."

"But you could have obtained it. You spoke to him last night, did you not?"

"My aunt Midmain informed that if I did not marry you, she would send me up to York to take Aunt Nan's place there."

"Lady Midmain would have made a better general than Cope, but I could wish that she had not interfered. Come now; admit that you are only objecting to the marriage out of perversity. You are a misfit here. As my wife you will have a good position in Society, will be able to travel, and will have the company of your Aunt Nan. There will be ample money for dress, your own sedan chair and the use of the carriage in Town. Your duties will not be arduous, for I have an excellent housekeeper, and your aunt will remain in charge of my son Thomas."

149

"Aye, there's the rub! You men are all the same. Wrap it up as you will, the bargain reads—for the privilege of acting as brood mare, one title and a wardrobe of dresses. How many times must I be brought to bed before I am considered to have fulfilled my part of the contract?"

"It would be the same in any marriage. Even Mr. Dalby would require that you bear him children."

"I would have served him with pleasure." She noted that his eyebrows contracted, and knew how best to hurt him. She chose her words with care. "He is, after all, young and pleasing to me."

There was silence, except for the rustle of coals in the grate. He walked to the fire, and leaned against the mantel. He took out his snuffbox and helped himself to a pinch. He stowed the snuffbox away, and dusted his sleeve with a handkerchief. Sophia smiled to herself, for she knew he only took snuff when he needed time to think.

When he spoke, it was to the carpet at her feet. "I have an heir already. Thomas is not strong, but with your aunt's help, he should see me out. So long as he lives, I need no other heir. If he should die before I do..." He shrugged. "Even so, I engage not to enter your bedroom without invitation."

She leaned back in her chair, and gave a sigh of satisfaction. If he had bought her, it was going to cost him dear. He would keep his word, of course. A second wife would normally wish the child of the first marriage dead, so that her own children would inherit; he must have thought she would neglect Thomas. But Thomas alive was her guarantee of his good behavior. Night after night she would drop off to sleep with a smile on her lips, thinking of his frustration. It would almost be worth marrying him to inflict such a punishment.

She studied him. He was well enough to look at, she thought. They would make a good couple, both being so tall. She would be able to get away from the Midmains, and have Aunt Nan...perhaps marriage would not be such a terrible fate, after all.

She pulled her lovelock up. "Take it. It is yours."

He took a pair of folding scissors from a leather sheath and cut off the lock, stowing it away in his pocket. She felt a pang at parting with it. She stood up and looked at herself in the mirror. Her neck looked bare without it. She set her teeth. She could always coax another lock forward, or would that be cheating? She rather thought it would be. No, she would have no lovelock in future. A Tarrant must always pay her debts.

Shortly after her betrothal Sophia was reunited with her Aunt Nan. They clung to each other, and laughed, and cried, and started sentences which had no endings, trying to tell each other everything that had happened in the months of their separation.

Presently servants brought in a dainty luncheon, and Sophia dried her eyes and admired her aunt's rustling black silk dress.

"Philip had three beautiful dresses waiting for me, and I have a maid of my own, and this room is to be refurnished as I wish, and my bedchamber, and...oh, my dear; you don't blame me too much for accepting his offer, do you?"

"But dearest, can you be happy here, in the house of our enemy?"

"Poor Philip. Do you still think of him as your enemy? I don't. We brought the sale of Tarrant Hall on ourselves. Philip was in no way to blame for what happened to the Tarrants afterwards, although being Philip, he does of course accept the blame."

"I hadn't noticed it."

"No, dear. You are very unobservant when it suits you. Do try to understand; I was so very unhappy up in York, and not really needed as I am needed here. There is so much to be done in this great house to make it anything like a home. But indeed, if you think it would be awkward having me here once you are married, I will go."

"Oh, dearest; of course not. Nothing could reconcile me to this marriage more than having you under the same roof with me again. Do what you like. Change what you like. Order things as you wish. Philip has told me I need not concern myself about the running of the house, and I do not intend to do so. I will never willingly step into a kitchen, or order a meal again. I am going to enjoy myself, when I am married."

"Are you, my dear? Are you so much in love with Society?"

"There is nothing to compare with it," declared Sophia. "I shall dance every night, and have a new dress once a week, and my portrait is to be painted, and perhaps I shall take little Marjorie under my wing...did you know she was in Town? I met her, with Sir John, at the Buckingham's last night. She was wearing the most frightful dress, so antiquated and yet it must have cost a lot. I was quite embarrassed for her, and told her—very kindly, of course—that she must be introduced to my corsetiere, and she looked quite horrified. I had to hide a laugh, for really, her figure is so clumsy! Sir Benjamin said that she reminded him of a badly-trussed..."

"Sophia!"

Sophia bit her lip. Tears glistened at the corners of her eyes, but she brushed them away. "Will you show me over the house before I go?"

Three grave-faced men gathered at Mr. Stone's office to discuss the latest news from Scotland. Four French ships had slipped through the English blockade to land in the northeast of Scotland. They had been carrying money, volunteers and arms to the Pretender; all of which were much needed. Even more disastrous from the English point of view, was the news that a Monsieur du Boyer, Marquis d'Eguilles, was on board one of the ships and was currently acting as French Ambassador to the court of Prince Charles. His Majesty had taken the news badly. There had been scenes in the Closet. Newcastle had withdrawn in tears, because the King had accused him and his brother, Henry Pelham, of having forced the dismissal of Carteret. The King had worked himself up to such a pitch that he really believed he was being imprisoned in a constitutional trap which forbade him any independent action. Never before had the King's relationship with Newcastle been at so low an ebb.

"It is a ridiculous situation," said Mr. Stone. "Carteret commands no sort of following in the Commons, yet he imposes his will on the King at all times. He is throwing the kingdom away for the sake of personal glory."

"It would be best if the Duke could be induced to offer my uncle office," said Philip.

"No," said Mr. Stone. "The Duke will not do so, under any circumstances. We must think again."

Mr. Carramine was re-reading the latest dispatches from Scotland. "Nowhere does it say that this Marquis is Louis' official Ambassador. The volunteers are hardly an official French force, either. This is support drummed up by the bankers, I daresay."

"True," said Mr. Stone. "My French agent in Paris tells me that one of the bankers returned to France in the *Du Teillay*, went straight to Versailles, and made a big speech in front of everyone about the standard being raised at Glenfinnan, and the local support which came in. Louis has officially pledged French support, but as we know, that will take time to organize. Lord John Drummond, who commands the Royal Scots regiment in the French Army, has been ordered to prepare for embarkation, together with one thousand well trained men. If they should succeed in getting to Scotland..." He shrugged.

"How long do we have?" mused Philip, looking at the map. "Two months? How many men of our own shall we have by then?"

"This will end in civil war," cried Mr. Carramine.

Mr. Stone began to pace the room. The others were silent, studying the map before them.

"We are in danger of losing our heads over nothing," said Mr. Stone at last. "The Pretender cannot succeed in his rebellion, and Lord Carteret cannot succeed in regaining office. The odds are stacked against them. All we have to do is keep calm, and deploy what forces we have to the best advantage. We have been pushed onto the defensive, yet we have superior numbers, more able commanders, more money, and the country is behind us. We are behaving like children, panicking at shadows, when we should be thinking how best to destroy our enemies. Why shouldn't we take a leaf from Lord Carteret's book, and lure the Pretender out of his safe harbor in Edinburgh as we lured him out of France? I do not like to think of him sitting in the capital of Scotland, holding court, raising taxes, drilling his men. Are you with me?"

"Ahead of you," said Philip grimly. "You want another letter from Jasper Tarrant, confirming that he is raising support for the Pretender, and inviting him to come south now, before the winter sets in?"

"Precisely. We can forge such a letter, of course, but it is better to have the real thing where possible. I have intercepted just such a letter from William Watkyns in Wales, and here is another from the Earl of Barrymore, and one from the Duke of Beaufort. These are also genuine, having been intercepted by our men, who have been watching these Jacobites from the beginning. With two or three others which I can supply—we made copies of the seals on all treasonable correspondence as it was sent through our hands earlier this year—we should give the impression that the south of England is only awaiting the call to rise in favor of the Pretender. Will you arrange for your friend David Vere to get these delivered to the Pretender in due course?"

Mr. Carramine thumped the table. "It might work, it might, indeed. The Pretender cannot be comfortable in Edinburgh, with winter coming on, and his men in canvas tents outside the city. The Castle is still held against him, and inside the Castle is the city's wealth. These reports here say that he is finding his first attempt at administration difficult, and I daresay the Scots are not too happy about being asked to pay a second lot of taxes direct to him when they have already been taxed by their legitimate Government. If he had a wise, cautious head on his shoulders he would of course stay where he is, consolidate his position, and wait for the French to send official support, But he is a rash youth, and ill-advised by the men around him. I am sure he will come south, if the bait is well-laid."

"Yes," said Philip. "It should work. You will be greatly in David Vere's debt, if it does. I wonder what his price is?" Here he looked straight at Mr. Stone, who met his gaze blandly, but did not reply. Philip thought: He knows who David Vere is, but doesn't choose to admit it. Very well, we can wait.

Lord Lincoln burst into the room, brushing aside the attempt of two of Mr. Stone's clerks to stop him.

"You must come at once," he said, panting. "My uncle has gone mad, I think. He broke in on the King's hour with Lady Yarmouth, to advise that the King pack and depart for Hanover until the Pretender can be dealt with. There was no reasoning with him. The King shouted, Lady Yarmouth was all incomprehension, and my uncle wept unceasingly."

The three men rose in consternation. "If His Majesty goes," said Mr. Stone, "Then the Pretender can walk onto the throne without a shot being fired."

"He must be prevented at all costs," said Philip. "I will fetch my uncle. He will see that this will not do, and will be able to persuade the King against leaving at such a juncture."

"The Duke will never allow it," said Mr. Stone.

"Nonsense!" said Philip. "The Duke has lost his head. This is no time to talk about the cost of such an alliance; and in any event my uncle requires prestige, not cash, for his services. I will go to him at once, and I suggest you go to the Duke and remove him from the King's presence before he does any more damage."

"Is this wise?"

"It is necessary, or we all lose our heads."

Sophia exclaimed with delight as she entered her Aunt Nan's room. She had not been to see her aunt for several days, and the room had been completely redecorated, and furnished with pieces brought—as she saw—from Tarrant Hall. "Oh, your old chair...and the cabinet from the parlor ...and our own tea service and tea-chest...and the silver spoons!"

"Was it not a delightful thought of Philip's? He sent for these things as soon as he knew I was coming. That big chair over there is for guests. It used to stand in the hall, remember? All my men visitors love that chair. They sit there and talk, and I sit here in my own little sewing chair, and make the sort of inconsequential, encouraging remarks which men like to hear from their women, and we are so pleased with each other! Oh, my dear—such fun—their little secrets—I never thought to be the center of such intrigues at my age. I declare I feel quite ten years younger."

"What has Philip been up to now?" said Sophia, in a bored tone, as if she personally couldn't have cared less what he had been up to.

"You must ask him that, my dear."

Sophia shrugged. "When next I see him, perhaps. Or perhaps I won't. That is the great advantage of a marriage of convenience, that one need not pry into one another's secrets. We do not have to be in each other's company all the time. Just as well. Heigho! I declare I don't know how I would find the time to spare for him, if he were forever sighing verses in my ear. I am invited everywhere, you know, and he seems to have forsaken Society since he presented me at Court."

"He is very busy."

"Oh, don't think I'm complaining."

"Are you not, my dear?"

"Certainly not." Yet Sophia's cheeks were suspiciously red. She plied her fan vigorously. "Several people have asked me whether you are meaning to go into Society yourself."

"I, dear? No. What would I have to say to Society, or So-

155

ciety to me? I am happy here, and Philip brings his friends to call on me, you know, just as if I were someone of importance."

"Really?" Sophia did her best not to sound incredulous. She had perhaps been spoilt by the adulation lavished on her, and the thought of her crippled aunt going into Society had caused her some embarrassment. To give her her due, she was angry with herself for being ashamed of her aunt.

"Oh yes, dear. There is a Mr. Andrew Stone, for instance. He was very distant and civil at first, but improves on acquaintance. Mr. Carramine comes, of course; and yesterday Lord and Lady Lincoln came. They are a sweet couple, are they not? They invited me to a rout—whatever that may be—but I told them I prefer not to go out. They promised me they would seek out young Marjorie and bring her to see me next week. Mr. Denbigh often comes, of course; he is to teach me how to speak German with a good accent, and I am to help him with his book on poetry. And Thomas."

"Who is Thomas?" Then she remembered. "You mean, my step-son?"

"Philip carries him down here from the nurseries in the late afternoon, and we eat sweetmeats and drink hot chocolate, and I tell him a bedtime story. It is the only time he leaves his room, now."

"And does he have a secret, too?"

"Yes, my dear, he has. He has agreed to share it with me because I, too, have been afflicted with something which the doctors cannot cure."

"What? Is he that ill?"

"You are perturbed? Good. It is the first time I have known you express concern about anything but yourself since I arrived."

"Have I become so selfish?"

"Yes, my dear, I think you have. But perhaps it is only natural. Philip says that it is, anyway. He says that you ought not to be scolded at present, because you are not well."

"He—says—that? How dare he! How I hate him!"

Aunt Nan smiled at her niece. "Come and meet Thomas!"

Sophia opened her mouth to refuse her aunt's request, and then shut it again. What had she to lose by learning the truth about the boy? So she followed Miss Nan up the winding stair to the nurseries at the top of the house. The windows were tightly sealed, and the air was close and warm. A sea-coal

156

fire burned in the grate, tended by a nurse in white cap and apron. On the bed lay a slim figure with blond hair, restless in sleep.

Sophia dropped to her knees beside the bed. The boy was Philip all over again, but if Philip was slender, this lad looked as if a rough caress might break his bones. Philip was naturally pale, but this lad's skin was waxen, save for a flush high on either cheekbone. His hands were skeletal, and he looked older than his ten years.

He was lying in the same position as his father after he had fallen from his horse, the day Sophia had met him. She remembered it all too well. She had thought at first that the fall had killed him. His hat and wig had gone in the fall and his fair hair, cropped short, had gleamed bright against the turf. She had looked for gray hairs at his temples, for though his face was hardly lined, the bones were not padded with the full flesh of youth. She had seen many accidents and never lost her nerve before that day, but she had knelt over him in the field, and stared and stared and done nothing to help him, or to fetch help, until he had begun to regain consciousness. And then she had been brusque with him; she, who was never brusque with her patients.

Why? Why had she had to show that side of herself to him? He had been courteous in return, had apologized for troubling her, had managed to walk to the house even though she saw he could barely stand upright. He had disturbed her as no man had done, before or since. Her life had been well ordered until that time. She had known where she was going, and what she had to do. She had accepted the fact that she would have to marry Sir John, and it had not troubled her until Philip had put his arms round her, and kissed her. He had woken a craving in her which Sir John could not satisfy.

In fact, the thought of Sir John had been repugnant to her from that moment, although she knew that Philip was not for her. He had been quite open about it. He had not tried to deceive her in any way. She would have loved him; perhaps had begun to love him, until he had insulted her and she had revenged herself on him by inflicting such hurt as no man could easily bear. She remembered the look on his face when she had laughed at him, and the way he had bowed his head on his hands when he leaned on the stairs, afterwards . . . and how the sight of his humiliation had hurt her, until it had been almost as much as she could do not to run to him and put her arms round him, and tell him that she was his, and he might do what he willed with her....

There were tears on her cheeks. She brushed them away. The boy stirred, opened his eyes, and smiled up at her. Then he began to cough. Sophia lifted him in her arms. Aunt Nan proffered a bowl, and a handkerchief. The boy stifled his paroxysm at last, and let her take the handkerchief from his mouth. It was stained with blood. His head was hot. Aunt Nan gave him some soothing syrup, and he smiled at her. He was a nice child, and Sophia knew he was dying of consumption, and that there was nothing she could do about it.

"Don't look so sad," said the boy. His voice was hoarse, but his face serene. "Tell me a story, instead. Tell me about when you were presented at Court, and the King had to decide whether you were an Amazon or a Rose, and he said you were a Rose. I like that story. I didn't know what an Amazon was at first, but Mr. Denbigh read me some stories about Amazons and it was very interesting, but I like the way Father tells the story best."

"You know who I am?" Her hands pushed the hair back from his forehead, caressingly.

"You are the Rose. No one else could have such a lovely smile and such gentle ways. You are going to marry Father, and live with us and be happy ever after." He patted the bed at his side. "Will you sit with me for a while? Aunt Nan says you know lots of stories because you used to tell them to your brother. I wish I could meet him. Will you tell me about him, and about Tarrant Hall, and the Ram and the Rose?"

An hour later, Sophia followed her aunt downstairs. The boy had had another coughing fit, but was now asleep.

"How long has Philip known that the boy will die?" said Sophia.

"He will not admit it, even though I have persuaded the doctors to stop pulling the lad about. Thomas knows, of course. He is resigned to it. One day Philip talks of taking Thomas to Hanover, or Brussels or Stockholm with him, and the next he says it might be best if I took the boy to Tarrant Hall next spring."

Sophia shook her head. "I don't think he'll live that long."

"Neither do I." Aunt Nan sighed.

Sophia sank onto a chair. Her head drooped. The pressure of her stays on her body increased, and she jerked upright. Perkins was lacing her ever more tightly; each week her dresses were being taken in at the waist. She sighed. Had Philip known that Thomas was dying when he made his bargain with her? She thought that such double-dealing was not beyond him, but that in this case he had been sincere. It was hard to maintain a high level of hate against a man whom you had learned to pity. The thought of Thomas...his affectionate nature...Philip's love for the boy...Philip, lying on the ground, injured...oh, why had he not been someone as unimportant as herself? Why had all this to happen?

She said, "Philip comes to see you every day?"

"I sleep little, as you know. This room is so positioned that I can see everyone who comes up the staircase, or goes in and out of the library. If I am tired, I close my door and no one knocks; but if I am feeling lively, I leave the door ajar and then the gentlemen come in, if they feel like it, for a few minutes' talk before they go to bed."

"What do you find to talk about?"

"Politics, my dear. What else?"

"My aunt Midmain says no woman should talk politics to men."

"Hmph!" said Miss Tarrant.

"You think I should talk politics to Philip? I would not know what to say."

"You don't have to say anything. All you have to do is listen intelligently, and when he has learned to trust you, I daresay he will tell you everything, as a matter of course. To know a man's secrets is to have power over him, but Philip will not give you that power until he is sure that you will not abuse it."

Sophia's eyes narrowed. "Does he trust you with all his secrets, Aunt?"

"Are you jealous of me, child? He trusts me with some of his secrets, and others I have guessed, but I do not know everything yet. It is like peeling an onion; you take off this layer and then the next, until you arrive at the truth of a man. Given time, he will tell me all his hopes and fears, but you could find out what he is made of before me, if you so wished. You are in a privileged position, are you not?"

"I wish I had your privileges. I hardly ever see him, and when I do, it is in company."

"Then write and ask him to call on you at a time when you will be alone."

"We are to meet at the Dalbys' tonight, I believe. He is engaged to me for the second minuet. Perhaps I will ask him then."

But it was not to be. Before Sophia set out for the Dalbys', she had received a note from Philip to make his apologies, since he was unavoidably detained at St. James'.

While Sophia jolted across London in the company of the Midmains, Philip was walking up and down one of the galleries in St. James' with his uncle. The day had been spent in anxious consultations, interrupted now and then by hysterical outbursts from the Duke of Newcastle; the King was bewildered by the conflicting advice being given him. Carteret was so sure that His Majesty must stay in London—Newcastle was so sure that the King must flee—what was he to make of it?

Philip and his friend Henry Lincoln were quietly working to bring the two sides together in a coalition Government. If only Newcastle could be prevailed upon to give Carteret office, and if only Carteret would accept such office...the strength of the Duke in the Commons would match the influence of Carteret over the King and in foreign policy to make an unbeatable combination. Mr. Stone was cautiously encouraging, but not optimistic. The Duke's opinion of Carteret was not high, and Carteret's opinion of the Duke....

"A superior clerk, Philip. He is very happy fitting his friends into places here and there. He is very fit for that sort of drudgery, I daresay; if he spends his time deciding on the merits of this man or that for a bishopric, then I daresay he has learned something of that business. But what is it to a statesman who is made a bishop or a judge or whatever? Newcastle is incapable of taking the wider view. His knowledge of international politics is negligible. Why, you know very well that he will never go abroad with the King, because he is afraid of being seasick! He speaks no language but his own, and resorts to tears when pressed. And you ask me ...me!...to ally myself with such a man as this?"

"It is the very qualities which you despise which have made him master of the House of Commons," said Philip. "He bribes no one, but he places his friends to his own advantage. He has a solid majority in the Commons, who will vote whichever way he tells them to vote. The man who commands the Commons, commands the pursestrings of the nation, and in the long run that man must also command the King."

"I, and I alone, have the King's confidence."

"That is very true. You have the breadth of vision, the education, the mastery of foreign affairs which he lacks. The King needs you; the country needs you... but both King and country also need the Duke. There is no getting away from him, you know. The man is your inferior in many ways, I grant you, but could you not use him to regain power? An alliance with him would give you what you lack at present, which is command of the Commons."

"Out of the question! I could never share power with that... nincompoop! Only look what happens when he is in charge of events. Our armies beaten, and the King implored... yes, on his bended knees Newcastle implored His Majesty to run away! The man is an incompetent fool."

"He is not a fool, but he does lack your particular quality of statesmanship, I agree. Now if you accept Newcastle's offer of office in the ministry, then you are half way back to power."

"I, accept office under Newcastle? Under that sniveller? I thought you had more sense, Philip. Never. I would never demean myself so as to... Ah! I see what it is. You have been listening to that snake Stone. What? Has Newcastle suborned you? What offers has he made you? I knew how it would be when you offered for that Tarrant girl instead of fulfilling your contract with Lady Millicent. It is all plain, now. You have betrayed me for..."

"I have not betrayed you, Uncle. I work with Mr. Stone on the plan you made to bring the Pretender here, alone. It seems I have inherited a good deal of your liking for playing the puppet master. I cannot hope to become the master of international events that you are, but I entertain a modest desire to be in the center of affairs. Mr. Stone is capable and intelligent..."

"Which is more than can be said for his master."

And so it went on, hour after hour. Carteret would not move from his position, and neither, in the event, would Newcastle. Neither man would agree to serve with or under the other.

The King retired to spend the evening with his mistress, and nothing had been decided. Philip left St. James' only when the King had retired to bed; it was too late by then for him to go to the Dalbys', but he was heartened, on his return home, by the news that Sophia wished to speak with him in private. Perhaps his luck had turned.

His luck had not turned. That evening at the Dalbys', Sophia had been accosted by Lady Millicent, all dimples and false friendship.

"My word!" cried Lady Millicent. "Are we left all alone again? No Philip? I had heard rumors, of course, that he was spending all his time with another lady, but I had not believed that he would fail to turn up here at the Dalbys'. Does he not know that you have another admirer? Two, I suppose; if you count the gallant Sir John. What a monster of a figure he has, to be sure! And that daughter of his; positively crude. But what am I saying? Are they not friends of yours? Dear friends from the country? Ah, what one would give to be able to shed one's old friends with one's old clothes."

"What did you say about Philip?"

"Why, didn't you know? Oh, my dear, I see you know nothing! But that is always the way, is it not? We women are always the last to hear when our men are unfaithful to us. How pale you have gone! Won't you take a seat?"

"I am perfectly well, thank you. What is it you have heard about Philip?"

"Nothing more than anyone knows." She twirled her fan. "Oh, just look at that hooped skirt! Did you ever see anything more elegant? I declare she must have to go sideways through doors! Mine is not half so wide."

"What about Philip?" asked Sophia, through clenched teeth.

"He goes to a certain house in St. James' three times a week. It is run by an old friend of his; a very old friend of his. It is supposed to be a gambling establishment, but everyone knows that Philip doesn't gamble, and it can't be the company which takes him there, because they are most of them Jacobites, and so ... I hear she is very pretty, with sparkling dark eyes. She was a singer once, but has no need to sing for a living now, if you understand me?"

Sophia sat down. Her hands trembled so much that her

162

fan dropped to the floor. Lady Millicent picked it up, and set it on the couch by Sophia.

"Didn't you know? Dear me! I would never have told you, if I had thought you so completely in ignorance. It has been going on for years, you know. On and off. She was in Hanover this summer, and came back to London with him, or perhaps on the next boat. Quite romantic. Everyone is talking about it. How clever Philip is, to take everyone's attention off his *chère amie* by making out that he was in love with you. How soon are you to be married? Next week, is it not? Well, it is to be hoped, for your sake, that he ceases to visit her after you are married, but if he doesn't, I am sure you will have sense enough to pretend that you know nothing of the matter. After all, men will be men, will they not?"

"Yes," said Sophia. "Thank you for telling me."

"My dear," said Lady Millicent, sinking into a curtsey, "It was a pleasure, believe me."

Chapter Ten

"The Earl of Rame!" He came into Lady Midmain's drawing-room with a step which was lighter and swifter than usual. Even while he bowed over Lady Midmain's hand, his eyes sought Sophia's. His betrothed turned her back on him, and busied herself at the escritoire. Lady Midmain abandoned her newspaper to comment that it was later than she had thought and to bustle away, leaving the betrothed couple alone.

He took two steps towards Sophia, and halted, his hand outstretched. "You asked to see me?"

She picked up an invitation and read it with care. Would he notice that her hand was shaking? "I? Why should I wish to see you?"

His hand dropped to his side. "Your aunt said that..."

"Oh, that. That was yesterday. A thousand and one things can happen to change a woman's mind from one day to the next. I cannot even remember now, what it was that made me wish to speak with you."

"Are you angry with me because I could not be at the Dalbys' last night? Did you not receive my note?"

She shrugged. "I may have done. I really cannot remember." She drew some writing paper towards her, and began to write. "Please forgive me—I am very busy this morning."

He did not take the hint and go. Instead he walked around the room, picked up Lady Midmain's newspaper, scanned it, and threw it down again.

He said, "I am sorry if I have given you cause to feel neglected of late. The political situation is..."

"I do not feel myself neglected, I assure you. I have plenty of cavaliers to squire me around. What you call your 'neglect' has suited me admirably."

Still he did not go. "How do you find your aunt?"

"Very well, thank you."

"And Thomas?"

"Dying."

She knew she had hurt him, for she saw his eyelids contract. At the same time, she felt her own throat constrict with tears. He walked away from her to the window, and took snuff.

"Give me one good reason," he said, "Why I should go through with this marriage."

The quill slipped from her fingers. "It would make a scandal."

"It would be assumed you had not come up to expectations. You asked me to release you. You said you had other prospects of marriage."

"My aunt would lock me in."

"Not if the affair were handled discreetly. I have business in the north. I could leave tomorrow morning for an indefinite period of time. I could write to Lady Midmain, saying I was detained and that the wedding must be postponed. She could have no reason then for being angry with you. She would continue to take you out in Society. The wedding can be postponed again and again. Some time this winter I shall be sent abroad, but by that time you should have landed yourself another husband. What do you say?"

She stood up, and papers fluttered to the floor, unregarded. "It is too late...if I do not get away from this house soon...oh, my wretched temper!"

"Is that an apology?"

"I suppose so."

"Come..." He extended his hand. Slowly she joined him at the window. "Yes, I thought so. You have not been sleeping well. Is something worrying you?" She shook her head. Pride forbade her to complain of his mistress. "Ring for your maid, and we will take a turn or two in the Park. When did you last go out walking?"

Dumbly, she allowed him to summon her cloak and hat. They walked through the teeming, noisy streets to the Park, and sauntered by the lake. She looked at the ducks, and up at the trees, which had shed nearly all their leaves, and wished she were once more at home in Hamberley. They bowed to this acquaintance and that, but stopped to exchange words with few, for the Park was more or less deserted at this unfashionable hour of the day. At last he guided her to a bridge, on which he could lean and watch the leaves float on the water beneath.

"You see," he said, "it would be very easy for us to tear each other to pieces. If we do not marry, we will end up as mortal enemies. If we do...I do not know what will happen. I am not one of those men who marry a spirited woman in order to break her. I don't want my home to be a battleground. Yet I feel compelled to marry you, in spite of the danger. I tell myself that with a little forbearance on both our parts, with the exercise of common sense....Are you with me, or against me? If you are against me, then let us break off the match and say we are well rid of each other. If you are with me, then you must say so." He waited, but she said nothing, her eyes on the water below. "I will not force you to marry me against your will. If we can agree on terms, then..."

"Did you know that Thomas was dying when you asked me to marry you?"

"No. Or at least, I did not consciously know." He put his hand under her chin, so that she was forced to look at him. "Is that the cause of your anger? You think I tricked you? Yet you must know that I would not compel you to take me into your bed. I will swear it, if you wish. I will never enter your room uninvited, whether Thomas lives or dies."

She sighed, and lowered her eyes to the water again. "I do not know what I want. I do not know who I am. I used to know, but I don't any longer. I am so tired, I could weep. All I can think of is escaping from my aunt, whatever the cost. I will marry you, if you still wish it, and I will try to keep my temper under control." She knew she sounded unenthusiastic. She placed her hand on his, as it rested on the bridge. "There is my hand on it. I will try to be the sort of wife you want, although, come to think of it, I don't know what sort of wife it is that you do want. My Aunt Midmain says..."

"You need not take your tone from her, once you are married. She has done much for you; although I deplore her methods, the results are highly satisfactory. I doubt if there is another woman in Town who could have turned you from a hoyden into a fashionable lady in so short a time. However, you need see little of her once you are the Countess of Rame."

"But will that not be awkward for you, politically? Have you not arranged for Sir Gregory to get some post or other in the Treasury?"

"I did not recommend him for the position. He thinks I did, that is all."

"Then why is he getting it? He has been kind enough to me in his fashion, but he is a lightweight, when all is said and done."

"The Duke of Newcastle has given him the post, thinking thereby to earn my gratitude. He misjudged me, as it happens. It is a matter of indifference to me whether your uncle receives a post in the Treasury or nothing at all."

"The Midmains live beyond their income, and have spent a lot of money on me in one way or another. I suppose I owe them something."

"I don't think so. Lady Midmain will be amply repaid by being able to refer to 'my niece, the Countess.'"

"But why...I beg your pardon. My aunt has told me again and again not to talk politics to gentlemen."

"Not every man who moves in Society is a fool, as I said before. If you choose your company wisely, you may talk politics as much as you please—if it interests you."

"It interests you, and therefore it interests me. No, I am not being truthful. I find it a fascinating subject, and I have noticed that my aunt Midmain, although she deplores my speaking of it, is also interested in politics."

"Your aunt would have adorned the post in the Treasury which is to go to her husband. The Tarrant women have more than their fair share of intelligence and spirit."

"Then I may ask you questions? Yes? Then why does the Duke of Newcastle seek to attach you to his party?"

"Because I own a great deal of land, and can therefore influence the election of men to the House of Commons. It is as simple as that. Also, his party is weaker—not weak, but less strong—in the House of Lords, and he would welcome my personal influence there. That is why he encourages me to put forward my bill to increase the penalty for smuggling."

"I do not understand about that. You must know it cannot succeed, for too many men in the Commons have relatives or friends who benefit from Free Trading."

"True, it will fail. Nevertheless smuggling is an iniquitous practice, and one day will be stamped out by military action, if steps are not taken to deal with it through the Preventives."

"But why do you concern yourself with such a measure while the country is facing much greater problems?"

"I am concerned with those, too. Who is not? But what can I do?"

"Fight."

"No, my arm is too weak. You said so yourself."

"To command troops, you do not need to wield a sword," she said, scornfully. He bowed. She thought he smiled, but he had turned his head away before she could be sure. She bit her lip. "Oh, I am sorry," she said. "I have broken our truce again, have I not? Tell me this; do you mean to vote with Newcastle in future? I would not wish to make any faux pas, politically, as your wife."

"I am not sure. I would prefer to remain outside the party lines. I owe my uncle a great deal; certainly I owe him more than I owe Newcastle. Neither man is faultless, but both have their points. I hope very much that I need never choose between them, and if I am sent abroad soon the contingency need never arise."

"You are not anxious for power, then?"

"Not that sort of power. I lack my uncle's sweeping powers of invention, or Newcastle's love of administration. I like to be occupied, and to know what is going on; sometimes to pull a string here, or push a man into action there; but I do not want the center of the stage for myself." He smiled at her. "And before you say that I am not fitted for the center of the stage, I will do so. I need to be kept occupied, and by great good fortune, it appears that I shall be given a post which will occupy me without tying me to the fortunes of one party or the other. Now what of you? What is your goal in life?"

She looked up at the trees, and down at the water. She turned her back on him and looked all round her. She shook her head and sighed.

"I wish I knew."

The wedding day approached. Sophia was apathetic, but dutiful. She no longer felt the urge to lose her temper and scream, even at Philip. She went wherever her aunt Midmain was invited, and was mildly amused to learn that "the Tarrant Rose" had won a reputation as a charming girl. Her frequent visits to her Aunt Nan and to Thomas were put down to her credit, and greatly increased her popularity. She had become, in short, the latest "rage."

She saw much of Marjorie Bladen, because Sir John had taken to calling on Lady Midmain several times a week. The Bladens lodged with an elderly aunt of Sir John's in the City, and seemed determined to make a lengthy stay in Town. Sir John had spent a good deal of money on equipping his daughter with a new wardrobe, and made sure that she was seen everywhere. He made no secret of the fact that he wished to marry again, and that he felt a grown-up daughter was a hindrance to his plans. The sooner he could get her married off the better, he confided to Sophia; but not to just anyone; the man should have a title, or at the very least, a respectable fortune of his own.

Poor Marjorie did not seem to be enjoying her visit to London. She was not as adaptable as Sophia, either in mind or figure. She continued to behave in exactly the same way as she had done in the country, and to look like a rosy-cheeked milkmaid, dressed in someone else's finery. Her conversation was all of Hamberley and what the country might be looking like, and fears that Betty the cook might not have remembered to make enough rose-hip syrup against the winter. She went to the opera and said it reminded her of the doves in the dovecote at the end of her herb garden; she went to balls and said she doubted she would ever get the hang of the quadrille. She stared at Sophia's hooped dresses and wondered aloud how Sophia had learned to manage them.

"You'll never catch a husband at this rate," said Sophia, who was at once exasperated and amused by her friend's stolidity.

"I don't need to," replied Marjorie. "I am going to wait for Jasper. Oh, I know I may have to wait for years, and that it will be difficult to persuade Father to accept the match even then, but I don't mind forgoing my fortune, and Jasper doesn't mind, either."

"But your father has other plans for you, doesn't he? Did I not hear him talk about a match with young Lord Courtenay? He is very pleasant, I believe, and would make you a far better husband than my hotheaded rebel of a brother."

"He might," said Marjorie, folding her lips.

"Then there is Mr. Dalby, who is pining for a sympathetic

169

listener. Why don't you talk to him about farming, instead of sitting mum when he calls?"

"I shall marry Jasper, or die an old maid."

"Your father will not allow you to..."

"Some men never grow up," said Marjorie, with a wisdom beyond her years. "My father is just like a spoilt child. He wanted Tarrant Hall, and because he couldn't have it, he spoiled his chances of marrying you. He took a dislike to the Earl of Rame, because he conceived that Philip had made him look foolish. I have told him that it will do no good talking wildly about taking revenge on Philip, but he will do so. I blame that man Farrow in part. If he were not in my father's service, I am sure things would have been smoothed over long ago."

Sophia was silent. She did not like the development, either. Sir John had brought Mr. Farrow to Town with him, and talked to anyone who was prepared to listen about the unfairness of the former bailiff's dismissal. Mr. Farrow went with Sir John wherever his master went, and was frequently seen whispering in his ear. What was perhaps even more sinister, was the recent appearance of the "Death's Head," Greenwood, as a footman in Sir John's entourage. Farrow and Greenwood were very close. Neither Marjorie nor Sophia liked the men, but there was nothing they could do about the situation.

The two girls had been sitting alone in the drawing-room, but presently Lady Midmain came in, and company began to arrive. Sir Benjamin, Mr. Dalby, and then Mr. Carramine, with Sir Gregory Midmain standing on tiptoe to whisper in his ear...Mrs. Dalby locked in confidential talk with Lady Lincoln...Lord Lincoln looking somewhat jaded...and then the butler announced the Earl of Rame and Miss Tarrant, and the company fell silent.

This was the first time that Miss Nan had visited her married sister, although they had exchanged messages through Sophia. Miss Tarrant advanced into the room at the Earl's side, smiling, perfectly at her ease. Lady Midmain rustled to her sister's side, and they kissed each other's cheek. Miss Nan was looking very distinguished in her new black silk, her bright eyes and ready smile contrasting attractively with her white hair. Most of the company could already claim acquaintance with her, and as Lady Midmain introduced the rest to her sister, Sophia saw that she need not have feared what might happen if Miss Nan were to go about in Society.

"What a remarkable woman your aunt is," Lady Lincoln said to Sophia. "So sympathetic, so distinguished, and yet so self-effacing. It is no wonder that Philip adores her, but I doubt he will keep her. Dowry or no dowry, she will be mistress of her own home before long."

"Who? I don't understand?"

Lady Lincoln smiled, and indicated with her fan where Mr. Carramine was busily settling Miss Nan into a chair. "He is always to be found at Philip's house, nowadays. Didn't you know?"

No, Sophia had not known. The Tarrants had been close neighbors with the Carramines, they had constantly been in each other's company, and yet Sophia had never seen anything to indicate that Mr. Carramine was enamored of her aunt. Could it be so? Might the removal to London, the Earl's patronage, and the new dresses have opened Mr. Carramine's eyes to her aunt's attractions? It did look very much like it. Was Sophia pleased? She could not say. She thought her chief emotion was one of surprise.

There was no time to dwell on the matter, for here came Sir John Bladen to pay his respects. He bristled at the sight of the Earl, and put his hand on his sword.

"Good Gad!" said Sir John, with a jocularity which verged on insolence. "I hardly recognized you, my lord. Fine feathers, eh?"

Like Lord Lincoln, the Earl was in Court dress, having called at Lady Midmain's on his way to St. James'. Because he was in Court dress, he was not wearing a sword. Would he take exception to Sir John's tone? He decided not to do so. He raised his eyebrows, bowed, and turned away to speak to Sir Gregory.

Sir John could not let well alone. He caught at the Earl's sleeve. "Did you hear that I have taken on two men who used to be in your service? Your bailiff, and a footman who used to work for you. They have some pretty tales to tell of you. What do you say to that?"

"Merely that I hope they will serve you better than they served me." The Earl bowed again, and moved a step away from Sir John. It was apparent that he wished for peace.

"Talking of service," said Sir John, so loudly that everyone stopped talking to glance his way. "I hear you have been

paying attentions to my daughter of late. You will allow me
to tell you, my lord, that I find such attentions undesirable.
I will not have my daughter served as you have served Miss
Sophia."

"What?"

"What does he mean?"

Sophia saw that Sir John meant to be offensive. Had he
been drinking? The insult had been given in front of everyone, and must be answered. The Earl's hand had gone to his
side, as if seeking his sword. Marjorie had her hands over
her mouth, her eyes reflecting Sophia's horror. No one seemed
to know how to avert a duel. The Earl's arm was not strong;
Sir John would know that. Miss Nan caught Sophia's eye,
and indicated what she must do.

Sophia moved between the two men, taking Sir John's arm
in hers, and drawing him away to the fire. "Indeed, Sir John,
you must not be angry if Philip speaks with Marjorie, for he
does so at my request. Only see what a little polish has done
for us country mice. Do you like this new silk? It came from
Lyons, I believe. A glass of claret? It is your favorite. Come,
sit down beside me, and tell me all the news of home. How
did the harvest go? Did you need extra men?"

Out of the corner of her eye she saw Philip bend over
Marjorie, talking. The frightened look had gone from the
girl's face, and she listened, her hands clasped and eyes lowered. She frowned, and raised her eyes to the Earl's face,
seeming to ask a question without words. He turned his
shoulder on the room and maneuvered the girl into the window. Now Sophia could not see Philip's face, but she could
still see Marjorie's, glowing in sudden radiance. The girl had
both her hands on Philip's arm, and was talking...pleading
with him? Philip's head went from side to side. He moved
round, so that he could review the room, but everyone else
had plunged back into conversation. Marjorie still clung to
Philip's arm, talking. He was still shaking his head but smiling, too, as if with a little more persuasion he would do whatever it was she wanted. There; the minx had won her point,
and what was more, she had gone on tiptoe to kiss Philip's
cheek. How dared she! Sophia herself had never...and he
was actually laughing as he bent to receive her caress.

The Earl and the Lincolns were leaving. Marjorie stayed
by the window, looking out on the street. Philip was at her
side, bowing over her hand, saying something about haste.

He would leave his carriage for Miss Nan, and go with the Lincolns to Court. He had time for Marjorie, it seemed, but none for Sophia. Sir John bristled at her side. What could she do? She smiled, and said what seemed to be appropriate, and wondered how much more of his unfaithfulness she was supposed to accept. First the lady in St. James', and now Marjorie...perhaps Sir John had been right....

Sir Gregory was at the Earl's side, eager to establish himself as a man of importance. "What, off to Court again? Is the King going to Hanover? They said he would, yesterday, but today I hear the contrary. Are there to be celebrations for the King's birthday at the end of the month, or are there not? That is what I asked the Duke. Newcastle, you know. We are on the most intimate of terms. I can tell you, in confidence, that the Duke is a very worried man these days."

"What do you think of that, Philip?" Lord Lincoln's eyes were bright with mischief.

The Earl appeared bored. "By Gad, what should I think? I never meddle in backstairs politics." Lord Lincoln put his handkerchief before his face and emitted a sound which was something between a sneeze and a cough. The Earl's mouth twitched. "I have far more important things to think about than politics. My speech, for instance. I have to give my speech next week, and it is worrying the life out of me. Ought I to commit it to memory, that is the question? His Majesty was kind enough to ask me to read part of it to him last night."

Lord Lincoln winked at Sophia. "Almost burst a blood vessel, laughing."

The Earl shook his head. "I only hope that my peers will not give me the same reception." He bowed over Sophia's hand, and left with the Lincolns, still smiling.

"What was all that about?" Sophia demanded of Mr. Carramine, who was now waiting for her to turn to him.

"Don't you know? Ah. Perhaps better not. Your aunt Midmain's not a fool by any means, but your uncle might blab anything to anybody. First-class booby. No offense meant, of course. My congratulations; you handled Sir John well. Unnecessary and indeed inconvenient to have a duel at this moment. Besides, Philip might easily kill him."

"How? His arm is not strong?"

"The challenged person has the right to name his weapons, has he not? Philip is a crack shot, I believe." He nodded. "Keep Sir John cool, if you can. He's an ignorant man and

173

a fool, and I don't like his association with Farrow and Greenwood, who feed their master's ill-humor. They think they know something which might embarrass Philip if it were generally known. Perhaps they do. Perhaps they don't. Better not to bring it out into the open, anyway. Trust you to see that they do nothing foolish. Don't look so surprised. You could manage any man, if you so chose."

But not Philip, she thought. I don't understand him well enough.

It was the night before the wedding, and Lady Midmain was giving a formal dinner for all those most closely involved. Two courses, each consisting of ten dishes, were set on the board, and removed before sweetmeats. Everyone except Sophia, suffering in tightly-laced corsets, did justice to the food. Philip pressed her to eat this and that. His attentions to her were remarked on with smiles and, now and then, a bawdy jest. Sophia smiled and said everything that was polite, and wondered what would happen if she were to faint.

She did not faint, but it could not be said that she understood the business which was transacted in Sir Gregory's study afterwards. The lawyers explained the settlement which Philip was making on her and her heirs, she was told how much pin money she was to have...talk of reversions, of if's and an's and in the case of the death of...or alternatively in the event of...She smiled and signed her name where indicated, and gave her hand to the lawyers each in turn, and wondered why they all wore the same kind of wig. Were there two lawyers, or only one? No, there was only one. Why had she thought there were two?

Someone was holding a glass of wine to her lips. She drank. It was Philip, of course. He noticed everything. She looked up into his face and wondered what he was thinking. Had he turned to the lady at St. James', and to Marjorie Bladen, because his future wife had barred him from her bedroom? Had he done it to make her jealous? And if so, did she feel jealous? She did not know.

Her Aunt Nan was at her side, looking anxious. Sophia smiled, and said wasn't it foolish of her to feel faint, and ought they not to rejoin the guests? Then back into the drawing-room. A curtsey to a great-aunt here, a curtsey to Lord Carteret, who seemed to have forgiven her for not being Lady

Millicent, because he smiled at her.... Who was Lady Millicent? Sophia could not even remember what she looked like....

A chair was set beside her, and she sank into it. Philip, again. The noise was tremendous. She smiled, and said yes, she was a little tired. Faces came and went, but Philip stood over her, taking the burden of conversation on himself. Only then it was Marjorie Bladen's turn to pass before her, and there was something in the girl's face which made Sophia look up. The girl was smiling up at Philip, but the smile was not the sort of smile which you gave acquaintances or even friends; it was the smile of conspirators, or lovers. Yes, Marjorie's smile was full of meaning, and Philip—the traitor— was stepping away from Sophia's side, drawing Marjorie away, while he chatted to her lightly about the state of the roads...and the false jade was passing a closely-folded note to Philip, and he was taking it and sliding it into his pocket, still talking. No one but Sophia, watching so carefully, could possibly have seen it. Then Marjorie was bending to kiss Sophia, and Sophia jerked her head back. And Philip had noticed her rudeness, and Marjorie's start of surprise, and he was placing his hand on Marjorie's arm to prevent the girl from showing her alarm, and talking all the time. And the room grew hotter, and Marjorie's anxious face sank back among the guests and at last people were leaving, and Philip had gone, too. Where? To his mistress at St. James'? Or to meet Marjorie somewhere in the City?

Sophia lay in bed, listening to the clock strike hour after hour, looking up at the tester over the bed, and thought of Marjorie and Philip lying naked on a bed together, laughing at her....

A tall, wasp-waisted girl with powdered hair and painted face stood and looked at herself in the mirror. Her dress was of white satin with a faint stripe of silver running through it. The hoop was enormous, and the overskirt tied back with knots of roses and pink bows. There were more pink bows edging the elbow-length sleeves, and down the front of the bodice, too.

"I shall never wear pink again," said Sophia to her reflection.

"You must," insisted her aunt Midmain. "Remember, you

are the Tarrant Rose, and it is expected that you wear pink
and carry roses, always. You have set quite a fashion for it.
You are a legend."

"Then I will create a new fashion, when I am no longer
the Tarrant Rose."

Perkins fastened on heavy diamond earrings—Philip's gift
to his bride. "What would miss like, instead of pink?"

"Dark blue, very plain, with a small hoop."

Lady Midmain cried out in horror, but Perkins nodded.
"Miss has excellent taste. With her height and coloring, she
might succeed in setting a new fashion in simpler clothes."

A maid brought in a posy of white roses from her betrothed, and a last-minute present from Mr. Carramine in
the shape of a chicken-skin fan. Then it was time for her to
go downstairs. She took a last look around. She had been
very unhappy in this house, but at least she had known her
place. The future was a blank.

She turned sideways to maneuver her hoop through the
doorway, and followed her aunt Midmain down the stairs.
Aunt Nan was downstairs already; Sophia would have liked
Aunt Nan with her while she dressed, but Lady Midmain's
generosity did not extend so far as that. The sisters were on
civil if distant terms with each other. Sir Gregory appeared,
pulling at the collar of a new coat. He enquired if Sophia
were ready and asked his wife if she thought his new coat
becoming. Perkins shot down the backstairs. The servants
would all be lined up at the back of the drawing-room to
watch as Sophia was given in marriage to the Earl of Rame,
and Perkins would not wish to miss a second of her triumph.
It was no easy matter, as she told her fellow servants, to turn
a country girl into a Countess.

The stairs were slippery. She must not fall. Her uncle was
worried about some wine he had ordered. The double doors
into the drawing-room had been opened for them. Her uncle
was pinching her arm. It was hard to smile and smile while
he was pinching her arm. . . . There were banks of white flowers on either side of the doorway, and most of the furniture
had been removed from the room, to accommodate the guests.
The parson was waiting; his teeth were uneven, and his wig
didn't look clean, but he was a Man of God and able to tie
the knot.

Philip was wearing a scarlet coat, laced with gold. He
looked very stiff and remote. His hand was no warmer than

176

hers. She closed her eyes for a second, and the room seemed to rock under her feet. Philip's handclasp turned into a grip whose strength pulled her upright once more. Had anyone else noticed that she had almost fainted? A ring was slipped on her finger. It seemed too big. Instinctively she clenched her hand, pressing the ring down her finger with her thumb. Philip bent to kiss her cheek. It was gracefully done. She moved her lips into a smile, and curtseyed to him...and proffered her cheek again and again...Mr. Carramine...Lord Carteret with his dragon of a mother, Baroness Granville...the Lincolns....

Was that the time? It was amazing how time passed. Someone was urging that they witness the ceremony of bride and bridegroom being bedded, but Philip was laughing them away, saying that he had been through all that before, and wanted a little privacy this time.

Then...how did it happen that she was being handed into a coach when she could not remember having left the house? Had she said everything that was proper to her uncle and aunt? Yes, she must have done so, for they were smiling and waving from their doorstep. How odd to think that they would go back into the house and continue to talk of the wine and whether the second best silver would do for dinner, and if such and such an invitation might be looked for...

Whereas Sophia would be somewhere else, thinking of...what?

Her hoops took up all the space on one side of the Earl's carriage and so he sat opposite her. He was looking at his watch as the coach drew away from the Midmain's.

"Aunt Nan!" she cried. "Ought she not to have come with us?"

"Mr. Carramine has already taken her home. The heat and the noise were rather trying for her, and she was concerned about Thomas, who is not feeling very stout today. She will be waiting for you at your new home." His matter-of-fact air calmed her. She leaned back against the cushions, thinking that his coach was better appointed than the Midmain's.

She asked, "Did you wear your uniform to remind me that our marriage is to be a fight to the death?"

"You are hardly capable of bearing arms at the moment. I suggest that we resume hostilities only when you are restored to full health."

"A truce?"

"If you will."

"Yet I am sure you had some reason for donning a soldier's uniform today. If it was not meant as a warning to me, then..."

"Can you keep a secret?" He leaned forward and took her hand. She nodded. "In an hour's time Henry Lincoln and I, both dressed in the uniforms we wore when we served in Flanders, will stage a patriotic scene at His Majesty's levee. You picture it? Two ex-soldiers, recently married, on their knees imploring the King to take them back into his service...seeking permission to raise regiments...fight the Pretender single-handed, and so on. It is all arranged that Henry will do all the talking, for I am no hand at such fustian. All I shall have to do is kneel at the right moment, and pull the appropriate faces."

"But what a ridiculous thing to do! The King will never accept your offer! Everyone knows that he is far too fond of both you and Lord Lincoln."

"I sincerely hope so." He smiled. "Of course, it is all a sham, but such ploys have their uses. I shall not enjoy doing it, but if it means that other men will come forward to place their services at the King's disposal, then I don't mind. You said I ought to fight for the King, and this is my way of doing so; there are more ways than one of fighting, you see. To whip up patriotic sentiment, at a time when His Majesty is unsure of the feelings of the British, is surely worth a regiment or two."

"What if he takes you at your word? You do not wish to rejoin the Army, do you?"

"Henry has wagered his new hunter against my Prince that 'Someone' will rumble us before he is halfway through making his offer. Myself, I think we will be rumbled as we approach the King. He is no fool."

"You would leave me on our wedding day?" She gasped at his effrontery.

"Henry said that leaving you on our wedding day would make a very telling point in his speech. I shall explain that I have left you prostrate, in bed, with the doctors hovering over you."

"What nonsense!"

"It will be the truth. You are about to be handed over to your aunt and the doctors, to be dosed with physic and put

178

to bed and given sleeping draughts and plenty of nourishing food until you begin to look something like the girl I met in the spring."

"What?"

"And if you refuse to take your draughts, I daresay your aunt will hold your nose until you do. Or perhaps, if you ask very nicely, she will sweeten her potions to make them more palatable, since you are in such a very weak state." He was enjoying himself. "And as for your stays, your new maid has orders that they are to be let out six inches..."

"None of my dresses will fit!"

"...and she has two sempstresses waiting to alter your wardrobe accordingly. You should have at least two dresses ready to wear tomorrow, although your aunt thinks—and I agree with her—that it would do you good not to receive or make any visits for at least a week. It will be thought that your fatigue is the result of my attentions, or of my wish to leave you to rejoin the Army. Either way, no one will think any the worse of you if you do not appear in public for a week. You must be presented to the King again, in your new role, but that can wait until you are better."

She began to laugh. She was on the verge of hysteria. He took hold of her hands. Would he slap her? She thought he might. She fought for control. It would never do to arrive at her new home in hysterics. They were turning into the square.

She had beaten him in the country, and he had beaten her in Town. What would happen in the months to come? She stared at him with narrowed eyes, and he stared back. They were like wrestlers, studying each other's strengths and weaknesses against the resumption of the fight.

The coach stopped. A footman opened the door, and let down the steps.

"Welcome home!" cried Miss Nan.

Chapter Eleven

The winter nights were long and dark in Edinburgh, and now that the Jacobites had left the city, a slack feeling pervaded the streets. In the private room behind the tap of a small tavern near one of the city gates, two gentlemen sat over the remains of a substantial meal. The weather had taken a turn for the worse, and the clothes of the older man were travelstained. He was soberly, but well dressed; perhaps a merchant in a profitable line of business. The landlord heard him observe that he was lucky to have arrived in Edinburgh before the city gates had closed for the night. There was a Jacobite cockade on the table. The landlord thought nothing of it, for there had been plenty of them around recently.

The younger of the two men was neatly but poorly dressed in clothes such as a clerk might wear. Perhaps he was in the employ of the merchant? He wore a scratch wig, by no means new, and now and then he eased his shoulders in his drab coat, as if it were too tight for him. Few would have recognized the once elegant Sir Jasper Tarrant in this disguise. He had put on weight since the spring, and gave the impression of being much heavier and older than the lad who had so lightheartedly set out to make his fortune. He had gone under many aliases since that day, first in Britanny, and then in Scotland, and he was known to the Government department who employed him as David Vere.

"I'd hardly have known you," said Mr. Carramine, when the landlord was out of earshot.

"I've learned a lot, this last year," agreed Jasper.

"But not enough to trust Mr. Stone?"

"Not now. I know the kind of men I have to deal with—gallows birds, every one of his couriers. I feel safer, sending my dispatches direct to Philip. I can trust him to work for my interests, but who knows who might get the credit for my work if I sent my dispatches direct to Mr. Stone?"

"Philip charged me to tell you that you have done enough to earn yourself a commission. Why don't you return to London with me?"

"Not now. I want to see this thing through. You heard that the Pretender has taken our bait, and is quite convinced that a large number of English gentlemen are only waiting for him to cross the Border to rise on his behalf? You should have seen the letter I wrote to him, in my father's name. It was a masterpiece of suggestion and innuendo. I had a drinking companion called James Gordon, who is a lieutenant in the Pretender's Army. He's only a young lad," said Jasper, who was no older himself. "He was a fisherman by trade and one day his chief sent out men to round up everyone who could bear arms to fight for him, and hey, presto! James becomes a soldier. And a very bad one, too. He thought I was interested in joining the Pretender, and I had to laugh at his expression, for half of him wanted to convince me that the rebels were about to sweep King George off the throne, and the other half wanted to warn me off. Then I told him I was acting for some highly-placed gentlemen at the English court, and that I had orders to pass secret documents through to the Pretender. He was easily gulled. He went off with those false 'invitations' as happy as you might wish, and lo and behold, the Pretender and his Army marched out of Edinburgh two days later. I rode out to watch them pass, all five thousand of them."

"Did you find out where the rebels were going from Edinburgh?"

"Yes, that was easy. They said they were going this way, and then that, but the tents are going direct to Carlisle, so that's where they mean to end up. Did you know, the rebels didn't have any maps of England? They didn't know which towns were on the road to London, or even which road to take?

181

All they knew was that they had to go south and east."

"Carlisle? Well, all the Border towns have been sent reputable officers to take charge of their defenses, and Wade is ready and waiting." Mr. Carramine picked up the Jacobite cockade. It was formed of five bows of white silk, tied in a knot. On it was printed a laurel wreath, and the words *With Charles our brave and merciful P.S. we'll greatly fall, or nobly save our country.*

"Now the rebels have gone," said Mr. Carramine, "you might discover for us exactly how many of these have been made. Also, how many pairs of shoes were extracted from the citizens of Edinburgh, and how much money was handed over."

"Not I," said Jasper. "I'm off after the rebels in the morning. You can get someone else to tie up the loose ends for you."

"But Philip said..."

"I'd do much for Philip. He showed me how to turn the situation to my own advantage, and at the same time led me into the biggest adventure a man could wish for. He doesn't understand me, though. He thinks that when this affair is done, I'll be happy to go back to Tarrant Hall and lease it from him. I told him clearly enough that all I want out of life is to make my own way in the Army, and that I'll never take his charity."

"What about Miss Marjorie? Has she no place in your plans?"

Jasper was silent. Mr. Carramine sighed, put his hand in his pocket, drew out a folded note, and handed it to the lad. Then he rose from the table, and went to peer out of the window, in order to give Jasper a chance to read his letter unobserved.

Rain beat against the curtainless window. Underneath his feet the flagged stones were chill. Mr. Carramine shivered. He had not particularly wished to make the trip to Edinburgh, but Mr. Stone had heard that food was being sent over from Ireland to the Jacobites in large quantities. Also, there were some men in Edinburgh whom it seemed politic to interview. Exactly how much money had the Pretender managed to extract from the city? That was the question.

It had been impossible for Philip to leave Town while the King was still so undecided, and yet someone had to go. Mr. Carramine had volunteered for the mission, because he had

182

wished to persuade Jasper to return to Town with him. Perhaps Miss Marjorie's letter might succeed where he had failed.

Jasper's voice broke across Mr. Carramine's reflections. "What is this about trouble between Philip and Sir John? And is Marjorie really being pressed to marry someone else?"

Mr. Carramine returned to the table. "Sir John is drinking heavily. I think perhaps he has become a little unbalanced. He dreams of wedding his daughter to a peer, or a man of immense fortune. He has taken a dislike to Philip and makes slighting remarks about him, which Philip has so far chosen to ignore. It would be extremely awkward if he were involved in a duel now, when so much depends on him. Sir John mistakes Philip's forbearance for cowardice, and calls him 'Philip the Bold,' in a sneering tone."

"No one but a fool would believe that Philip is a coward."

"There are always plenty of fools about, ready to believe the worst of those in the public eye. Moreover, Sir John has taken two of Philip's ex-servants into his own employ, and thereby has learned something—not much, but something—of what happened at Hamberley in the spring. Sir John misunderstands the little he knows, but rumors are beginning to spread about Town that Philip was involved in some shady transaction or other. Then your sister let slip that Philip and Lord Lincoln had planned their supposedly spontaneous plea to lay their swords at His Majesty's feet."

"Sophia? What has she to do with this? I thought—there is something in Marjorie's letter—are Sophia and Marjorie on bad terms?"

"I'm afraid so. Your sister misinterprets Philip's kindness to Marjorie."

"But he is quite old!" Jasper shouted with laughter.

"Miss Marjorie may think so, but I doubt if the Countess does."

"How odd to hear her spoken of as 'the Countess.' Does she grace her new position?"

"She goes everywhere, and is greatly admired, but she is escorted by Mr. Dalby and Sir John, rather than by her husband. We have ceased to use the library of his house for our conferences, because Philip does not feel she can be trusted."

Jasper reddened. "You insult my sister, sir."

"Jasper, I have known you both since the day you were

born. I love you both, but I am aware of your faults. Sophia is acting like a spoilt child. Philip requested that she see less of Mr. Dalby and Sir John, and she ignored his request. He confided in her about Lincoln's ploy, and she blabbed of it to Marjorie for one, and possibly to others."

"Marjorie would not betray us!"

"No, I do not think she would, but she may have told her father, or he may have forced the truth out of her. She says not, but..." He shrugged. "Either way, Sir John got to hear of it, and made fun of Philip because of it. It is not pleasant for a man like Philip to have Sir John mock him. Setting hurt pride on one side, Philip thinks it would be unwise to let Sophia have access to our secrets at this moment. Suppose he told her everything, and she considered she had cause to be angry with him, and told what she knew? We cannot afford to have our spy system a household word, and above all, we cannot afford to let the Pretender know that he has been duped as to the number of active Jacobites in England. If he learned that, he'd turn straight round and come back to Edinburgh, to wait until his brother Henry and the French are able to invade these shores some time next year. In such case, we would be let in for a long, costly and terrible civil war." He laid his hand on Jasper's shoulder. "My boy, you have done enough here. Will you not come back with me to London, and see what you can do to help?"

"What? Leave the field of battle to solve Philip's matrimonial problems? What nonsense. Tell him to beat her. That's what my father used to do when she got out of hand."

"I never noticed that a beating improved Sophia's temper in the old days, and I don't think Philip is the man to beat his wife. Promise me you will think over what I have said. We have other men able to take your place here, but we cannot replace Philip."

Jasper laughed, to hide his hurt. What? Was he of less account than a man who hid behind a desk in London? A man who avoided a duel with Sir John, because it was politically inexpedient?

"I will think about it," he lied, "and send you a letter with my decision."

Sophia, Countess of Rame, strode across her daintily-furnished drawing-room in a temper. Her silken skirts caught the leg of a fragile table, and it overturned. "Damn!" she cried, and jerked her silk free. She did not like the room, with its countless mirrors, each reflecting her angry face, and still less did she like the owner of all this magnificence.

"He tricked me!" she said. "I wondered why everyone was looking at me and then nodding to each other, knowingly. Lady Millicent—the cat!—told me why this morning. Everyone thinks I'm pregnant, because I am now going about with a natural, instead of a pinched-in waistline! Philip made such a point of saying that tight-lacing was bad for my health, and now...oh, I could kill him!"

"Could you really, dear?" Miss Nan placidly sewed away by the window. "Well, it's your own fault if you're not pregnant, isn't it?"

"Oh!" Sophia stamped her foot, and then ran to her aunt's side and sank to her knees, burying her hot face in her aunt's skirts. "How is Thomas?" she asked, at last. "The doctor wouldn't let me in to see him last night or today."

"Very patient. He knows he's dying, but he's so tired that he doesn't mind. We do what we can for him, Philip, and Mr. Denbigh and I."

"Everyone but me. Since I am not pregnant, I don't see why I shouldn't be allowed in his room." Miss Nan said nothing to that, but continued to sew. Sophia fingered the hem of her aunt's dress. "Do you know what Lady Millicent told me today, Aunt? She said that that woman in St. James' Street whom Philip visits is going to bear his child in the spring. It's not fair, is it? He's put me in an impossible position. He's proved he can sire children, and now he's made everyone think I'm pregnant, and I'm not, and when people realize that I'm not, they're going to point the finger at me and say I'm barren, and that he ought to get rid of me."

Miss Nan made a sound half way between a cough and a hiccup. "Really, dear? Then you'd better change your tactics, hadn't you?"

Sophia wriggled, but did not reply.

"For a start," said Miss Nan, "you'd better stop seeing so much of Mr. Dalby and Sir John. Then you might do something to make this house more comfortable for Philip, and arrange for food to be available at any hour that he comes in, cold and tired and hungry."

"It's his own fault if he's not here for meals."

"He is a very busy man. He has handed over the management of the household to you. I cannot look after the house and manage the sickroom as well."

"I don't see why he has to pretend he's so busy now. He's given his speech, and been heartily laughed at for a fool."

"Sophia!"

"Well, it's true," said Sophia, in a muffled tone. "Everyone says so."

"By 'everyone,' you mean Sir John and Sir Benjamin and suchlike fribbles. They know nothing of politics. Men of substance—yes, and the newspapers, too—reported on his speech respectfully. He is not a natural orator, I agree. He found making a speech in public a great trial, but it had to be done and he did it. Far from making a fool of himself, I am reliably informed that the speech did him a great deal of good politically. As for Sir John, old friend though he is, I am become almost ashamed of him. His jealousy of Philip leads him into saying the wildest things. Was it he who told you of Mrs. O'Dell?"

Sophia lifted her shoulders. "Perhaps. Is that her name? An Irish adventuress, I suppose. They say she is fat and forty. What Philip can see in her, I don't know."

"A sympathetic personality, I suppose. You don't exactly make him welcome when you see him, do you?"

"Ought I to do so? A man who spends his days locked in his library and toad-eating the King, and his nights in another woman's arms?"

Miss Nan smiled. "I must say, I would like to see Philip toad-eating anyone. Child, child! Whose words are you quoting? You don't really believe them, do you? Philip has been occupied with arrangements for celebrating the King's birthday. I am sure he would have been delighted to tell you about his work, if you had asked. As for Mrs. O'Dell, rumor lies if it says she is his mistress. Now why don't you ask him to spend an evening with you?"

"I'd sooner die," said Sophia through her teeth. "Why, he's made it clear he thinks I told everyone the truth about his playing at being a soldier."

"Didn't you, dear? You looked so guilty when he spoke of it that..."

"I told Marjorie, that's all. Who else did I see that week? I was kept in bed, as you know, and fed on pap until I could

186

have screamed. I had no opportunity of telling anyone else. Admit it! I only told Marjorie because I thought it would make her see Philip for what he really is, a double-dealing..."

Miss Nan raised her hand sharply. Sophia stopped. Noiselessly, Miss Nan crept to the door, and pulled it open. There was a scuffling sound outside on the landing.

"Who was that?" asked Sophia, staring. "Someone was listening to us?"

"Perhaps that was how the tale got about," said Miss Nan, frowning. "She was too quick for me. I only saw a woman's skirt as she whisked around the corner. I think I'd better mention it to Philip."

"Will you tell him that it was not I who told Sir John they were only playing at being soldiers?"

"If I am right, and there is a spy in the household, then Sir John would not have known, if you had kept your mouth shut. But I will do what I can for you, if you in turn will be kinder to Philip."

"Perhaps I will; perhaps I won't." The Countess of Rame inspected her image in the mirror over the fireplace. "I can't make up my mind whether to powder my hair or not, when I sit for my portrait. What do you think?"

For once, the Earl and his Countess were to dine and go on to a ball together. Philip was about to go up to his room to dress, when a messenger brought in an urgent dispatch from 'David Vere.' The rebels had crossed the Esk into England on November 8th. By riding hard, Jasper had reached Carlisle ahead of them, but had nothing but bad news to report. A certain Captain Durand had been sent from London to take charge of the city's defenses for the Crown, but although he was by no means incompetent, he could not reverse the neglect of years in the short space of time left to him. Once upon a time, Carlisle had been a well fortified Border town, but the recent period of prosperity and the union with Scotland had made it seem unnecessary to keep the city's defenses in good repair. The walls were crumbling, and although there were guns in the castle, children had been allowed to play on and around them, and in consequence certain vital components were conspicuous by their absence. Captain Durand was not young, but he had driven himself and everyone else hard in his efforts to put the city into a state of defense, hampered by inertia on the part of the inhabitants of Carlisle. The local militia, hurriedly called together, were as badly armed and trained as the Jacobites and far less enthusiastic about fighting. The soldiers on garrison duty were superannuated invalids who had fought under Marlborough and Eugene in the days of Good Queen Anne, and were either halt, blind or lame. In short, if the Pretender's spy system were anything like as good as the Government's, Carlisle was as good as lost, unless....

"Bad news?" asked Mr. Denbigh, hurrying into the library. "I heard that another dispatch had arrived."

"Bad news," confirmed Philip. "I must take this to Mr. Stone at once. If we can get Wade moving in time, then we can save Carlisle. If not, the city is lost."

"My God! Carlisle? One hardly credits that an English city can be conquered. I can hardly believe it. Yes, yes; you must go. But...were you not going out with the Countess this evening?"

Philip debated with himself whether he might safely entrust the dispatch to someone else to deliver, but decided against doing so. Mr. Stone might be easily run to earth, or he might not. If the Duke of Newcastle were to get the dispatch straight away, action might or might not be taken; the probability was that nothing would be done, while the Duke worried the problem around for a day or so. If Mr. Carramine had returned from the north...but he had not. No, there was nothing for it, but that Philip must go.

"I suppose the fate of Carlisle is of more importance than my attendance at a ball," said he, fingering the note which Jasper had enclosed with his dispatch. Marjorie Bladen was to be at the ball tonight. It was a thousand pities that Sophia was no longer on good terms with the girl. He must find some means of getting Jasper's note to Marjorie tomorrow, but he could not possibly call at Sir John's lodgings. If only Sophia could be trusted....

It was Martinmas Saturday, November 9th. The town woke early, not because the Jacobites were said to be in the vicinity, but because it was a feast day and a market day, and the citizens of Carlisle saw no reason why business should not go on as usual. The country-folk trooped to town

188

as usual; it did not occur to them that the Jacobite army might use the same roads.

Some of the clergy had climbed the cathedral tower with a spyglass to see what there was to be seen. They were pleasantly excited, but not unduly worried by the approach of the Jacobites. It was all in the nature of a holiday treat to them, for General Wade was known to be nearby to protect them from harm.

Jasper climbed the tower, too, and asked permission to join the clergy. He was so obviously a gentleman—though judging by his clothes, one in poor circumstances—that they did not object. Besides, a small party of mounted Jacobites was coming into view, pushing through the countryfolk on their way to market. The clergy told each other that they'd soon see some action, but after a while this scouting party withdrew. Jasper, who had brought his own glass with him, looked grim. From his vantage point he could appreciate how hard Captain Durand's task was. If the Jacobites chose to march into Carlisle through the countryfolk, then how could the captain bring his guns—those that were working—to bear on the rebels? It was a farcical situation, but one with sinister undertones, as the men of Carlisle would eventually discover.

After a while Jasper left the tower and wandered through the town. He knew he was being reckless, and he did not care. His instructions had been clear enough; he was to glean information at second-hand from reliable Whig gentry, and report daily at pre-arranged rendezvous where Mr. Dodge or one of his team would be waiting to collect his dispatches. Philip had forbidden Jasper to risk personal encounters with any more Jacobites. If Jasper were caught and his identity established, or even if he were brought face to face with one of the rebels he had met in Edinburgh, then he would be hanged as a spy.

Unfortunately, the love of adventure which had bedevilled the Tarrants from time immemorial beckoned Jasper on. He knew perfectly well that he ought to get out of Carlisle before the Jacobites entered, but he simply could not tear himself away.

When he was weary he made his way to the outskirts of the city, collected his horse from the inn at which it had been stabled, and ambled out into the country. He was to rendezvous that night at a hedge tavern some five miles south of

Carlisle, but if he took the long way round, he might see something of the Jacobite army before he finished his report. Carlisle was still safe, but aware now of its danger. No lights were to be lit in the streets that night, but a candle was to be put in the window of the rooms next the street. The city gates closed for the night. Jasper raised his head and sniffed. There was a clammy feel to the air. There would probably be a fog before long. He rode on, his pistol loose in its holster, and his ears stretched for movement....

A bulky form rode out of the dark towards him, and the two horses reared. There was a white cockade in the hat worn by the newcomer, so he must be a Jacobite; and well-mounted, so he must be an officer.

He swore at Jasper, and his accent was Scots.

Jasper apologized, all meek servitude. He managed a reasonable version of the local accent, which apparently was good enough to deceive the newcomer, for he demanded directions to the seat of the Barrymores, a local family of great influence and Jacobite sympathies.

Jasper proceeded to give lengthy and involved instructions, although he had only the slightest idea where the Barrymores were to be found. The Jacobite lost patience with Jasper's mumbling. He was in a hurry, he announced, and would pay Jasper well if he would deliver a letter to the Barrymores for him. Jasper could hardly believe his luck. The Jacobite turned his horse, and held out the letter and a coin. Jasper moved nearer to take them, and in so doing his face and form became lit by the distant glow of the city behind them.

"Haven't I seen you before somewhere?" asked the Jacobite, still retaining the letter.

"I don't think so," said Jasper, forgetting to speak in dialect. He could not recall seeing the officer before, but the latter now appeared to regret the bargain he had just made. He frowned, and said perhaps it would be better if Jasper were to guide him to the Barrymores' place, even though it meant a further delay. Now Jasper was in a quandary. He did not know the way, and once the Jacobite realized that he had been duped....

Jasper leaned forward, snatched the letter, and dug his spurs into his horse. The Jacobite was facing the wrong way, and had to turn his horse to pursue. Jasper's horse was a good one, and swift, and easily outpaced the horse on which the Jacobite was riding. The darkness swallowed the Jacobite, and Jasper turned his horse in the direction of his rendezvous with Mr. Dodge.

Together they eased the seal off the letter and spread it out on the table. It was a call to arms, penned by the Pretender to Lord Barrymore.

> .... *This is to acquaint you with the success we have had since our arrival in Scotland, and how far we are advanced without repulse. We are now a numerous army, and are laying siege to Carlisle this day. After this we intend to take our route straight to London, and if things answer our expectations, we design to be in Cheshire before the 24th instant. Then I hope you and all my friends in that county will be ready to join us, for now is the time or never.*
> *Adieu. Charles P.R.*

"Pretty good," commented Mr. Dodge. "That'll take my lord Barrymore to the Tower, that will. He'll look pleasant, when his head's lodged on a spike."

"No need for that," said Jasper. "Our lord and master in London made me memorize details of the Jacobite families I might encounter in my travels. I seem to remember that while Barrymore himself is a Tory and Jacobite sympathizer, the son is an ardent Whig and Hanoverian. We'll arrange to have this letter delivered to the son—after we've taken a copy of it, of course."

"But..."

"We don't really want any more Jacobites swelling the ranks of the Pretender's Army, do we? Barrymore's son will probably burn the letter. What the eye doesn't see, the heart doesn't grieve over. I'm sure you agree?"

"Then you'd better keep out of reach of the Jacobites, my young cockerel. You're crowing too loudly for my taste nowadays. It's all very well to have plenty of courage, but a spice of fear might slow you down. A man who takes avoidable risks in our trade doesn't live to collect his pension."

"Oh, I've a charmed life," said Jasper. "What news of Wade?"

"The blithering old hen is stopping where he is, waiting for reinforcements to arrive by sea. I doubt he'll move before Christmas."

"Then Carlisle is lost. I suppose there is only one route which the Pretender can take, if he intends to press on to London?"

"So Carlisle has fallen." Philip seated himself wearily in the chair which had tacitly become 'his' in Miss Nan's sanctum, and stretched out his long legs. "His Majesty is furious, of course. There was a christening party today at St. James'— yet another of the Prince's offspring—the cooks had outdone themselves and created a centerpiece for the table in the likeness of Carlisle Castle. All the guests pelted it with sugarplums, to show their contempt for a city that could allow itself to be taken so easily. Yet I have some sympathy for the men of Carlisle. They were ill-equipped, practically defenseless, and besieged by what must have seemed to them to be an overwhelming Army, who were making scaling ladders and throwing up entrenchments...all very alarming to a generation who have never known war in England. Then Wade sends them a message that he won't be coming to relieve them, after all, but will wait for the Pretender in Lancashire. They say Durand was like a hen who'd had her neck wrung, dashing hither and yon, squawking. His garrison didn't feel like standing a siege, knowing how poorly they were equipped. Some of them went over the Castle walls, and some forced open the gates which Durand had ordered closed. There was confusion in the streets, with civilians mixed up with rebels. As for the militia: hopeless! They didn't want to fight at all. If there had been a full garrison of trained soldiers in Carlisle, it might have been a different story, or if Durand had been appointed two months earlier.... The Stuart boy, having learned his lesson in Edinburgh when he gained the town but was unable to take the Castle demanded that Carlisle surrender the Castle together with the town. And so it was."

"Jasper is safe?"

"Yes. He sent word he would try to obtain lodgings in the city of Carlisle itself. I think that would be folly, but there is no arguing with the lad at the moment. He is drunk on the smell of powder. You have not told Sophia what Jasper is doing?"

"No, but I wish you would tell her. She has learned her

lesson, I think. She was jealous of your attentions to Marjorie."

"A poor excuse. If I couldn't trust her with such a small secret, how can I trust her with anything of importance? Granted that it was not Marjorie who broadcast the tale, but..."

"I am pretty certain that the spy is Sophia's maid. I have seen her skirt disappearing round corners once or twice, after I have been talking to you. I think we are safe in here, now that I have had that heavy curtain draped over the door—it keeps the drafts out so nicely, too—but I think you ought to have her watched."

"I will set Mr. Dodge—or better still, Chivers—on to her. If the Jacobites were to learn what Jasper is doing, his life would not be worth a rush. On the other hand, if I wanted to feed the Jacobites some misleading information, I could tell Sophia and leave the rest to her."

"For shame! You do not mean that, Philip!"

He shrugged, but his color rose. "Perhaps. Perhaps not. She is behaving very badly, you will agree. I have asked her to take over the management of this house, and she has declined to do so. I have asked her to be more discreet with Sir John and Mr. Dalby, and she is seen everywhere with them. I confided my political ambitions to her, and she has mocked them in public and in private, calling me Philip the Bold, and Philip the Cold and suchlike names. I tell myself that I can afford to ignore her pinpricks, but..."

"But they hurt," said Miss Nan. "Of course, you understand that she is merely trying to attract your attention, and that the more you ignore her the more outrageous she becomes? Why don't you woo her? Why don't you take her in your arms and tell her that you love her?"

He inspected his fingernails. "What makes you think that I do?" She did not reply. A coal rustled itself into a new position in the grate. He said, as if every word hurt him, "I did try to tell her, once. She laughed at me. I deserved her scorn. I wasn't offering her marriage, at the time. I offered to make her my mistress. It was before I thought marriage between us might be possible, and I wanted her so badly that..." He clenched his hand, and then relaxed it. "Anyway, she made it clear that she did not reciprocate."

"You insulted her, and she retaliated. Well, that is quite clear. Why did you marry her, then?"

193

"Guilt, for depriving her of her home and a suitable marriage? Perhaps out of revenge, also, because she detested me."

"Does she, now?" said Miss Nan, in a meaning tone. "Believe me, she wouldn't go to all this trouble to annoy you if she were indifferent to you. I wasn't going to tell you at first, but now I think I will. She has arranged to go with Sir John to a masquerade at Ranelagh tonight."

"She told me she was going to a card party at Lady Midmain's."

"Exactly. Now I think that a good quarrel between you two would clear the air. You must put her over your knee, or rape her, or slap her; anything to prove to her that you are her husband, and not 'Philip the Cold.'"

"Madam, I am not in the habit of forcing myself on women who are not attracted to..."

"Philip! And you so wise about other people's problems.... The girl is swooning for you. It is your duty to exercise your matrimonial rights. I suggest that you send to the stables at once to countermand her instructions as to having the coach brought round at nine. Sir John, being a careful man with his money, prefers to use your coach on these occasions... so stupid of him! If he had hired a coach, I might never have heard of the venture, but Chivers naturally told me, the moment he heard."

Philip bent over her hand. "Thank you, my dear. I will do as you suggest; and you may tell Hugh Denbigh that I think he is a very lucky man."

Miss Nan blushed to the frill round her very becoming cap, and told him to be about his business.

"I hear you've countermanded my instructions to the servants! How dare you!" The Countess of Rame swung through the double doors of the drawing-room and slammed them shut behind her. She wore a domino of dark blue over a low-cut dress of pale blue silk. The Earl was engaged in writing a note at the desk in the corner of the room. He looked up, and advised her to moderate her voice if she did not wish to have the servants pry into their affairs.

"The whole Town shall hear," she threatened. "It must be all over the house already that you have prevented me from going out tonight. What will everyone think?"

"That I'm being very sensible. It is raining, and Ranelagh is full of riffraff nowadays. I dare not think what insults you might have had to suffer if you attended a masquerade there."

"But...I was going to a card party at my aunt's."

"Dressed like that? By the way, you need not worry that Sir John will fret; I am sending a footman round to his lodgings to inform him that you are indisposed this evening."

"Indisposed! Yes, I am sick—sick of you!"

He folded his letter, and began to write the superscription. "Do pray moderate your tone. You sound like a fishwife."

"A fishwife?"

"You repeat yourself, I think."

She picked up a paperweight from a nearby table, and lacking a more appropriate target threw it into the fireplace. It did not break, but rolled back onto the carpet. "Oh!" She beat both hands against the panniers of her dress.

"Temper!" remarked the Earl.

She looked around for something else to throw. A book lay on the table. The temptation was too great. She threw it at his head. He caught the book and set it down with care. "A good shot, for a woman."

She ran at him, fingers raised and crooked. He rose, but not quickly enough. His heel caught in the leg of his chair and they both went over, onto the floor. Clawing, biting, her nails seeking his cheek, she closed with him. Her aim was to mark his face, and at first he was content merely to defend himself without hurting her. She put her weight on his weak arm, and felt pleasure as he gasped. He had recovered his usual strength, but rage lent her energy. Their breathing became short and sharp. A table went over. It winded her momentarily, and he secured her right arm, holding it above her head. She groped around on the floor with her free hand...something round...another paperweight...she threw it at his head; it missed, and a mirror shattered behind him. They were both on their feet, glaring at each other. He had cut his hand, and lost his wig. The lace at his throat hung loose and one sleeve had been torn from the shoulderseam. She pointed at the blood which was dripping from his hand, laughed, and picked up a fallen chair to use as a weapon. He caught the chair and deflected it onto the floor, following through to grasp her elbow and twist it, using his weight to throw her to the floor once more. She struck at him with her free hand. He caught that, too, and held it above her head, forcing her to lie flat on her back...she could not move her arms. She kicked, and he sat on her. She had a hand free...raking at his face...her hand was caught again...her wrist! He was crushing her wrists...and then her skirts were being pulled up, billowing up...and then....

His weight was more than she could bear. She could not bear it. She could not shift him. She tried to scratch, but he had both her wrists fast in his grasp. The blood trickled down his cheek onto hers. She twisted and turned, but her body was no longer her own to control, and..."Oh!" she cried, in a breathless voice that she did not recognize. "Oh!" Then with a shudder he was still, lying across her, and his grip tightened, and then relaxed, so that her hands fell apart on the carpet.

Her hair had come down. His cheek was warm against hers. She could feel his breath hot against her lips.

He rolled off her. She was free to get up. She didn't want to move. She continued to lie there, with her hands above her head, her hair half over her face, and her skirts round her waist. After a while she heard the door open, and then close. She turned her head, then. It cost her a great effort to move even her head. The room was empty. He had gone.

Presently she got to her feet. Her knees trembled. Her skirt was ripped from side to side, and bruises were coloring up on her arms and wrists. There were bloodstains on her hands. She looked at herself in a mirror, starred where she had broken it, and her reflection stared back, split into a dozen segments, none of which matched its neighbor.

A sound attracted her attention. Several of the servants were at the door, peering in. She walked through them and up the stairs into her bedroom. She would not explain. There was, perhaps, no need to explain. It must be obvious to everyone what had happened, and the news would be all over Town tomorrow.

Philip felt humiliated. He had been trained never to let his temper get the better of him, and yet he had beaten and raped a woman whom he had sworn to respect. One moment he told himself that he must beg her forgiveness, and the next he was recalling with guilty pleasure the moment her body had responded to his. As had happened before in his dealings with Sophia, he was ashamed of the line he had taken, and aware that he would do the same again if need be.

Sophia avoided him for two days, and then sent him a note asking if he meant to go with her to the Lincolns' that evening. Never before had an olive branch been so eagerly accepted, but as he was dressing to go out, a footman brought a note from Lord Carteret, summoning Philip to dine.

Philip understood very well that this was an order. Normally he would not have hesitated to obey, but...tonight of all nights...what would Sophia think if he refused to accompany her at the last minute? Could he afford to jeopardize his chances of reconciliation with Sophia? No, decidedly he could not.

He tore his uncle's note into small pieces and let them drop into the fire. Then he sat back and indicated that Chivers might paint his face. The summons from Lord Carteret was unexpected; what did the old devil mean by it? There was something at the back of it, of course. But what?

Philip closed his eyes, and thought hard.

"Your coat, my lord." Philip shrugged it on, and inspected himself in the mirror. Gone were the days when he had not cared how he looked.

"Her ladyship is waiting for you in the morning room."

"I must make my apologies. I have to go to my Lord Carteret's, instead." Chivers managed to convey his disapproval without uttering a word.

Philip said, "Yes, I, too, am disappointed." He sighed. How many more times must he put duty before pleasure?

Chapter Twelve

It was exactly as Philip had thought, and Lord Carteret was planning a coup which would return him to power. Over dinner Lord Carteret talked fluently of the balance of power in Europe, of "Antimac"—and the treaty which had recently deprived France of her biggest ally, and of subsidies and armies and of the future, when he, Carteret, should once more be in power.

"For who can withstand me now?" The question was intended to be rhetorical, for Lord Carteret could not conceive of there being any opposition. Had he not been proved right? Was he not the greatest statesman of his generation?

Philip listened, drank sparingly, and watched the clock. What would Sophia be doing at that moment? She had returned him no answer to his apology for not being able to accompany her. If only he had the right to go to her room, and talk to her quietly as he talked to her aunt. She had given him certain rights by marrying him, but he had forsworn them, and then been forsworn. He had broken his word to her. She had every right to despise him...and yet...how lovely she had looked in her rage....

"...and so," concluded Lord Carteret, "I believe the time is now ripe to strike. The King will dismiss Newcastle and his followers, and invite me to form a new ministry. The Prince of Wales has promised to support me; one or two of his followers will have to be accommodated...that man Bute, for instance....But for the rest, we will have men about us

198

who know what they are doing; men of culture; men who understand the broader point of view. I shall, of course, take charge of Foreign Affairs once more, and you Philip..."

Philip sat up straight.

"...you shall have Harrington's place, the Secretaryship for Northern Affairs. What say you to that?"

Power was at present divided between the two secretary-ships, one held by Newcastle, and the other by Harrington. Effectively this meant that Carteret was offering Philip the second highest office in the land. For a moment Philip was tempted. It even crossed his mind to wonder whether he were capable of doing the job. He decided that he probably was. Then his common sense reasserted itself, and he shook his head.

"I regret—I very much regret that I must decline."

Lord Carteret drew in a hissing breath, but he was not yet angry. That was to come later.

The clock on Miss Nan's mantelpiece chimed the hour of midnight.

"...and so I left him," said Philip. He was seated in "his" chair, sipping a posset specially prepared for him. The house was quiet around them. "There will be a fight, of course. There will be scenes in and out of the Closet, but if I do not back him—and even if I were so foolish as to do so—the result would be the same. My uncle cannot grasp the fact that the nature of politics has altered, and the power now lies not with the King, but with the Commons, who control the purse-strings of the Crown. Newcastle understands that. I hold no brief for Newcastle, but he is honest and painstaking and he understands the party machine. I respect him, although I cannot admire him. Without money, the King cannot con-tinue to reign, and therefore, no matter how many tears are shed and threats uttered, Newcastle will continue in office."

"Which means that you have been forced at long last to choose between your uncle and Newcastle. You must have hated that."

"I hope my uncle will forgive me in time. At the moment he accuses me of having sold out to Newcastle, in order that I may go as Ambassador to The Hague, or wherever. I am ungrateful, treacherous—what you will!"

He gazed into the fire, deep in thought.

"What do you see in the fire, Philip?"

"I was thinking how chance had altered my life. If you had told me, a year ago, that I would one day turn down an offer to be Secretary of State, I would not have believed you. I was tempted. I have a certain capacity for administration, and for interfering in other people's lives which I had not suspected in myself, even a short time ago. I thought I could remain aloof from politics, but a bungled robbery on the highway, a girl jumping out of a hedge, and the course of my life is altered." He sighed, put his cup down, and remarked that it was more than time that Miss Nan was in bed.

"I have been thinking about Jasper," she said. "I, too, was looking into the fire, and I thought I saw...perhaps I was mistaken, but I thought I saw Jasper in a dark room, with his wrists in gyves."

"He is well, so far as we know," said Philip.

She tried to smile. "I know that. I would rather you did not tell Sophia. She has not been quite herself these last few days."

His face burned.

"I have decided," said Sophia to her aunt, "that I must bear him a child. It is my duty to do so. On the other hand, I see no reason why I should countenance his visits to that Irish adventuress, and to Marjorie. If he will give them up, he will find me a dutiful wife. I will even stop seeing Sir John and Mr. Dalby, if he so pleases."

"Enjoyed it, did you?"

Sophia colored. "That is not the point. Women marry to supply their husbands with heirs, and at the moment I am not fulfilling my part of the contract. I shall tell him so, when next I see him."

"I would advise you to do so soon. He is a busy man, and it won't be long before he realizes you are pregnant, and then your argument will fail to hold water, won't it?"

"I'm not!" gasped Sophia. "Well, I suppose I might be, but it's far too early to..."

"Another thing. You'll have to do more than say you've changed your mind to get him into bed with you. You've said some hard things to him, by all accounts. You'll have to coax

200

him a little. Don't look so shocked! Sit on his knee, stroke his cheek, pull off his wig and ruffle his hair. Find out where he likes to be kissed, and whether he's ticklish or not. You know the sort of thing I mean."

"I...do...not!" declared Sophia. "I'm surprised at you, Aunt. Where have you been learning this? Have you been making love to a man, behind my back? Yes? Why, who the devil could it be! Ah, it's Mr. Carramine, isn't it? He's forever in the house."

"Don't be absurd, Sophia." Miss Nan almost ran from the room.

Sophia knelt down by the fire and stared into it. Presently she blushed so deeply that she had to put her hands over her cheeks to cool them.

"I couldn't," she said to herself. "Not with Philip. It would be impossible...."

Sophia bit the end of her quill, and considered the note she had penned to her husband. Several times over the last few days she had tried to bring about a reconciliation with him, and failed. She realized that she was herself largely to blame for this failure, for her temper was uncertain and tears sometimes rose to her eyes without warning. She would begin by saying something soft, and then spoil the effect with a jibe at which he would turn on his heel and leave the room. Therefore she was now resorting to pen and ink to state the terms on which she would be willing to receive him into her bed.

She had not seen him that day, for he had been out until quite late. He had not come home, in fact, until after the evening meal had been cleared away. Then he had gone up to see Thomas, while Sophia had paced the drawing-room, rehearsing what she wished to say to him. He was dressing to go out for the rest of the evening; so much she had gleaned from Chivers, who was proving unexpectedly sympathetic. If he went out without seeing her, it would mean the loss of another day, and she didn't think she could bear it. She rang the bell, committed her note to a footman, and began to pace the floor again. She paused to check on her appearance in a mirror. She had ordered some of the mirrors and most of the knicknacks to be cleared from the room. She thought it looked better without all that clutter, but she still did not admire the decorations. The fire had burned low, so she put some more coal on. Now she had got her hands dirty. Damn. She knew she ought to have rung for a servant to make up the fire for her, but it was difficult to remember to ask servants to do things when she was perfectly capable of doing them for herself.

Philip came in, dressed in a new coat of gray satin. His wig and ruffles gleamed white. He was all gray and white, Philip the Cold. Her heart sank. Where was the man she had found lying in the field, the man whose ardor had caused her to turn from marriage to Sir John Bladen? Where, even, was the man whose kindness and consideration had upheld her through the difficult time of her debut in Society?

"You desire a truce?" He gave no indication as to whether he liked the idea or not.

"I desire merely to fulfill my duty as a wife."

He took out his watch, and compared it with the clock on the mantel behind her. She put her hands behind her back, hoping he would not notice how dirty they were. Only now did she notice that she had an inkstain on her skirt. Of course he would notice, and despise her.

"I have an appointment this evening. Perhaps we can discuss the matter tomorrow."

"You go to see Mrs. O'Dell? If you came to my bed instead of hers, you would save yourself the cost of maintaining two houses."

"You are mistaken."

"I think not. My sources of information are good."

"Lady Millicent Fairweather? Sir John Bladen? They are biased, you know. The lady in question keeps a gaming house, not a brothel."

She allowed her incredulity to show. "I am told you are allowed to visit the lady's sanctum every time you go there; a privilege accorded to no one else."

"It is true that Mrs. O'Dell and I are old friends, and that once upon a time we were somewhat closer than...This discussion could easily degenerate into an undignified squabble. Please take my word for it that our present relationship is purely business."

She did not believe him, but as he had pointed out, shouting at him would get her nowhere. "What about Marjorie?"

"I fail to understand why you object to my befriending the girl your brother wishes to marry."

"Sir John will never agree to the match. Even if Jasper comes through this campaign, he will be a proscribed rebel with no Tarrant Hall behind him, and no prospects but that of a traitor's death on Tower Hill."

"I have told you before that Jasper is not with the rebels. I believe he will make a good soldier, and that he and Marjorie are well suited."

"You are being unrealistic. Sir John is arranging another match for her, with my erstwhile suitor, Mr. Dalby."

"Poor girl, she will need a friend now, more than ever. Sophia, if you will be Marjorie's friend, I will gladly promise to abjure her company. Will that satisfy you?"

"Yes, I suppose so."

"Very well. Now, I..." He stopped and looked behind him, at the door, as if he had heard something. He resumed his speech, at the same time striding back to the door, and jerking it open. "...I have an appointment this evening, as I said...Ah! So I've caught you at last, have I?" Sophia's maid had evidently had her ear to the keyhole, for she tumbled into the room, on her knees.

"Was she listening?" asked Sophia, doubtfully. "How very odd! Aunt Nan said she thought someone was listening at her door the other day, but I couldn't understand why anyone should bother to..."

"To report on your actions to Sir John Bladen." Philip grasped the maid's arm, and drew her upright. "You are in his pay, are you not? Answer me. You have been seen in the street, talking with Greenwood, a rogue whom I dismissed months ago, and who is now in Sir John's employ. What were your instructions? To foster discord between your mistress and myself?"

The woman stared back at him, open contempt showing on her face. "I was set to watch a traitor at work," she said.

Philip caught his breath. "What?" he asked, quietly.

"You know!" she said meaningly. Her gaze traveled to Sophia. "There is more going on in this household than meets the eye, my lady. You should ask him why he needs to lock his library door every day, and where he goes each night. It is not for the usual purposes that he visits this Mrs. O'Dell, but..."

"Out!" said Philip. He opened the door, and gestured the woman to leave. "You are dismissed. Your wages will be paid up to date, but I never want to see your face in this house

203

again. Is that clearly understood?" The woman hesitated. Philip rang the bell, and Chivers appeared. The maid reared her head, shot Philip a poisonous glance, and left.

"Chivers, that woman's belongings are to be searched before she leaves this house—which she must do within the hour. She is not to have converse with any of the other servants before she goes. Perhaps Mr. Dodge will assist you."

Chivers' bow contrived to indicate that he approved of the maid's dismissal. He closed the door behind him.

Philip said, "I am sorry that you should have been exposed to such a situation. I have had my suspicions of the woman for some time, and so has your aunt. I fear Sir John's mind has become unbalanced through jealousy, or drink, or both. Perhaps this woman is more a victim than a villain, for by corrupting her into his service, Sir John has caused her to lose her place."

"But why did she talk so mysteriously—and call you . . . what she did call you?"

"A traitor." Philip sighed. "I really don't know what is the best way to deal with Sir John's slanders. It is farcical. He wants to believe something to my discredit, and therefore he fantasizes until he comes to believe—yes, I really think he believes that I am engaged in something mysterious. He cannot imagine any fate worse for me than to be a traitor, and therefore I must become a traitor. His reasoning is that of a madman. It would be laughable, if it were not serious. His friends should have him confined to Bedlam, but then, he appears to have no friends, and no relations apart from this elderly cousin with whom he is lodging. I do not wish to fight him, because he is a sick man and not responsible for what he says; also because I might easily kill him, and I do not want that on my conscience."

"Why did you order the woman's belongings to be searched? Why did you not leave it to me to question the woman and dismiss her if need be?"

"It was a precaution against her taking something which did not belong to her. A woman who takes bribes may also take property. Have you missed anything recently?"

"No, I don't think so. It had not occurred to me to look. You are right, of course. The woman must go. I shall be somewhat relieved, in fact, for I cannot help feeling that she disapproves of what she calls my 'country habits' of doing things for myself."

204

"I will find you someone more discreet. You do not want every word that passes between us to be relayed to Sir John, do you?"

"No."

He extended his hand. "Come, then; let us be friends."

She hesitated to give him her hand, remembering that it was dirty. She saw him stiffen. No doubt he thought she was repulsing him, and she could not allow that.

"My hand is dirty," she said, showing him. "I put some coal on the fire myself, instead of calling a servant. I am sorry."

His lips twitched, but he managed to restrain himself. He took a handkerchief from his pocket, wiped her hand more or less clean, and then kissed it. Her fingers tightened on his. They looked at each other, speculation in their eyes.

"You were on the point of going out?" she asked.

"I will send someone else," he said, "if you..."

"Yes. I mean, no. I mean, I had ordered some of your favorite dishes to be served in my room. You have not eaten. I thought...perhaps...you might stay with me this evening, and then...perhaps...if you felt able to..."

"Very much so," he said, and kissed her hand again.

Sophia's new maid scratched on the door of her ladyship's bedchamber, and entered with the morning pot of hot chocolate. Two forms lay sprawled in the bed, the remains of supper were on a table by the now dead fire, clothes laid a trail from table to bed, and his lordship's wig had come to rest, rakishly, atop one of the bedposts. Sophia's maid regarded this evidence of depravity with an indulgent eye. A widow, and a connection by marriage of Mr. Dodge, she was country-bred, and had been brought up in the tradition that happiness in marriage was brought about by four legs in a four-poster bed. In this, as in much else, she was very much in agreement with Chivers, who followed her with his master's dressing gown. Two footmen came in, bearing great cans of hot water, and a maid cleared the grate and laid a fire while Chivers drew back the window curtains, and Sophia's maid picked up discarded clothes.

The Earl opened one eye, and demanded to know what time it was. On being told, he groaned, and raised himself carefully to a sitting position. His lady was barely visible under the bedclothes at his side.

Sophia's maid, whose name was Polly, caught Chivers' eye. She did not smile, for she was well-trained, but Chivers' lips quivered as he set a table at the bedside, and poured out the hot chocolate. Undoubtedly the Earl and his Countess had spent an active night.

Sophia sat up, yawned, and sniffed. "Hot chocolate!" she said, turning a peculiar shade of green. "Take it away, do!"

The Earl was about to insert himself into the dressing gown which Chivers was holding out for him. He paused, and looked at his wife. Everyone else also stopped what they were doing. A silence as thick and satisfied as cream spread round the room.

The Earl snapped his fingers. "Leave us," he told the servants. "Tell the chef that my lady would prefer tea, or barley water in the mornings in future."

Chivers bowed, and shepherded the other servants out of the room.

Sophia sat up and tossed back her hair. She looked both defiant and guilty. "It must have been something I ate last night. Do we go to the Lincolns tonight?"

"It is over a month since you invited me to share your bed. You may or may not have been pregnant then, but you are certainly pregnant now."

"Is it really a whole month?"

"At this point," said Philip, pressing her hand to secure her attention, "my late wife always advised me that my services were no longer required."

"Oh, well. There's no accounting for tastes."

The Earl smoothed out a smile. "I wouldn't wish to impose myself on someone who found me repugnant."

"Did I say that? How I've changed."

"That's the trouble. First you smile at me, and then you laugh at me. I can never be quite sure of you. If only I could trust you to be the same every day...."

"No woman can be the same, day after day."

He withdrew from her, not only physically, but also mentally. She saw the ardor die out of his eyes, and cursed her flippancy. She had not meant it. Little by little he had lost his reserve and begun to be at ease with her. He had even begun to speak to her of his political ambitions again, and to explain to her why it was taking so long to confirm his appointment abroad. Now...tears sprang up to her cheeks, but he did not see them, for he had gone to take his bath in the dressing room next door.

Sophia sat up and reached for her hairbrush. Most ladies' maids would be annoyed if their mistress brushed out their own hair, but Sophia knew that Polly would be amused and not sullen when she found out. Sir John had denied that he had ever set Sophia's first maid to spy on her, but his manner had not carried conviction. He had been laid up with the gout recently, and she had hardly seen anything of him. She was inclined to think this a good thing, for there was no denying that he was jealous of Philip, and that going about in Society was less wearing in his absence.

Philip returned from his bath, freshly shaved, and dressed—except for his coat, shoes and wig. "Have you seen Marjorie of late?" he asked. "I am concerned for her, and so is Jasper. He hasn't heard from her for nearly a month. You promised you would let me have any notes she might give you for him, and he wonders whether you have forgotten to do so."

"There haven't been any notes. I've called at their lodgings twice since Sir John was taken ill, and both times they told me that she was confined to her room with a heavy cold. Sir John was walking in the Park yesterday, and I spoke to him about Marjorie and Jasper, but he was adamant; he will not hear of the match. He says Mr. Dalby has proposed to make a handsome settlement on Marjorie, and that they will be wed before Christmas. I am sorry for Jasper, but what can he expect if he goes off and leaves the girl like that?"

He looked vexed. "Jasper is the sort of young fool who gets careless when he is emotionally involved. I've asked him to leave the Jacobites and come to London on two occasions, but he says he can't leave until their cause is dead. He says he trusts me to look after his interests where Marjorie is concerned. When the marriage with Mr. Dalby was first proposed, Marjorie told me categorically that she had no intention of agreeing to it, but I could see that she was troubled by fear of what her father might say or do. He is a violent, unpredictable man. Do you think he has confined Marjorie to her room because she has refused to marry Mr. Dalby? Do you think she is suffering not from a cold, but from a series of beatings? For my sake—and for Jasper's sake—will you call on her once more, and this time insist on seeing her?

You could choose a time when you knew that Sir John would be out."

It was the first time he had asked her to do anything for him, and it had to be for that whey-faced Marjorie! If she refused, he might show his displeasure; perhaps he might even refuse to go on sleeping with her.

"If I visit her, will you continue to visit me?"

He sighed. "Do you always have to make bargains? Can you never find it in you to grant a favor without asking for one in return?" She dropped her eyes from his. She was ashamed, but persistent.

"But will you come?"

He laughed, without mirth. "You know perfectly well that I will."

Jasper glanced at the calendar in his pocket book and added the date to his report before he signed it and stowed it for safety in his boot. December 5th, 1745, and a night to remember in the history of the city of Derby. There were bonfires in the streets, lit for the benefit of the rebel army, who wandered around the town at will. It was not yet seven o'clock, and Jasper was restless. He felt he could not stay in his lodgings, although he knew it was unwise to move about among the Jacobites. He was not due to meet Mr. Dodge until eleven that night, and he thought that in the dark and confusion that reigned in the town he might learn something to add to his report. Sometimes the Pretender walked out at night, alone. Jasper toyed with the idea of assassinating the Pretender, which would undoubtedly end the rebellion. Then he could go back to London, and see what was the matter with Marjorie. It was over a month since he had heard from her. Philip's excuses rang hollow, as Jasper had told him in his report. Who was this Mr. Dalby, anyway?

He primed a pistol and put it in his pocket. His orders had been very clear, to observe and not to interfere with the course of events.

He shrugged. Well, he would not tempt Providence, but he would go armed, just in case.

The Pretender had his headquarters in Exeter House, a handsome building with a large garden behind it. A couple of respectable-looking milliners stood in the street on the opposite side of the road, looking at the house, and Jasper joined them. Like him, they wished to catch a glimpse of the Pretender, and were happy to have his company, which protected them from the attentions of the soldiery. After some time Charles Stuart came out. His color was high, and his gestures expansive; perhaps he had been drinking again. The two milliners exclaimed at the Pretender's height and good looks. Jasper teasingly suggested that they should make themselves Jacobite cockades, and the women laughed. The reaction of the civilian populace to the invasion seemed to be the same everywhere; they treated it as a sideshow at a fair, something to be watched with varying degrees of wonder and incredulity, but not to be taken seriously.

There was a bustle in the street. Lord George Murray strode up, all grim purpose, and accosted the Pretender. There was an argument; the Pretender wanted to walk around the city, and Lord George wanted to call a council meeting. Lord George won, and the two men went into Exeter House and closed the door. Other Highland officers began to arrive, which seemed to indicate that Lord George had commanded their presence before he had spoken to the Pretender about the meeting. If only Jasper could eavesdrop on their councils!

The two milliners decided to go home, so Jasper went down the street, looking for a wall or gate which might give access to the garden of Exeter House. Presently he found an alleyway which might serve his purpose, but it was guarded by a rebel soldier. Jasper fitted himself into the shadow of a doorway nearby, and waited. Presently a crowd of young people came along the alley. They surrounded the guard, teasing him to tell how they might catch a glimpse of the Pretender. The sentry's back was turned to Jasper, and he took a running jump at the wall, felt the glass shards on the top bite through his gloves, hauled himself up, stood, and jumped down into the garden. He crouched, listening. There was no alarm. He could not have been seen.

Gradually his eyes grew accustomed to the patches of light and shade in the garden. The first floor was brilliantly lit. Some of the windows were closely shuttered, but others had been left ajar. The windows on the first floor were brightly illuminated. These windows were high, surmounted by elegant mouldings, indicating the presence of a reception room of some importance. It was likely that this was the room in which the council was being held.

Jasper avoided the gravel paths, which might have betrayed his footfall, and made his way to the house via the flowerbeds and the lawn. A thick, lead drainpipe debouched onto the terrace at the back of the house. He looked up. All the windows of the first floor room were shut, except for one. He could hear a voice speaking in measured tones and thought he recognized it as Lord George Murray's. The voice faded and Jasper guessed that the speaker was walking round the room. He tested the drainpipe. It was fixed to the wall with brackets at intervals, and looked secure.

He did not have far to climb—perhaps ten or eleven feet—and then he had a foot on the architrave of a ground floor window, and his ear to the sill of the window above. Grasping the sill, he edged round until he could see past the half-open shutter into the room. Intent faces were angled to the right of Jasper. Someone was saying that it was madness to engage the Hanoverians with the forces they had at their command, that the Duke of Cumberland was waiting for them to the south, that Wade was at Wetherby, and the militia at Finchley. Until the French sent reinforcements, it would be best to retreat to Scotland, where they might recruit more men.

Another voice broke in; a younger, impetuous man. The Pretender? Jasper wished he could see further into the room. He shifted his grip, but did not improve his view. The new speaker was excitable, declaring that he had firm promises of support from many gentlemen in the south.

Something caught Jasper's ankle. He kicked. There was a shout of "I've got him!" His other ankle was caught. He lost his grip and fell down onto the terrace. The window above him was thrown open and heads looked out. He saw them looking down on him as he was borne, struggling, to the ground, his fall broken by the men underneath. There were three Highlanders in the garden, and they explained to the heads at the window that a sentry inside the garden had seen someone come over the wall, and raised the alarm; that as soon as they saw the spy's head silhouetted against the lighted window, they had crept up on him, and seized him in the very act.

Jasper's hands were wrenched behind his back and tied there. At a word of command from above he was taken into the house, prodded up the stairs and thrust into the council chamber. It was a dining room, wainscotted with ancient oak, dark and handsome. Jasper had wanted to see into the room, but now he had his wish, he would have given anything to be elsewhere. Rough hands searched his pockets and discovered his pistol. Ah, a pistol! So he was planning to shoot their Prince through the window, was he? He was silent. They found his Jacobite cockade and a map showing the route from Macclesfield to Derby. Jasper bit his lip. Philip had told him to burn everything, the moment he had finished with it. Money...his money was removed from his pockets and thrown onto the table. His handkerchief...the monogram had been unpicked long ago, to conceal his identity.

What is your name? David Vere.

Are you with us, or against us? Neither, I was curious, that is all.

Why did you have a cockade with you? It was a souvenir.

What about the pistol? I carry a pistol to protect myself on the roads.

"Cockades!" One of the officers snapped his fingers. "That's where I've seen him before. I didn't recognize him at first. It was in Edinburgh. He was hanging around, asking questions about the number of cockades we had ordered."

"I'm not sure, but I think I've seen him before, too," said another man. "He was in a different wig and a suit of brown fustian, such as farmers wear. I asked him the way to my lord Barrymore's, and he took the letter to deliver for me." The man would not admit he had allowed Jasper to snatch the letter from him.

What bad luck! Should Jasper deny everything? "It could not have been me, sir, on either occasion. I've never been north of Macclesfield in my life. I was visiting my uncle there, and now I'm on my way home to Lichfield. My uncle gave me the map because I was not sure of the way. I heard you were in Town, and it seemed a lark—I mean, I was curious to see..."

"I am certain this is the man I saw in Edinburgh," said the officer who had first spoken. He was appealing to Lord George Murray.

"What is the name of your uncle, and what business did you have in Macclesfield?" asked Lord George.

"Mr. Pouncey," said Jasper, thinking hard. "My mother and I are not well off, and he invited me to stay for a sennight..."

211

"I know no one of that name in Macclesfield," said a man who had not spoken before. Jasper cursed under his breath. Of all the luck!

"I am certain this is the same man," said the man who had seen Jasper in Edinburgh. "I had a good look at him then, and I never forget a face. He has nothing on him to prove his identity, and that in itself is suspicious. If he was who he said he was, he would have papers on him to prove it. My vote says he is a spy. Have you searched his boots?"

Jasper was thrown to the floor, and his boots removed. He closed his eyes and began to pray. The game was up now. To the accompaniment of a buzz of alarm and speculation, his report was handed round the table.

"A spy, all right," said Lord George. "Take him out into the street and hang him from the nearest lampbracket."

Chapter Thirteen

"Wait!" The Pretender held up his hand, and cast a look of dislike at Lord George, presumably because the latter had failed to ask his permission before ordering the disposal of the spy. "The man is a spy, but we may be able to learn something from him. You..." he addressed Jasper. "What is your name? David Vere? Well, Mr. Vere, if you will accommodate us with some information, we may accommodate you by commuting your death sentence to one of imprisonment. Do you admit you are a spy?" Jasper did not reply. "Who is your contact? Are there any others of your kind in the vicinity?" Again, Jasper kept his mouth shut. One of the Highlanders hit him across the face. Jasper's face burned, but still he kept silent. "What do you know of Cumberland's plans?"

Jasper's throat constricted with fear at the thought of death, but it was not that which held him silent. He had been caught because he had disobeyed orders. He had deserved to be caught. He would go to his death in silence. It was the least he could do now. He would not betray Philip, whatever happened.

"This 'Marjorie' whom you mention in your letter; who is she?" The Pretender was studying Jasper's report. "And 'Mr. Dalby'? Are these code names, do you think?"

"Dalby?" A sharp-looking gentleman spoke for the first time. Jasper recognized him as a certain Mr. Townley, one of the Manchester recruits, and a respectable gentleman in civilian life. "I knew someone called Dalby once. He lived near my sister's place. His widow lives in Town now, with her son. I don't believe they are politically-minded."

"Is this the same Dalby?" Jasper stared ahead and made no response. He thought: I've handed Marjorie over to Dalby, when I could have done as Philip said and gone to London before this. Sweet Marjorie....

"This girl of yours cannot mean much to you if you are prepared to die without leaving her so much as a farewell note," said Lord George, his cold eyes now on Jasper, and now on his report. The temptation was great. He could write a note, bidding her farewell. But now, it would never reach her. Sir John would intercept any letter sent by the common post, and he could not send it by Philip, for that would tell the Jacobites the name of the man who had played such a big part in engineering their downfall. He could send the note to Sophia; but no, that would not do, either, for he would have to say that Sophia was his sister, and someone in the room would be bound to know that the Countess of Rame had been Miss Sophia Tarrant.

Jasper tried to think clearly. Would it matter very much, would it harm Philip or the Hanoverian cause, if the rebels were to learn his true identity? What would they say if they knew he was Sir Jasper Tarrant? That he had duped them with false letters of invitation? Surely the time for concealment of the fact was past? The rebels had been drawn down into England, were cut off from Scotland, which was the only part of Great Britain to support them, and they were wondering what to do next. Suppose he told them....

"If he will not answer, take him outside and hang him."

He was being dragged to the door. "Wait!" he said. They paused, their hands still on his arms. He tried to consider all the possibilities at once. If the rebels turned tail now, would that be a good thing, or a bad? Jasper had heard the French were poised to invade, but if the Pretender fled back to Scotland with his troops in disarray, then what would the French do? Would they still invade? Surely not. So....

"We cannot wait for ever," said Lord George. "Take him out and..."

"I will tell you something of great importance, if you will spare my life," said Jasper.

"A dead spy requires no food, or guards to watch him," said Lord George. "You will have to let us be the judge of whether your information is worth a life or not."

214

"Suppose I tell you something which will help you decide whether you should press on to London, or retreat to Scotland?"

"Is Cumberland upon us?"

The Pretender was more optimistic. "The south of England has risen for me?"

"It will not do so," said Jasper. "You see, my name is not David Vere, but Sir Jasper Tarrant. My father was the Sir Richard Tarrant with whom you used to correspond. He died a year ago, and since then it is I who have been writing to you in his name. I am no Jacobite, but a true supporter of our rightful King, George II, and the letters I wrote you were devices to lure you first into this country without proper support, and then to bring you down south, where you could be defeated with the minimum of effort. Let me be perfectly frank with you; none of the gentlemen who promised to rise for you will be doing so. Oh, some are still Jacobite in sympathy, but none of them are prepared to lose their heads for a lost cause. Has William Watkyn joined you? Or Barrymore? Or any of a dozen others who promised to do so?"

The Pretender's mouth worked. "I don't believe you. This is an invention to..."

"Compare the handwriting in my report, to that of the letters you received from 'Sir Richard Tarrant,' and you will see that they are the same. If anyone here knows the county of Sussex, I am prepared to give them chapter and verse of all the gentry who live within twenty miles of Tarrant Hall. Our crest was the Ram and the Rose, and it was to that sign that you sent your letters, and it was with that sign that I sealed my replies. The 'Marjorie' in my letter is Miss Marjorie Bladen, the niece of Sir John Bladen, our neighbor in Sussex. He does not approve of my wishing to marry his daughter, and is trying to force her into marriage with Mr. Dalby, who until recently was courting my sister Sophia. Mr. Townley may have heard something of that matter."

"Was she not known as the Tarrant Rose? There was some talk—my sister wrote me a tale about the King's interest in her. Did she not marry someone else? Ah, I have it. She married Rame, a nephew of Carteret's. If you know so much, what is Rame's Christian name, and what does he look like?"

"His given name is Philip; he is tall, fair of complexion, and has been a soldier. His crest is a Swan. Is that proof enough, gentlemen, or would you like me to describe Tarrant Hall to you, room by room?"

"I don't understand," said the Pretender. "How could you, whose father and brother both served the Jacobite cause, believe in the Hanoverians?"

"My father and brother drained the estate in the Jacobite cause to such good purpose that I had to sell Tarrant Hall to pay their debts. Allegiance to a lost cause has cost the Tarrants dear. I am just as much a soldier of fortune as they were, but I have picked the winning side. Oh, you may hang me or not, as you choose, but it will not alter the fact that you have lost this throw. There is no support for you in England. There never has been, and there never will be. You had better run for safety while you can."

Everyone started to talk at once. At a sign from Lord George, Jasper was dragged out of the room and taken down the stairs. Would they hang him now? Oh, Sweet Jesus, have mercy! His boots had been left behind in the upstairs room, and the floors were chill. He was thrust into a cellar and thrown to the floor. His feet were tied. The door was slammed shut, and bolted on the far side. The window was small and barred and high above his head. He was safe for the night.

"It's all the fault of that traitor, the Earl of Rame," said Mr. Farrow, refilling Sir John's glass. "You remember I told you he was secretly working for the Jacobites?"

Sir John looked up, bleary-eyed. He was frequently the worse for drink nowadays, and his memory was beginning to go. His temper, however, was as fresh as ever.

"You remember Greenwood's story of the letter that the Frenchman gave the Earl, and how he concealed the true facts of the ambush from you? You had every right to be told the truth as Justice of the Peace, did you not?"

"That's right," said Sir John loudly. "He made a fool of me."

"That was only the beginning, though. He's been working in secret for the Jacobites ever since, hasn't he? Doesn't he have suspicious-looking men hanging around in his hall, night and day? And letters which arrive by couriers who have ridden hard and fast? Haven't we had these couriers followed, and don't they all go north? Why should he need so many letters from the north, when his estates are in the east? And why, if he is not engaged in treasonable activity, does he need to guard his papers so carefully? That woman we bribed—the Countess's maid—she reported that she could only once catch a glimpse of the library, but that the walls were covered with maps."

"He shall be exposed as a traitor," nodded Sir John. "I shall denounce him, before everyone, in public."

"I have a better idea," said Mr. Farrow. "You don't want to run the risk of his calling you out..."

"Never fear," said Sir John. "The man's a coward—twice refused to fight me, though I as good as gave him the lie. He's behaved very badly to Sophia, you know. Her maid said...badly bruised. The brute! Making eyes at Marjorie, too...though I soon put a stop to that, didn't I? Marry Dalby, or stay locked up till I take you back to the country, I said."

"She still hasn't consented to marry Mr. Dalby?"

"The little idiot! Haven't I gone to enough trouble for her already, persuading him that she was the very wife to help him with his farms? Ungrateful...teach her a lesson...teach her a lesson every day until she promises to obey me."

"Better be careful," warned Mr. Farrow. "You don't want the girl's death on your hands. If someone sees her with those bruises, there will be talk of the wrong kind."

"'S all the Earl's fault," said Sir John, dissolving into tears. "Damn his eyes! Putting ideas into my little girl's head...never would have disobeyed me, otherwise."

"Yes, yes. We must bring him down, but we must do it properly. Giving him the lie in public is one thing, but a better way would be to denounce him as a traitor to the newspapers. Think of it! He would wake up one morning to find his treachery a household word. Everyone would shun him. He would have to resign his place at Court and flee the country to avoid arrest."

"No, let him be arrested," said Sir John, breathing fast. "Let him be hung, drawn and quartered on Tower Hill, and then I will rest easy, and my little girl will marry Mr. Dalby, and..."

"And the Countess of Rame will be a widow, and very rich." Mr. Farrow raised his glass to Sir John. "To your future happiness."

Sir John's eyes narrowed. "Do you think she would? Sophia? Beautiful creature, but hard to handle."

"I think you could have her for the asking, once her husband is out of the way. Now, I shall need some more money."

"Haven't you had enough?"

"Not for this. We must have at least one piece of paper, one map, or letter, or dispatch out of the Earl's library to prove our case to the newspapers. I have sounded out a man, a carpenter, who carries out all sorts of jobs in the Earl's household, and he is willing to pick the lock of the library door, if we will pay him well enough to do so. We will have to choose our time carefully, for the room is almost always occupied, if not by Mr. Denbigh, then by Mr. Carramine or the Earl. Also, that gallows-faced valet is always on the lookout. But it can be done. The son and heir is dying, and this means extra people in the house, doctors, surgeons, nurses, and visitors. Mr. Denbigh is often up in the sickroom for hours at a time. We will watch and wait, and then...."

On the morning of December 6th, the Highlanders marched out of Derby, taking Jasper Tarrant with them. He had lost his hat and boots, and his hands were still tied behind his back, but one of his guards had bound his feet with rags so that he should not fall out of the column for lack of shoes. No one seemed to know where they were going; perhaps to fight Wade at last, or perhaps to meet Cumberland at Lichfield. The men were looking forward to a battle.

Jasper was on the lookout for Dodge, who would have become alerted to the fact that something had gone wrong when he failed to arrive at the rendezvous. A group of rustics stood at one side of the road, watching the Army march out. Jasper saw that Dodge was standing among them, but made no sign. He let his eye pass over the group to the horizon beyond. Thoughts of a rescue attempt flitted through his mind, and were rejected. What could Mr. Dodge do against so many rebels?

Presently the Jacobites began to recognize landmarks which they had noted on their way into Derby. They were marching north, not south. They were not going to give battle to anyone, but were retreating. Their mood became ugly.

* * *

That very same morning, Friday, December 6th, the news reached London that the Jacobites were in Derby. Everyone panicked. It was the first time that Londoners had felt in danger, for after all, Derby was in the Midlands, and who knew how soon the rebels might be in London? There was a run on the banks, which began paying out in sixpences to gain time. No one paused to reflect, but rushed about making plans to flee the country, or to arm their households.

The Government reacted with unusual firmness and promptitude, offering a six-pound bonus to any man who would enlist, and making arrangements for them to join the militia on Finchley Common. Various noblemen were already under oath to form companies of their own, and this notion caught on, so that it seemed every other man either had or was about to offer his services. His Majesty remained calm, and showed himself as usual, in the company of his favorites, Lord Lincoln and the Earl of Rame. It was rumored that Lord Carteret had actually been seen conversing amicably with the Duke of Newcastle, but this was generally felt to have been a figment of someone's imagination. What was true was that Baroness Granville, Lord Carteret's mother, was dying, and that he would shortly acquire her title. How annoying for everyone to have to remember that Carteret must now be addressed as Granville.

By the evening of Black Friday the panic had subsided, and the polite world attended the rout which the Earl and Countess of Rame were giving. Earlier in the day Philip had feared they might have to cancel the event, but the rooms were crowded with people all talking at once. They said that the Countess looked sweetly pretty in her white gown, and was that the one she had worn at Court when she was presented the other night? And didn't they make a handsome couple, but what a pity that the son was said to be dying, although with Sophia being so young and well—buxom—perhaps it was just as well. That they didn't know what the world was coming to, and yes, their brother was wild to join Lord M—'s regiment, and thank goodness that the Duke of Cumberland was still between London and those dreadful Highlanders; they eat babies, my dear!

The Countess touched her husband on the arm during a pause in the reception line. "Have you heard from Jasper lately? I hadn't thought of him for days, but last night I woke

219

up with the most extraordinary feeling that he was in trouble."

"You, too?" said Philip, keeping his voice low. "Your aunt is in the same way. If anything has gone wrong, we will hear of it soon enough."

Sir John Bladen came, although he had not been invited, and stood around looking angry and speaking hardly at all. It was said that the attack of "gout" which had laid him up recently was really debility brought on by drink. People tended to move away when he looked at them.

Marjorie did not accompany her father, and Sophia promised Philip that she would call on the girl the very next day.

Sophia was shocked by Marjorie's looks. The girl had no color in her face, and there were greenish-yellow bruises on her wrists. Miss Bladen, her aunt, sat nearby, grimly attentive to everything that was said.

Sophia suggested that as Marjorie looked pale, the girl might be permitted to accompany her for a half hour drive in the Park. The request was refused, on the grounds that Sir John did not wish his daughter to leave the house at present. Sophia said yes, Marjorie did look ill, and what did the doctor prescribe? Miss Bladen said that there was nothing wrong with her niece which marriage wouldn't cure. Marjorie looked down at her hands, neatly folded in her lap, and Sophia began to chatter about the rout party the previous night, and a new dress that she had ordered, and the progress of the portrait which was being painted of her.

Presently a servant came in to speak with Miss Bladen, and Sophia took the opportunity to draw Marjorie out of earshot into a window embrasure.

"What ails you, my dear?"

"I am in great trouble. They are trying to marry me to Mr. Dalby against my will. For Jasper's sake...for old time's sake...will you not give me sanctuary?"

"You would run away? What good would that do? He has the right, legally, to...come, child! Mr. Dalby is not such an ogre, and he will take you away from all this into the country where you can be happy again."

"I cannot be happy unless I marry Jasper."

"You know your father will not hear of the match. I have

tried to soften him, but he is quite determined. You must make up your mind to it, and take Mr. Dalby. It is not so bad to be married to a man who has a good position in Society."

"Our cases are different. You were not really averse to marrying Philip, even though you pretended indifference."

"Believe me, I hated the very idea, but it has worked out well enough."

"I am not like you. I cannot change. If I cannot marry Jasper, I will marry no one but die an old maid. Will you not help me? I will watch my chance, and slip out of the house at dusk, perhaps. I can make my own way to you. I am not afraid of passing through the City at night, although I know there are many around prepared to offer insult to a lady unescorted. But I will do it, if I have to. You would only need to hide me for a night, and then..."

"Yes, and what then? Your father would demand you, and we would be forced to give you up, and there would be a scandal."

"Philip will think of something. He will find somewhere for me to go, where I will be quite safe."

"It is out of the question!" said Sophia. Was she guided to refuse the girl because of the reference to Philip? "No, my dear. You must resign yourself. We women cannot always marry as we choose, but on the whole the system works well. Now, I really must go. If you have a note for Jasper, I will take it with me."

"I wrote one, but my father found it when he beat me, and he burned it. I have not been able to obtain any paper since then."

Sophia hesitated. Ought she to offer to help by lending Marjorie her own tablet, and... Miss Bladen dismissed the servant and swept down on them, her eyes suspiciously examining them for traces of wrongdoing. Indeed, she was a formidable lady. Sophia curtseyed, and excused herself, saying she had an appointment with her dressmaker.

Marjorie stood in the window, watching until her friend emerged into the street and climbed into her carriage. Then, snatching at something on the floor, she exclaimed that the Countess had dropped her handkerchief, and ran out of the room and down the stairs, calling her name. Miss Bladen decided to reprove the girl for going on an errand more suitable for a servant, but it was too late. The girl was out in the street, bareheaded and without a cloak. The only servant who had seen her depart was too slow-witted to understand what it was that Marjorie intended to do. An hour later, Sir John returned to find the servant in tears, and Miss Bladen white-faced with anger. Marjorie had not returned.

Miss Nan bathed the spittle from the dying boy's lips. He smiled up at her, game to the last, and asked if his father had returned.

"Not yet, dear. He went for a ride in the Park. Shall I send a footman after him?"

"No. He will come as soon as he can, I know that. It must be lovely in the Park, with the leaves coming out. How I wish I were in the country again." Thomas's room was filled with the flowers that he loved so much, and now and then he thought spring had come.

"Soon, dear. Soon."

"The Rose? Is she here?"

"Downstairs, dearest, with her dressmaker. She wanted to sit with you for a while, but the doctor doesn't think it wise."

"I wonder if they will call the new baby by my name."

"Would you like that?"

The boy shook his head. "I'm me," he said. "I don't want them to use my name. They wouldn't, if I were still here when the baby is born. I did want to see it, but I'm so tired...."

Hugh Denbigh slipped into the chair at the side of the bed, and smiled at Miss Nan. She pressed his hand, or perhaps it was he who pressed hers. Then, strengthened by this moment of contact, Miss Nan went out to wait for Philip's return. She did not think the boy would last another twenty-four hours.

Lord Lincoln had also been riding in the Park. Philip and he had a satisfying canter, and then walked their horses back, exchanging news. Lincoln would shortly finish his present term of waiting at Court, but in view of the national emergency had decided not to leave Town at present. Philip commended his decision.

"Oh, it's far too exciting a time for me to leave," said Lincoln. "How goes it with Mr. Nelson?"

"Cautiously. He is of a suspicious nature, and if one hint of what we are doing were to reach the newspapers, I think he would disappear again. However, he is happier to have discussions on a friendly basis round the fire in my library than to be received in Whitehall officially. The news that the Jacobites are on the retreat from Derby made a considerable impression on him. He had given us to understand that the French had twelve thousand men under Richelieu waiting to embark, if we did not agree to such and such terms; I doubt if we will hear any more of invasion plans now, and his demands will be moderated. If only we could smash the Pretender...but Wade is a broken reed."

"Be of good cheer. My uncle tells me the Navy has captured a French ship which was taking money to the Jacobites, and that two more were wrecked. The rebels are isolated. I can't understand why his forces haven't disintegrated before now."

"They keep together because they are mostly Highlanders far from home. What will happen once they are over the Border again is anyone's guess." The Earl indicated the swirling, crowded streets beyond the Park with his riding crop. "I wonder how they would all behave if the Highland Army were to march into London at this moment. Come to that, how would we ourselves behave? Would we simply stand and stare like everyone has done in the north? Or would we fight?"

"I hope we would fight. Nay, I am sure we would."

"That's what the people of Carlisle and Derby said, but when the time came, they dispersed peacefully. They don't like the Stuart cause enough to fight for it, but they don't think it's their business to fight it, either. This affair will be decided by hired troops from Flanders, which leaves a bad taste in my mouth. If the Pretender had had access to funds, or had been supplied with French troops, would he not have been in London by now, instead of fleeing north?"

"I believe that bringing foreign troops over here would have united the country against the Pretender. Philip, this is not like you. Have you forgotten that there will be upwards of ten regiments raised by volunteers to fight the rebels? How do you fit their patriotism into your pessimistic view of the situation? And what of the demonstrations in favor of the King?"

223

"Ought I to believe in my own propaganda?" Philip forced a smile. "Forgive me. I did not sleep last night. Thomas is not well, and I was sitting up with him until...Sophia came to call me away to bed, but I could not sleep, even then. He is dying, you know. The last of my children."

"Not the last," said Lincoln, pressing his friend's arm. "You must not give way to despair. The Countess is young and healthy. Put your trust in her."

"I wish I could," murmured Philip.

"What did you say?" Lincoln had not understood.

"I mean, yes, I should."

Philip handed over his horse's reins to a groom, and mounted the steps of his house at the same time as a sedan chair was borne to the door. Sir John Bladen erupted from the chair, his wig awry, hatless, and brandishing a cane.

"My daughter!" he cried. "Where have you hidden her, traitor?"

Philip half turned, paused in his ascent, and looked around. Was Sir John addressing him? Sir John left the issue in no doubt, but pounded up the steps to Philip's side, and thrust his empurpled face into that of the Earl.

"Where—have—you—hidden her?" he demanded.

"I beg your pardon?"

"My daughter—Marjorie—your whore! You have her somewhere." He lunged forward, brushing past Philip and the astonished footmen into the hall. "Where is she?" He raised his voice, and hollered her name. "Marjorie! Come here, I say!"

Philip followed into the hall, and shed his hat, gloves and riding crop into waiting hands. He looked amused, but a keen eye would have noticed that he was also very alert. "Your daughter, Sir John? Is she visiting us? I had no idea." He summoned the butler to his side. "Is Miss Bladen within?"

"There have been several visitors, my lord. Mr. Nelson is waiting in the library with Mr. Carramine. Mr. Dodge has just arrived and is wishful to speak with you urgently. Lady Midmain called some time ago, but I do not believe she was accompanied by anyone but Mrs. Dalby. They did not stay above half an hour."

Sir John stamped with rage. Doors were opening above

and around them. Miss Nan's anxious face appeared on the landing above, and behind her came Sophia.

"Will you produce her, sirrah?" cried Sir John, "or do I have to lay information against you to the nearest magistrate?"

"I am not in the habit of detaining ladies in my house against their will," said the Earl, losing his smile. "What, man! Do you think I have abducted your daughter? For what purpose, pray?"

"For the usual purpose, my lord. Your reputation is against you, as I am sure the magistrate will agree."

"Oh, have done!" said the Earl, with a flash of anger. "If Miss Marjorie is indeed here, it is without my knowledge. You have heard my butler give you a list of those who have called in my absence, and now if you please, I have some business to..."

"Oh yes, your butler has given a list of those who have called, but not of those who have stayed. Where have you stowed her?" He began to mount the staircase.

Miss Nan stepped forward. "I assure you, Sir John, that..."

"Out of my way, Cripple! I intend to search every room of this house until I find my daughter, and when I have found her, I shall take her to the nearest magistrate and swear out a warrant against this libertine, this seducer, this traitor!"

"Sir John!" Sophia stood before them, straight and tall. Sir John stopped, on the step below her. "I saw your daughter only this afternoon. We talked at some length, and..." She put her hand on his arm, and gestured that he precede her into the drawing-room. "Will you not come this way? You will not wish to discuss the matter in front of the servants. I will have some Madeira sent up." She nodded over her shoulder to the butler, who had followed close on Philip's heels, up the stairs; two other footmen hovered, their eyes watchful. She shook her head slightly at Philip, indicating that she felt able to deal with Sir John. Surprisingly, he succumbed to the pressure of her fingers on his arm, and walked heavily at her side towards the drawing-room. They were almost there. Someone was running up the stairs behind them. The butler exclaimed something, but the newcomer was not to be denied. It was Mr. Dodge, travel-stained and beaming. His smile was a harbinger of disaster.

"My lord, a word with you!" he said, both hands clasped over his ample stomach.

"Jasper!" gasped Miss Nan. "Not dead?"

"No, no, ma'am."

"Captured," said Philip, flatly, as if he had known it already.

Sophia paused, her hand to her heart. She saw Mr. Dodge nod, and clutched at the bannister for support. So her rebel brother had been caught by the Hanoverians, and would doubtless die on Tower Hill. She had known it! She had known for several days that something terrible was about to happen.

Sir John was slipping away from her controlling grasp, his anger reviving. She could not, for the moment...to be dizzy at a moment like this! She took one deep breath, and then another. Her sight cleared. She was not going to fall, although she still felt as if there were no bones in her legs. Where was Sir John? He was not at her side.

The double doors leading to the library were flung open, and Mr. Carramine appeared from within, agitation in every line of his body.

"Philip! Thank God you've returned. I've been waiting for you this hour. I must speak with you, urgently, but Mr. Nelson arrived just after I came, and I suppose he must be attended to first....Christ in heaven! What is the matter with you all?"

"Philip, you must come up to Thomas; he is asking for you."

"My lord, a word with you..."

Sir John thrust through the group at the head of the stairs and made for the open doors of the library. "Just as I thought! You have hidden her in here, have you?"

Philip had pressed his fingers to his forehead. Sophia wondered if he were ill. She forced herself to take two stumbling steps, and was at his side. Out of the corner of her eye she saw Mr. Carramine try to prevent Sir John rushing into the library, and fail. Then Philip was clinging to her arm, or she to his. For a moment, she had all his attention.

"You are all right?" he asked. "Believe me, I will do everything I can to obtain Jasper's release."

Jasper was her brother, and in peril; but Philip was her husband, and he also needed her help. "I shall be all right.

I trust you to do what can be done. What would you like me to do?"

"You are offering to help me?" Fatigue had dulled his reactions, which were usually quick. His clasp on her arm tightened. She read admiration in his eyes; for the first time he was proud of her. He looked around. The servants hovered, waiting for orders. Mr. Dodge was muttering in Miss Nan's ear. She was wringing her hands, and there were tears on her face. Mr. Carramine was holding his ribs, where he had been winded by Sir John's thrust. Mr. Denbigh was descending the stairs from the nursery, looking distressed, and at that very moment the door knocker sounded, and a footman announced the arrival of Lady Lincoln.

"I hardly know where to begin!" said Philip. "Of all the preposterous..."

A voice was raised from within the library, swearing fluently in French, Mr. Nelson protesting at Sir John's invasion.

"Oh, my God!" said Philip. "Mr. Nelson! Of all the..."

Nodding to collect the butler and one of the footmen, Philip made for the library, only to be met by Sir John, retreating onto the landing, with his hands in the air. The furious face of a well-dressed, middle-aged man appeared over Sir John's shoulder, and the point of a sword flickered this way and that around Sir John's wig, keeping him at arms' length.

"But the man is mad! He insists I have his daughter! He must be locked up! This house is not safe! I leave, this instant! I do not stay, not for one moment!"

"The man is mad, I agree," said Philip, stepping between Sir John and the Frenchman. "He shall be removed, at once." A flick of his wrist, and the butler and footman closed in on either side of Sir John. "He believes I have hidden his daughter somewhere in my house, and I cannot convince him otherwise."

"Do you deny that you encouraged her to run away?" demanded Sir John. "You sent her notes, singled her out in public!"

"Of course I deny it," said Philip. He held the library door open for Mr. Carramine, and turned his back on Sir John. "Mr. Nelson, I very much regret that I was absent when you arrived. I trust that Mr. Carramine has looked after you properly." His eye flicked to the butler. "I am not at home to anyone else this morning." And went on to Sophia. "I am

227

sure we wish to give Sir John every assistance in our power to enable him to find his daughter. Perhaps you will obtain the full story from him before he leaves? I much regret that I have a business matter to attend to." His eye went on to Mr. Dodge. "Mr. Dodge, you will kindly wait below. I will ring for you when I am at leisure." And to Miss Nan, "I will come to Thomas as soon as I may. Will you tell him that?"

"But...!" said Sir John. He said it to a closed door.

He turned on Sophia. "This will not do," he said.

"No, indeed it will not," she said. She put as much sympathy in her voice as she could, and took his arm again. "We must look into it for you. Here is Lady Lincoln come to pay me a call. My dear... you have caught us in the middle of a domestic crisis, as you can see. Dear Aunt, I will come to you presently, but for the moment...?" Mr. Denbigh took Miss Nan's elbow and retired with her up the stairs. The butler darted angry glances at the staff, who melted away in this direction and that.

The doorknocker fell again, and the butler looked at Sophia for instructions.

"I am not at home, and neither is the Earl. Some light refreshments please, in the drawing-room." She held her hands out to Lady Lincoln and Sir John. "Come; let us sit near the fire. I am half perished, standing in this draft."

"Do you wish me to stay?" Lady Lincoln asked.

"Two heads are better than one," said Sophia. "It seems that Miss Marjorie has disappeared; I only saw her this afternoon, and Sir John quite naturally thought that she had returned here with me, but unfortunately it was not so. I thought the child looked very pale, and I did offer to take her up in my carriage for a while, but Miss Bladen said Sir John did not wish Marjorie to leave the house until she was in better health, so... Yes, take that chair, Sir John. Come nearer the fire, Catherine."

The butler brought in wine and biscuits, but Sir John would not relax. Neither Sophia nor Catherine Lincoln could get a word out of him. He drank, and looked at the fire, and grunted when addressed by either of the ladies. Presently Catherine gave her friend a look of comical despair, and took her leave. As soon as she had gone, Sir John caught her arm, and put his mouth to her ear.

"Traitor!" he whispered. "He is a traitor!"

"I wish you would not say such things," said Sophia. "No wonder that the Frenchman thought you mad."

"Ah yes, the Frenchman. And what is a Frenchman doing in his library at this present time? Business, he said. Treasonable business. 'Mr. Nelson,' he called him, but that wouldn't be his real name, would it?"

"I really have no idea." It was odd, of course, but Philip would have an explanation for it.

"So he hasn't told you what he's up to? I've wondered, now and then, if you knew. I didn't think you'd knowingly marry a traitor, even if your brother was out with the rebels and your father and elder brother had been rebels. I thought better of you than that, Sophia."

"Philip is no traitor. He is devoted to the King."

"He is a Judas. He smiles and pretends devotion, and all the time he is betraying his country to the French. Oh, you may laugh, but when I tell you what I have seen and heard, with my own eyes...and what other people have seen and heard..."

"I do not wish to hear."

"I insist that you hear me out. I have made a serious allegation against your husband, and you have said that you think I am mad, but you have not heard the grounds on which I base my claim. For instance, did your husband ever tell you how he disturbed some highwaymen in the act of robbing a French courier, when he was on his way down to Sussex? Did he never tell you that the Frenchman gave him a letter to deliver, and that he subsequently concealed that letter from me, the magistrate dealing with the matter? Did he not tell you of the secret meetings he had with your rebel brother Jasper, down at the mill at Hamberley, and in other places? I can bring witnesses to the letter, and to the meetings. Did not this treacherous man worm his way into Tarrant Hall under a false name, and while he was under your roof, being nursed by you, betray your hospitality by persuading Jasper to join the rebels? You knew that he did this, and yet you were so blinded by his money and his high and mighty air that you refused to admit it. Did he not subsequently steal Tarrant Hall from Jasper, in the guise of buying it at a low price? At a price which anyone with a particle of business sense would have known was fraudulent. He stole, and cheated, and lied his way into your affections, and then left you to go off to Hanover and his mistress for the summer.

You knew that Mrs. O'Dell was in Hanover this summer, didn't you? He went straight from Tarrant Hall to her arms, and when he returned to London, she came back with him. He married you not because he loved you, but because you are from a Jacobite family."

"No, that is not true!"

"What other explanation fits the facts? Has he ever been open with you about his affairs?"

"Why, yes; he has spoken of his political ambitions once or twice. He told me about..."

"That ploy of his, when he pretended he wanted to raise a regiment for the King? Is that not typical of him? The man is not what he seems. Let us take one more example; the man Dodge. Now I happen to know that this is the very man who took part in the ambush of the French courier. How can you explain his presence in this house, and the trust which the Earl reposes in him, unless you postulate the presence of a guilty secret between the two of them? Mr. Dodge is a blackmailer, my dear; the Earl is paying him to hold his tongue. Perhaps the man Dodge has become a willing tool of the Jacobite spies, since he has brought the news of your brother's capture by the Hanoverians. What other construction can you put on what you have just seen with your own eyes?"

"I do not know." Sophia pressed her hands over her mouth. She felt ill. She could not believe this of Philip...and yet...

"It is not as if he had any sincere regard for you," continued Sir John. "His continued visits to Mrs. O'Dell prove that, as does his pursuit of my poor daughter Marjorie. He has convinced me that she is not in this house. Very well. I see now that it would have been stupid of him to bring her here, where you would see her. No, he has taken her elsewhere, or arranged for her to be taken elsewhere, and later on today, or tomorrow, he will go to her. She is lost, disgraced. She is no longer my daughter. I renounce her. My chief regret is that in making a whore of my daughter, he is insulting you."

Sophia cried out, and put her hands protectively over her body. She was carrying Philip's child, and he was unfaithful to her.

"He ruins everybody with whom he comes into contact," said Sir John. "Jasper, Marjorie, you...and even Mr. Carramine; my old friend Mr. Carramine is working with him to bring down the King."

Sophia stood up. Inaction was unbearable, but the pain

did not ease with movement. "I cannot believe it!" she cried. "You are mistaken. There must be some explanation..."

"What explanation?" asked Sir John. He stood up, too. "My dear, there is only one explanation. The man is a traitor, out of ambition, out of spite, perhaps. He loves no one but himself. He will bring us all down, unless he is stopped."

"Proof! You have no proof!"

"I have given you proof. What more do you need? Shall I tell you what I saw in that library of his? Maps, my dear; marked with the route taken by the Pretender and his forces, and also marked with the route taken by Government troops. How comes he by such things honestly? And there are documents piled high on tables, which I did not have time to examine, for that thrice-damned Frenchman came at me. Give me one paper, or one map from those tables, and I will set your husband on the road to Tower Hill...."

"No!"

"...and execution. Do you not want to free yourself from this mockery of a marriage? Do you not want to free the country from treason? Is it not your plain duty to do so? I will tell you what to do. There is a man in your employ; a carpenter, who will open the doors of the library if given ten minutes alone with them. You will see that he has all the time he needs, and take what evidence we need, and then you will leave this house of lies for ever. Go down to Tarrant Hall. Your aunt Midmain says that the Earl has given it to you, as part of your marriage settlement. It is only natural that you should wish to visit it. You may safely leave the rest to me."

He bowed. He was gone. He trusted her to help him. Philip trusted her to help him. She sank onto a chair and wept.

Chapter Fourteen

Sophia shivered, and rang the bell for a footman to make up the fire. She had been sitting in the corner of the settee, or pacing the drawing-room for nearly three hours, and was no nearer a decision than when Sir John had left her. The afternoon sky was growing darker by the minute as the smoke from the coal fires rose to the low clouds overhead. Perhaps it would rain. She went to the window and looked out over the square. Down below was a hired sedan chair, with its bearers standing idle. Inside the chair she saw a man; he leaned forward to speak to someone standing beside him, and she saw that the man in the chair was Sir John Bladen, and the man standing beside him was Mr. Farrow, once bailiff to Philip. They were waiting, presumably for her to act.

She shivered again, and asked the footman if the Earl were still in the house. The footman replied that the Earl had left the house some time ago, with his guest, Mr. Nelson. Miss Tarrant was upstairs with Mr. Denbigh in the sickroom, and Mr. Carramine had just stepped out for a breath of air.

"I wish to speak with Mr. Dodge. Will you send him to me, please."

She could not believe that Philip was a traitor, and yet...Philip in Mrs. O'Dell's arms, Philip hiding Marjorie from her father....

He had denied it. It must be false. And yet...

She would not spy on him. She would not enter his library for proof of his iniquity, but she could and would ask Mr.

Dodge certain questions. He came, full of apologies for having blurted out his news in such an indiscreet fashion and thus upset the ladies.

"Never mind that, now. I want the truth about my brother. How was he captured? Was he a spy?"

Mr. Dodge was silent. He beamed her an apology, but made it clear that he did not feel able to speak.

"Don't be afraid," said Sophia. "I know what my husband has been doing. I know you ambushed the French courier, and that the courier gave Philip a compromising letter. I know Philip involved Jasper in his ploys. I know everything, except what has happened to my poor brother."

"Begging your pardon, my lady, but better be safe than sorry, as the saying goes. Well, I don't know precisely how the young cock was caught, but I'd say he was asking for it in some way. Reckless, he was. I don't hold with reckless men, because they lead others into danger, too, most often. The truth is, I didn't see his capture, because I wasn't there. All I knew was that I was supposed to meet with him just outside Derby, and he didn't turn up. So I hung about for a while, and then did the rounds of the taverns, and sure enough I heard after a while that a spy had been picked up. I thought they'd hang him outright, but no one said anything about hanging. I watched next morning, and he walked past me, under escort, as calm as you please. His hands were bound, and he'd lost his hat and boots, but otherwise he looked fit enough."

She sank onto a chair, her hand to her heart. "What will they do with him?"

Mr. Dodge weighed his words. "No point mincing words, my lady. They'll hang him, most like, but they may not get round to it for some time. They'll want to question him, and they can't do that so easily while they're on the march. Before I started back, I set my mate Peter to watching the column. If they leave him hanging on a tree, then Peter'll cut him down as soon as he can, and stow the body safely so's you can bury it properly later on. Maybe—just maybe—they'll be so pressed for time they'll forget about him; they won't let him go, but they'll keep him safe and sound till they have breathing space. Now if that happens, we've got a chance of getting him back, by exchange. We have one of their spies, they have one of ours, and we exchange them. The Earl had a quick word with me before he went out, ma'am, and he told

233

me to send the word along that we value your brother. Oh yes, while there's life, there's hope, as the saying goes."

Sophia inclined her head in token of dismissal, and Mr. Dodge left her.

So it was all true, and Philip was a traitor, and so was her brother and her aunt, and everyone she valued. Where would it end? On Tower Hill for Philip, and on the branches of a leafless tree for Jasper? And what of Aunt Nan, and of the child in her body? Sir John had been right; she must leave this house and return to Tarrant Hall...it was like Philip to have given her back her home...he was so unfailingly kind, always courteous and considerate...and a traitor not only to his King, but also to her.

Her wanderings had taken her back to the window. Sir John was still there, waiting for her to send him some piece of incriminating evidence to convict Philip. Well, she would not do so. She would not help to bring him to the block, however much he had deserved it. She would leave the house next morning, and never see him again; she would write him a letter telling him exactly why she was leaving him, and then she would go.

Aunt Nan must go with her. But what of the boy Thomas? Aunt Nan would never leave the boy. But he was dying. Oh, it hurt to think how Philip had tricked her into bearing him a child....

She went out onto the landing and looked about her. It was as if she had never seen the house before; the gracefully proportioned pillars, the cream and gold of the walls, the heavily-framed portraits, and the softly shining wood of the double doors of the library. Her aunt's door was closed. Should she go in? Might she be able to think more clearly there?

There was an altercation on the landing behind her; her maid was scolding someone. It was the little carpenter, who had no doubt come to open the library doors for her. The maid was objecting to his presence.

Sophia said; "Let the man be. I ordered him to attend to the lock on the library door. It is stiff."

The maid hesitated. Sophia outfaced her and swept to the library door. The carpenter followed, grimacing. He was a nervous little man, but he did not take long to open the door. All the time, Sophia's maid stood in the background, clasping and unclasping her hands. At last the door was open. Sophia slipped inside the room, and shut the door behind her.

234

The shutters were open, but the room was dusky. Heavy curtains hung at the windows, and the fire had burned low. There were candles set in candelabra here and there, but they had not yet been lit. She saw what Sir John had seen, and closed her eyes, leaning against the door for support. Maps, and yet more maps; marked as Sir John had described. She lit a branch of candles, using a taper from a box on the mantelpiece. There was a crumpled piece of paper on the hearth, one side of which was singed. Someone had thrown it at the fire, it had rebounded and fallen onto the hearth. She picked it up, and smoothed it out, recognizing Mr. Carramine's neat handwriting.

"In haste," she read. *"The girl came to me an hour ago after having wandered half way round the Town. She refuses to return to her father. I took her to the address in Crooked Court that you know of. She is in great distress. I promised you would visit her as soon as you could. C."*

So it was all true. She could doubt no longer. Philip was Marjorie's lover, and Sophia's life was finished.

She would not weep. The time for tears lay in the future, in the long years to come without a husband or friends. She had a duty to perform. She would not give Sir John the evidence he needed, because Philip was her husband, and because of that she would not betray him to death on Tower Hill. She would warn him, as soon as she could, that his activities were suspect, but she would not betray him.

Marjorie, however, was a different matter. She must be restored to her father, who would know how to deal with her. If she were married to Mr. Dalby before the scandal broke, then perhaps the girl's reputation might be saved.

She left the room with the note in her hand. Her maid was still standing outside on the landing.

"If you please, my lady, but his lordship does not wish anyone to go into the library."

"I know," said Sophia. "I will see him when he comes back."

She went into the drawing-room and rang the bell. When a footman came, she gave him Mr. Carramine's note, and told him to deliver it to Sir John Bladen, whom he would find waiting outside in a sedan chair. She watched from her window as the note was delivered. The footman was being detained. Why? Ah, he was being given a note. Yes, he was returning. She went to the fire, and tried to warm herself.

She was shivering once more. The footman scratched on the door, and delivered the note. She read it, and dismissed him.

"Make sure he forgets to take his pistols with him. J.B."

She shivered again. "Make sure..." Did that mean that Sir John meant to challenge Philip to a duel? Of course, if Philip did not go to see Marjorie, he would be in no danger. But if he did go, then he would be bringing his fate upon himself.

She began to pace the room once more. She had not meant to betray him into Sir John's hands, even though he were guilty a hundred times over. If he were to keep his marriage vows...yes, and his pledge to her not to visit Marjorie...then he should be quite safe.

He came in. She was startled, and cried out.

He smiled, and took her hand in his. "Are you well? You did bravely, calming Sir John. I was proud of you."

She snatched her hand away. "I know what has been going on. I have been in the library, you see."

"I know. Your maid came to tell me, as soon as I returned. I am sorry I could not tell you before. I wanted to do so, many times."

"Why did you do it? You, of all people!"

"Why did I suborn Jasper? Yes, I wish I had not, now. Yet it seemed the only thing to do, at the time. Do you blame me very much for it? Yes, I see that you do. If it is any consolation, I blame myself for it, too. Listen to me. Don't turn away. I must go out."

"To see Marjorie?"

"Why, yes. She does not know, yet, about Jasper."

"Is it only for Jasper's sake that you go? Not for your own?"

"You are angry. Why? You know why I used to see her."

"That tale won't do, when you have coaxed her to run away from home."

"I had no idea that she was going to do so."

"I beg of you not to go!"

"Why? Sophia, why? But I must! The girl is half distracted. I promise I will not stay with her more than half an hour. Thomas needs me, and your aunt, not to mention..."

"I understand. You put everyone before me. Marjorie, Jasper, my aunt, Thomas, Mr. Carramine—even this mysterious Frenchman, Mr. Nelson. Go, then—and on your own head be it."

Would he argue? No, he was tired, and would not quarrel.

236

She watched him shrug, and move away from her. He was at the door. She had only to lift a finger to bring him back. No, she would not. Pride forbade. She must warn him to go armed. He had opened the door. He was passing through it.

"Philip!"

The door shut, and he was on the other side of it.

She hesitated. Should she run after him? She would have to warn him in front of the servants, and how would that sound? It would sound very odd. He would not believe her. She could give him the note. Where was it? She had put it down somewhere, when the footman had given it to her. Where?

It was in the hearth. She picked it up, and sped after him. She reached the foot of the stairs only to see the butler closing the front door. He had gone.

The servants were staring at her. She knew she was behaving oddly. She turned round and went upstairs to her bedroom, and rang the bell for her maid. She would occupy the time until his return with packing her things.

It was only then she realized that Sir John meant to kill Philip.

The address to which the Earl directed his coach was near the Fleet Prison in the City. Crooked Court was one of a warren of alleys and passages in that part of London, chosen by Mr. Dodge as a suitable area in which to dwell, partly because a man could easily elude pursuit if he knew the area, and partly because it was cheap. No coach could pass through those alleys, so the Earl alighted nearby, and directed one of the footmen to take a lantern and lead the way. There were supposed to be street lanterns at prescribed intervals along these alleys, but some were broken, and some unlit. The Earl picked his way between piles of refuse and wished himself elsewhere. A grimy hand—probably a child's—clutched at his cloak. A baby cried unceasingly. White faces peered from the entrances to alleys as he passed, and he was conscious of being watched from every side. He had changed his riding dress for a suit of sober hue, and thrown a light cloak overall, but he was aware that his clothes, hat and shoes were objects of envy to the ragged creatures who lived hereabouts. His eyes alert to the slightest movement, he swung his cane, and wished he had thought to bring his pistol from the coach. It was lucky that Chivers had pressed his sword-stick into his hand as he left the house....

A strangled cry, and his footman dropped his lantern. There was a sound as of a foot slipping on refuse behind him. Philip whirled, to see the point of a sword snaking for his throat. He ducked, his right hand twisting at the top of his sword-stick. A cudgel whistled through the air, and he jumped back, withdrawing his sword from the cane-sheath...wondering how many assailants there might be; one to deal with the footman, and two behind him?

He set his back to the wall of a house nearby and sent out a cry for the Watch. The alley was dark. Darker than when he had entered it? Had there not been a light on a house some fifteen yards behind him? It was darkened now. The only light which entered the alley came from the mouth of the street, some fifty yards away. He could hear someone breathing hard, and thrust at the sound. His swordpoint met something soft, and someone yelled. Again the cudgel whistled, and this time caught his bad shoulder. He leaped to one side, but this took him away from the wall, and into the open. Refuse was under his feet. He must be careful not to slip. He began to move further from the wall, crouching low. If he could see them against the light, then he must take care not to be seen in the same way. What cursed luck to be attacked on such an errand! He knew footpads and Mohocks abounded in this part of the City. It was his own fault; he ought to have brought several men with him.

There was a rush of feet, the thud of a descending weapon, and a man swore. The Earl smiled. The enemy had engaged with itself. Enchanting! Then his smile faded, for he thought he had recognized the voice of the man who had sworn. Not footpads, not Mohocks out for a spree....

Cat-like, Philip retreated step by step down the alley, his swordpoint at the ready. He tried to breathe lightly, so as not to betray his presence. His breathing was far too loud. No, it was not his own breathing that he heard, but someone else's.

A sword sprang out of the darkness, catching the light, making for his heart. He had been seen. He engaged his assailant. His own sword was far too light for this kind of work, and he was not and never had been expert with the foils. His opponent was no expert, either, but he was a heavier man in every way. The swords slithered, dipped, disengaged and met again. Philip was younger and in better condition than his adversary, but he had had little sleep and much anxiety of late. Also, his shoulder ached. His feet caught on something yielding, and he slipped. The large man gave a shout of glee and shortened his arm to drive his sword home. Philip rolled to one side, towards the wall. Again he called for help, even though he knew it was unlikely anyone would come to his rescue. Prudent citizens left the victims of such attacks to their fate.

The big man had lost sight of him. He circled, facing this way and that. Philip recognized him, now that his eyes were growing accustomed to the gloom. Sir John Bladen. How had he come by, so opportunely? There was only one answer possible. Sophia had been in the library, had seen Mr. Carramine's note, and had betrayed him.

Philip was still holding the cane of his swordstick. He thrust it between Sir John's legs, and brought him down. Sir John fell heavily. He appeared dazed. Philip got to his feet slowly, looking around for his other assailants. The alley was silent, watchfully so. Philip bent over Sir John, and as he did so, someone leaped onto his back. A cloud of bad breath announced that his assailant had rotten teeth. Fingers crawled around Philip's throat and began to squeeze...he was done...he staggered back against the wall, throwing himself against the brickwork...the man would not be dislodged...Sir John was getting to his feet, looking around him, finding his sword, and shortening it to strike home...Philip threw out his arms...he had lost his sword...There was a drumming noise in his head...no, feet running...a muffling roar and he dropped to the ground.

There was a buzzing in his ears. Light, flashing, unbearably bright. One last heave, and the fingers around his throat slackened. The weight was off his back, but someone else was coming at him, iron bar raised, teeth grinning in a death's head of enjoyment. How ever many of them were there? He staggered to his feet. He had no weapon with which to defend himself. He avoided the first onslaught with feet which seemed weighted with lead. He tore off his cloak, and as the man came at him again Philip threw it over his head...and suddenly there was more light....

A door in a house along the alley had opened, and a gigantic man came out, arms outstretched to catch the man with the cudgel around his waist and swing him once ...twice...thrice...against the nearby wall. The man went limp, but the large man continued to swing...a fourth...fifth...sixth time. The man with the cudgel ceased to cry out after the third blow.

The Earl turned into the shadows and leaned against the wall.

"Are you all right, my lord?"

It was Chivers, smoking pistol in hand, and two footmen at his back. He spoke in a hushed voice, and looked scared. "My lady sent me after you. She insisted I take your pistols, but lordy me, I didn't know if I could hit a haystack, never mind a man! Only see what I've done, my lord! Will this mean the nubbing cheat for me?"

"That's my bully boy!" cried Mr. Dodge, throwing his victim against the wall and dusting off his hands. "A notch for you, and a notch for me, and his lordship that moithered he doesn't know whether to say 'Good Lord,' or 'Thank God!' Come into my house and have a drop of something while I get this place cleaned up. It won't do to have the bodies found here, will it?"

The Earl looked around him. The footman who had lighted his way down the alley was getting to his feet, looking dazed. The man Greenwood, who had wielded the bar, lay sprawled against the wall, his head flattened by repeated contact with the bricks. He was undoubtedly dead.

There was a huddled form at the Earl's feet; Farrow, his fingers still clutching, but this time at empty air. There was a hole in the back of his coat, and he was also very dead.

"This means the nubbing cheat for me," said Chivers. The pistol in his hand shook. "I saw him trying to throttle his lordship, and I aimed high, as I thought, to frighten him."

"You leave the pistols to his lordship and me in future," said Mr. Dodge, in fatherly fashion. "Now don't take on so, man! No one's going to the nubbing cheat for this affair, are they, my lord?"

"Not unless I join you on the gallows," said Philip, pointing to a gross body which was trying to heave itself to a sitting position a couple of yards away. Philip's sword was lodged fast in Sir John's body, although the fat man was trying to withdraw it with hands that slipped on his own blood. "I can't remember it," said Philip. "I must have impaled him without realizing it, when Farrow got me round the throat."

240

"He's done for, anyway," said Mr. Dodge, with a detached, even kindly interest. "Sir John, Farrow and Greenwood. As pretty a trio as were ever brought to justice."

Something bubbled at Sir John's mouth. He had his eyes fixed on Philip. He was pawing at his coat sleeve—there was something white protruding. Philip bent down and extracted it.

"She betrayed you," whispered Sir John. A look of malevolent glee contorted his face. He began to laugh, and died.

Philip did not need to read the note to know what it contained. "I know," he said. "She betrayed us both."

Chapter Fifteen

It was nearly ten in the evening before the Earl returned home. Sophia sat on the edge of a chair in the drawing-room, and watched the clock. Twice her aunt had been down to ask if Philip had returned; Thomas was worse and asking for his father.

She heard the stir in the house when he arrived, but she did not go out to greet him. She was afraid of what he would say. Presently he came to her. He had changed his clothes, and there were scratches on his hands, but otherwise he looked unharmed, if weary.

He did not greet her, but threw Mr. Carramine's letter about Marjorie onto the carpet at her feet.

He said, "You betrayed me, and then you betrayed him. I hope you are satisfied. He is dead, together with his two companions, Farrow and Greenwood. Their bodies will be found in that den of thieves, Seven Dials, tomorrow, or perhaps later than that, if the Watch is negligent. I doubt if there will be any query about their death...a quarrel between master and servants...everyone knows Sir John was unbalanced."

"I sent Chivers after you, as soon as I realized what Sir John intended. I could not find Mr. Dodge or Mr. Carramine. I am glad you are safely returned, even if you have been false to me and to your King. Sir John wanted me to give him evidence of your treasonable activities, but I refused to do so. I hope that you will have sense enough to cease corresponding

242

with the Pretender now, but...it is no affair of mine. I leave for Tarrant Hall tomorrow, and I do not intend to return."

"So that is what you think. It had crossed my mind as a possibility, but I had rejected it out of hand. Go, then. I have finished with you." He was not even angry with her.

Could she have been mistaken? No...it was unthinkable. She raised her voice. "I see you dare not explain your activities to me. What else can I believe?"

He hesitated, looked at the clock, and then spoke rapidly, as if his mind were elsewhere.

"My uncle Carteret devised a scheme to trap the Pretender into an ill-timed and ill-prepared invasion. He asked me to help him. At first I refused to do so, but a letter fell into my hands which, though it forwarded my uncle's plans, might incriminate its recipient. That letter was addressed to someone at the sign of the Ram and the Rose. It was meant for your father, who had been an active Jacobite. My uncle wanted me to persuade Jasper to take his father's place in the chain which linked the Pretender to these shores. Jasper was refused a commission and was ready to do anything to see active service, and so I recruited him to act for the Government as a spy—a double agent, if you like. He did not go under his own name, of course, but under that of David Vere, and under that name he has earned the gratitude of the Government.

"Mr. Carramine joined me in setting up a system to obtain information on the Pretender's doings, and conveying it to London quickly. Mr. Dodge and his men are all in the pay of the Government, but have been seconded by Mr. Stone to work with me on this assignment. My presenting a bill in Parliament was but a cover for the work I have been doing in private, both here and at Court. During the course of this last month I have been offered ministerial posts both by my uncle and by the Duke of Newcastle, but I stand by my original ambition, to be appointed Ambassador abroad. It is also rumored that I am to receive the Order of the Garter, but I will believe that when it happens."

"And Jasper? He is in the hands of the Jacobites, and not of the Government troops?"

"It appears they are making for Carlisle. I doubt if the rebels will be able to hold Carlisle, but even if they do, it is no matter, for this morning I agreed on the terms of a peace treaty with the French agent, whom you may know as Mr. Nelson."

"I thought he was a spy."

"I assure you his credentials are impeccable. As to the lady in Mayfair, of whom you have been so jealous, she really is a spy of a sort. She is an old acquaintance of mine, but devoted to her permanent and very wealthy protector. She runs a select gaming establishment. Gamblers are expansive both when they have lost or when they have won. She is adept at extracting information. Her speciality is acquiring information as to the movements of prominent Jacobites in London. I went there for information and also, to be fair, for food. She keeps an excellent table."

"And Marjorie?"

"She knew what Jasper was doing and was prepared to wait for him. She regards me in the same light as Mr. Carramine, as an aged but still mobile uncle. Sir John pressed her to marry Mr. Dalby; she refused. Sir John beat her; she applied to you for help. You refused. She could not think of anything else to do but run to Mr. Carramine and solicit his help. He lives in lodgings, and he could not think what to do with her, so he took her to Mrs. Dodge. The girl is now returned to her aunt, who has been warned to say nothing of the girl's absence today. Marjorie should inherit Sir John's estate, but Mr. Carramine will deal with it for her until Jasper returns. I would have brought her back here with me, but that it might have caused gossip, which is the last thing we want. I believe Lady Lincoln will hold her tongue about what she heard and saw this morning, but the servants may not. Marjorie wants to return home, but at the moment there is no one who can be spared to take her." He paused. Evidently he meant Sophia to offer her services, but she was still too confused to understand.

She said, "My aunt and Mr. Denbigh—do they know all this?"

"Of course. I would trust them both with my life."

"But you would not trust me."

"Time has proved me right, has it not? It does not matter what you know, now. The manner of Sir John's death you will undoubtedly keep to yourself, for fear of exciting contempt at your part in it. The rest is, or soon will be, common knowledge. I hope you will be happy at Tarrant Hall. I shall not, of course, request you to accompany me when I am sent

244

abroad. It is not likely that we shall meet again for some years, if at all. Indeed, I hope we do not. The lawyers will see to it that you have sufficient money, and if you wish for an official separation, I will agree, provided that I can have the child."

He was going. She could not bear it. She would fling herself at his feet and beg for forgiveness. Someone had come into the room; it was her aunt, with tears on her cheeks.

"Thomas," she said. "Oh, come quickly."

Philip put his arm round Miss Nan, and led her from the room.

"No!" shrieked Sophia. But there was no one to hear her.

Shortly after ten next morning, Thomas had another hemorrhage and died. Only then did his father lay the boy down. Sophia was waiting outside the room; he passed her by without speaking, and went to rest for an hour before departing for Whitehall and another meeting with Mr. Stone. Sophia paced the drawing-room for hours, and then gave the order for her bags to be unpacked. She would stay.

Miss Nan and Hugh Denbigh were both tired, but they did not seem to want Sophia. They sat together in Miss Nan's room, now and then smiling at each other, now and then reaching for a handkerchief, and although Sophia could hear them talking when she was outside the room, they always stopped when she went in.

She was in agony. Philip's words had stripped away all her self-deceptions and conceits. She saw her folly, and bitterly regretted it. Desiring mastery, she had lost his regard. Her pain was all the greater because the breach between them was of her own making. She had declared that she would leave him, and he had agreed. He took his meals in the library, and when they met he was civil, but made it clear that he was surprised to find her still in Town. The mourning which made Sophia feel drab, suited his height and elegance. It was remarked at the funeral that the Countess looked poorly—poor dear, was she breeding? There were Christmas roses and holly on the coffin, exactly as Miss Nan had foretold.

The Jacobite Army began to march out of Carlisle on the morning of December 19th, leaving behind a small garrison

245

of men under the joint command of Colonel John Hamilton and Colonel Townley. The Highland Army's morale was no longer what it had been; the men were in despair at their failure to press on to London from Derby, and had begun to plunder the countryside as they passed through it. Cumberland's cavalry harassed the retreating columns, the Pretender had more frequent recourse to his bottle of cherry brandy, and it was only through the superhuman exertions of Lord George Murray that the Army still held together.

Lord George had already mounted his horse when Jasper was brought out of the dungeon in which he had been stowed. Jasper's wrists were in irons, he was filthy, unshaven and hollow-eyed. He had not been interrogated since he had been captured.

"Hang him," ordered Lord George.

Jasper was marched to the nearest lampbracket, and told to stand on a wooden cask. A rope was dropped around his neck, and the free end secured.

He could not believe that he was to be hanged. He looked up at the rope, and then around him. The Jacobites were filing out of the Castle. The cask was kicked from beneath his feet, and the rope tightened around his neck. He was not killed outright, but began to jerk his legs, dancing in the air. He saw his aunt's face as if in a dream, and Sophia's, and the meadow above Tarrant Hall, and sweet Marjorie....

As soon as Lord George Murray had passed out of sight, Colonel Hamilton signed to the nearest soldier to cut Jasper down. "He's only been hanging ten minutes, and there are still signs of life in him."

They cut Jasper down, and laid him on his back on the ground. He came to himself at length, and looked around him. Colonel Hamilton bent over him.

"You're still alive, man, and likely to stay that way, if you behave. An acquaintance of mine in the town here tells me you're worth more to the Usurper's Government alive than dead. We need you as a hostage, for I doubt if the Prince will return with reinforcements before Cumberland gets here."

Early in the New Year, with the rebels retreating further and further north towards the scene of their inevitable destruction, His Majesty appointed the Earl of Rame Ambassador to The Hague. There were those who wondered why Philip had attained this position at such an early age, but most set it down to Lord Carteret's influence. To this statement they would hastily add, how difficult it is to remember that Carteret is now Earl Granville!

Philip, elegant in black and silver, received the congratulations of Society with becoming modesty. There were some—notably Lady Millicent Fairweather—who commented on the absence of the Countess of Rame, but most people were happy to accept that the doctors had advised her to have a period of rest in the country. "So she must be breeding, my dear!" Sophia had gone into the country in the New Year looking white and strained.

There was plenty to divert Society at this time. The antics of Lord Carteret—that is, Earl Granville—at Court had set up a tug-of-war between the diplomat and Newcastle, with the King as the prize. Society found this all the more amusing as there was not the slightest doubt that Newcastle would win.

Then there was the affair of little Marjorie Bladen—very pretty, of course, but positively no style, my dear! Her father's death had been set down to a drunken quarrel and Society, which had never really adopted the girl into its ranks, now made something of a pet of her. This might possibly have had something to do with the fact that the girl was now a considerable heiress. It was known that Mr. Dalby had tried and failed in the attempt to storm the fortress of Miss Bladen's heart. Society was not surprised at his lack of success, but they were somewhat piqued when a complete outsider appeared on the scene and bore off the prize. Who was this Sir Jasper Tarrant, anyway? Oh, a brother of the Radiant Rose? Well, that explained much...but had he not been out with the rebels? Not, of course, that one didn't know one or two people who had expressed sympathy with the cause of the King across the Water, but actually to fight for them....Oh, he had fought *against* them, and was now a Captain in the Army—you mean, the Hanoverian Army? How very patriotic of him. A very grim-looking young man, I must say; not at all comfortable to have around, but of course if he had known the Bladen girl since childhood, and what with him being penniless and wanting to buy back Tarrant Hall from the Earl...it made a sort of sense. And of course it was only

247

natural that the Countess would make her home with the young married couple while her husband was abroad.

Another wedding also caused Society comment. On a dark day in January the Earl of Rame gave Miss Nan Tarrant in marriage to his old friend and erstwhile tutor, Mr. Denbigh. It had been an occasion for tears as much as for laughter, for it signalled the end of a long and happy relationship between the Earl and his former tutor. Philip could not keep Miss Nan at his side, for her place must be with her niece, and he could not retain Hugh Denbigh's services when his old friend had lost his heart so completely to Miss Nan. Society might— and did—say that it was very odd of the Earl of Rame to allow his aunt by marriage to marry so much beneath her, but they presumed he knew his own business best, and of course if Mr. Denbigh did ever bring out the book of poems on which he was said to have been working for some years, that would be some kind of distinction to justify it. The Earl had settled a pension for life on both parties, and it had been arranged that the Denbighs would make their home with the Countess, either at Tarrant Hall, or on the great estate at Rame, during his absence.

There had been two other witnesses to the marriage of the Denbighs: one was Mr. Carramine, who was now a permanent employee at Mr. Stone's office, and the other was Mr. Dodge, who had been made very happy by the Earl's gift of the freehold of his house in Crooked Court.

"I never expected it," said Mr. Dodge, "but I don't deny that a bird in the hand is worth two in a bush, as the saying goes."

A fortnight after the Denbighs' wedding, Philip Rich, Earl of Rame, stepped into the pinnace which was to row him out to the packet *Amanda,* moored down river. The wind was favorable, and with luck he would be able to enter into his new duties at The Hague tomorrow, or the day after. The King had been most kind at their farewell interview...he was sorry to leave the old man, even though he would continue in his service. Chivers handed the Earl a heavier cloak, in exchange for the light one he had worn to Court. The black and silver of his suit was relieved by the light blue ribbon of the Garter. As Chivers had often remarked recently, The Earl was a man who repaid care in dressing.

Chivers was fidgeting in the boat. Philip supposed that his valet was nervous about the crossing, although he had done it many times before.

Philip himself sat still, with his eyes on the *Amanda,* and his thoughts far away. Perhaps he ought to have been thinking of his new duties, of the difficulties of working with our Dutch allies at The Hague, of all the problems there which had caused Lord Chesterfield to exclaim with relief when he was finally released from his post. Instead, he was thinking of his estranged wife, and of Jasper's new maturity, and of Cumberland's fury at being asked to negotiate for the captured "David Vere" who was nothing but a spy and deserved to be hanged, by God! And then again, Philip thought of the dignity which Sophia had shown in her last weeks in Town. The idea of Sophia Tarrant being dignified ought to have been risible, and yet...he had been so tired after Thomas's death...grief, remorse that he had neglected the child so much...Sophia's indiscretion had seemed like a betrayal, and yet she had done her best to atone, had seemed to be maturing at last....Had he been right to let her go to Hamberley? Could he have prevented her going there? Would she not have laughed at him again?

To tell a reserved man that he is cold ties his tongue. Philip lacked the Tarrant capacity for expressing emotion. He had seen their loving and giving way of life, had bought it, and had paid for his presumption by losing not only Sophia and Nan but also Hugh Denbigh.

The pinnace had reached the *Amanda.* Philip climbed the ropeladder, and congratulated himself because his shoulder had not complained. Chivers besought him to step below; the cabins were small, he said, but supper had been brought abroad for his master.

"I am not hungry," said Philip. "I will stay on deck for a while." The tide had turned, the anchor was up, and they were slipping down the river. He watched the lights recede. The sky was red and gray, from sinking sun and the smoke pall that hung over London. It would be a long time before he saw it again. He would not regret going if it were not that his new life were going to be so lonely. The Tarrants had brought warmth and gaiety into his life, and now they were gone, and Hugh was gone....Perhaps he could write to Sophia from The Hague; a friendly note, merely ... and if she were to reply ... would she consider coming out to him? No, of course she would not. She must be feeling the weight of her pregnancy by now, and no one could expect her to travel under such circumstances.

If she had ever loved him, of course, it would have been different. It had been mostly his fault, he saw that now. He had expected too much of a country-bred girl, unused to Society. Indeed, she had learned so quickly that he had been amazed, and that short time when they had been as one person....

The memory hurt him. Perhaps he should buy a dog?

Chivers interrupted him. The ladies and Mr. Denbigh awaited him below. Would he not come to supper?

The *Amanda* heeled in the wind. He must have misheard Chivers. He followed his valet down the companionway, along a passage and into a small cabin, lit only by the fast-sinking sun. The door closed behind him. He could see nothing but the sun through the porthole. The wainscotting was dark. Hands took his cloak and hat from him, and laid them aside. He could sense someone behind him, and smell her scent. He would have turned, anxious to see her face, but she set her hands on his shoulders and urged him towards a table, which was set for two. A tall woman; not Miss Nan. Not—? He sat. There was a branch of candles on the table, unlit. He reached for it, but a white hand put the candles beyond his reach. She sat at right-angles to him, her eyes down. She was dressed in some dark, rustling, loose robe, which was cut low at the neck. In the twilight she was all white and dark blue, her hair piled high but unpowdered.

She said, "It was my duty to come with you."

Was she mocking him?

She removed the cover from the dish in front of him, and poured him some wine.

She said, "You can have no business to attend to for several hours. No one will come in; Chivers will see to that. He has arranged everything beautifully, has he not? We must be well out to sea by now, so you cannot send me away. It would be cruel to send me to join my aunt and Uncle Hugh, for their cabin is even smaller than this, and my poor aunt is totally occupied with Uncle Hugh, who says he has never felt seasick before, but is undoubtedly so now. Isn't that strange? Neither my aunt nor I have so much as seen the sea before, yet neither of us feels the slightest qualm."

"Sophia, I..."

"Let me speak first. I promise I will not rant and rave, but I want to say something to you before you decide what to do with me. If you decide that we must continue to live apart, then I will remain on board the packet and return to England." She laid her hand on his. "Look...look at my hand on yours." He looked, and saw nothing more significant than her white, elegant-fingered, capable hand laid over his.

"You have forgotten," she said. "Yet I have not. You remember the day we met? I thought you were dead. I saw you, and I wanted you. I had not known what it was to want a man before. I was Miss Tarrant of Tarrant Hall, and men had talked of love to me, but their words had meant nothing, until I saw you. I put my hand on yours, and I noticed for the first time that mine was rough-skinned and red. Your hand was smooth and white and well cared for. The contrast frightened me, because it indicated that our lives were different. I did not know, then, how different. I was nothing but a stupid, ignorant girl, who thought herself a cut above her neighbors. I told myself that I was as good as you, and all the time I knew I was not, and that you would discover the truth about me sooner or later. I knew I was going to be hurt, even before you opened your eyes. I was angry with you, laughed at you, because I feared you. I could not believe that you loved me, that you could ever love me, because my hands went everywhere with me, telling me the truth...

"Then I came to Town, and everything I saw reinforced my fear. I learned to be fashionable, which ought to have lessened the gap between us, but you were changing, too. By the time I had learned to be like Lady Millicent, you had spurned her, and were as far from me as ever."

"I did not ask that you change...."

"Consciously or not, you wanted me to change. You wanted me to be a political hostess by day, and a whore by night."

His face burned. She was right.

Her voice was gentle. "My hand looks like yours, now. I am no longer ashamed of it. Are you still ashamed of me? I would not blame you if you were. The higher I climb, the farther you seem to be ahead of me. I foresee that you will end up as one of the greatest men in the kingdom, and I acknowledge that my temper is still not...not absolutely

251

under control. I have changed, though. I didn't know how much until I went back to Tarrant Hall. Marjorie is chatelaine there now, and Jasper upholds her in all things domestic. My neighbors talk of pigs and potatoes, and I read, and wonder what nonsense Henry Lincoln is up to, and what Lord Carteret—Earl Granville—will do next, and how your shoulder is, and oh, everything about our time together. I had not wanted to leave you, but my aunt said that I should show you I could be an obedient wife if I tried; but it was so dull without you, I could have wept! The knowledge that it was all my own fault made it worse, for if I had not been so jealous, and so stupid... I thought you would never forgive me, and then you sent my aunt and Uncle Hugh to live with me, and care for me, and I knew how much they meant to you, and I dared to hope..."

He pressed her hand to his lips.

She said. "I have been very stupid. I ought never to have left you."

"No, you were right to go. I deserved punishment for my arrogance. If I had not behaved so coldly towards you... I wanted to write to you... to tell you... but I was not sure if you would listen..."

"Philip the Cold," she said. She laughed, but her laughter no longer hurt him. "Philip the Bold. Philip the very, very stupid." The last rays of the sun caught the tears on her cheeks.

"That makes two of us, who are very, very stupid?" he said.

"Probably. It is expected that a gentleman should confess his foolishness first, is it not?"

"Probably," he echoed. "But then, I am notoriously slow in such matters. My wife may have to teach me the words."

He moved toward her, or perhaps it was she who moved toward him. Who knows? His arm was where it had long wanted to be; and yet she held him back, with her hand upon his breast.

"You must say it, first."

He removed her hand, and kissed it. "In a minute, when it is dark."

It would be easier to say it in the dark.

ABOUT THE AUTHOR

When six years old, Veronica Heley was sent away to boarding school. She was most unhappy there, and so began to make up stories in her head. She has continued to do so ever since, though it was not until after the birth of her daughter that she felt she could retire from office work and learn how to become a writer.

Born in 1933 she is married to a Probation and After Care officer, who has never read any of her work, except by accident.

She had five romantic thrillers published before she turned to her first love, historical romance. This is the third story of Old Time England to be accepted for publication.

Let COVENTRY Give You
A Little Old-Fashioned Romance

☐ **AURORA**   50160 $1.75
   by Joan Smith

☐ **THE WANTON FIRES**   50159 $1.75
   by Meriol Trevor

☐ **MILADY HOT AT HAND**   50161 $1.75
   by Elizabeth Chater

☐ **NOT QUITE A LADY**   50162 $1.75
   by Sara McCulloch

☐ **THE TARRANT ROSE**   50163 $1.75
   by Veronica Heley

☐ **SERENA**   50164 $1.75
   by Mollie Chappell

NEW FROM FAWCETT CREST

GREAT ADVENTURES IN READING